# Lessons from School Psychology

*Lessons from School Psychology* presents practical advice and evidence-based strategies for school-based professionals and parents to utilize when dealing with challenging and worrisome behavior in children and adolescents. Structured around a series of timely topics facing schools today, chapters cover everything from bullying and racial incidents to substance abuse and suicide prevention. This unique resource integrates proven models and strategies from school psychology practice in an accessible format that highlights key takeaways and valuable lessons for teachers, counselors, social workers, administration, or anyone looking to help a young person in their life.

**Gayle Macklem, MA, LEP, NCSP,** practiced as a school psychologist for 30 years and is currently an adjunct professor at William James College. She is the author of four textbooks.

**Arlene Silva, PhD, LEP, NCSP,** is chair, director, and associate professor in the School Psychology Department at William James College. Her professional interests include consultation, supervision, and culturally responsive practice.

# Lessons from School Psychology

## Practical Strategies and Evidence-Based Practice for Professionals and Parents

**Edited by Gayle Macklem and Arlene Silva**

Routledge
Taylor & Francis Group
NEW YORK AND LONDON

First published 2019
by Routledge
52 Vanderbilt Avenue, New York, NY 10017

and by Routledge
2 Park Square, Milton Park, Abingdon, Oxon, OX14 4RN

*Routledge is an imprint of the Taylor & Francis Group, an informa business*



*Library of Congress Cataloging-in-Publication Data*
A catalog record for this title has been requested

ISBN: 978-1-138-29356-4 (hbk)
ISBN: 978-1-138-29357-1 (pbk)
ISBN: 978-1-315-22933-1 (ebk)

Typeset in Sabon
by Wearset Ltd, Boldon, Tyne and Wear

Visit the eResource: www.routledge.com/9781138293571

This book is dedicated to all those who advocate for our children.

# Contents

# Contributors

**Joan Axelrod, MEd,** is the Director of the Academic Resource Center at William James College and an adjunct member of the School Psychology Department faculty. She has been evaluating and teaching about children with learning and developmental disorders for many years and has worked with local school systems to develop programming for these students. Her primary area of interest is reading and written language development. In her work at William James College, she has focused on the literacy needs of post-secondary students.

**Terry Bontrager, PhD,** has special interests in cross-cultural issues as well as in working with English language learners. After a stint in the Peace Corps in El Salvador, he taught English to Speakers of Other Languages in Japan, Germany and on the Navajo Indian Reservation in Arizona. In a mid-life career change, he earned his doctorate in School Psychology from Texas A&M University. He served as Spanish–English Bilingual School Psychologist for the New Bedford (MA) Public Schools before moving to the University of Massachusetts, Boston. He retired from that institution in 2013. Dr. Bontrager speaks Spanish, German, and Japanese.

**June Bowman, EdD, LEP, NCSP,** was the Massachusetts School Psychologist of the Year in 2014. She is currently an adjunct professor at William James College and the school psychologist at Gann Academy, a private high school in Waltham, MA. She is also a member of the College Board Advisory Panel for Services for Students with Disabilities. She has worked in a variety of school settings, including 27 years at Brookline High School, where she was co-chair of the crisis intervention team. She received her master's degree from Harvard University and her doctorate from Boston University.

**John Desrochers, PhD, BCBA, ABPP,** is a licensed psychologist, board certified behavior analyst, and board-certified school psychologist. He earned his doctorate in educational psychology at Columbia University and also holds graduate degrees in remedial reading, behavior analysis, and marriage and family therapy. He has held leadership positions in the Connecticut Association of School Psychologists (recipient of Distinguished Service Award) and the National Association of School Psychologists (named 2007 School Psychologist of the Year). His practice centers on mental health issues, behavioral assessment and intervention, and counseling, and he is a frequent presenter and author in these areas.

**Bruce Ecker, PhD,** is an Associate Professor and Director of the child clinical concentration, Children and Families of Adversity and Resilience (CFAR), at William James College. He is also a clinical and educational psychologist with 30 years' experience providing service in schools, community clinics, and hospitals. Dr. Ecker was trained in School Psychology at the University of Minnesota. He received his PhD from the Clinical Psychology Training Program at the University of Massachusetts at Amherst. He was awarded the William James College Excellence in Teaching Award in 2011 and held the Mintz Chair in Professional Psychology from 2014 to 2016.

**Ronda Goodale, PhD, LEP,** is Adjunct Faculty at William James College, Chair of Early Education and Care at Cambridge College, and Senior Lecturer at University of Massachusetts, Boston. Dr. Goodale received her PhD from Boston College. She has extensive prior experience working with students with disabilities of all ages in the Boston Public Schools as a supervisor of psychologists, literacy coach, and teacher. Her major interests include diversity, second language learning, social-emotional support, and early education. She is a frequent author, presenter, and consultant, and has been a frequent radio guest over the last few years.

**Margaret Hannah, MEd, GCEC,** is Executive Director of the Freedman Center for Child and Family Development at William James College and Adjunct Faculty in the School Psychology Department. She works in schools, agencies, and businesses designing, developing, and facilitating leadership programs, parent support groups, and evidence-based prevention programs. She serves on the following groups within the Commonwealth of Massachusetts: Academy of Pediatrics Mental Health Task Force, Governor's Commission on Post-Partum Depression, Commission on Behavioral Health and Upstream Prevention, and the Children's Behavioral Health Initiative Advisory.

**Daniel B. Jacobs, PsyD, MBA, EdM,** is an Assistant Professor in the William James College School Psychology Department. He earned his EdM from Harvard University, his MBA from Salem State University, and his PsyD in clinical psychology from William James College. His private practice, Jacobs Psychological & Consulting Services, is in Lexington, MA and he has treated adolescents and adults with dual diagnosis concerns, and has presented over 200 professional trainings, in the past 20 years. Dr. Jacobs is a licensed psychologist and HSP and was formerly the Director of partial hospital programs at Salem Hospital in Salem, MA.

**Jason P. Kaplan, PhD, LEP, NCSP,** is an Assistant Professor and Director of the School Psychology PsyD Program at William James College. He earned his PhD in School and Counseling Psychology from Northeastern University and is a licensed psychologist and HSP. Prior to joining William James College, Dr. Kaplan was a school psychologist for 14 years. In addition, Dr. Kaplan has worked in community mental health treating children, adolescents, and adults, and as a high school teacher for children with learning disabilities. His research interests include systems change, the assessment and treatment of children with learning and emotional disabilities, and supervision.

**Robert Kinscherff, PhD, JD,** is a clinical/forensic psychologist and attorney with more than 30 years of practice with youth, schools, juvenile courts and juvenile justice systems, and behavioral health care systems. His professional practice and research areas include violence risk assessment and management, clinical and forensic behavioral health with youth at risk or already involved in juvenile/criminal justice systems or forensic mental health systems, law and neuroscience, and legal and ethical issues in clinical and forensic practice. Dr. Kinscherff is widely published and he teaches and consults nationally and internationally to clinical professionals, educators, legal professionals, and policy-makers.

**Ronald Lee, PhD, BCBA-D, LABA,** is the director of the Master of Arts in Applied Behavior Analysis program at William James College in Newton, MA. He received his doctorate in psychology from the CUNY Graduate Center with specializations in learning theory and developmental disabilities. He has been a clinician and administrator for programs for people with autism for over 20 years. In addition to clinical work and teaching, he has conducted research and presented on a variety of topics, including response variability, conditioned reinforcement, and staff training.

**Gayle Macklem, MA, LEP, NCSP,** is a Massachusetts Licensed Educational Psychologist and a Nationally Certified School Psychologist. She has developed a number of prevention programs for schools and has worked as a curriculum developer and writer for the Open Circle Social Competency curriculum. She is the author of four textbooks. She is currently an adjunct instructor in the School Psychology training program at William James College in Newton, Massachusetts and is Senior Curriculum Writer for the School Climate and Social Emotional Learning Certificate Program in the Freedman Center for Child and Family Development at William James College.

**Colleen Meigher, PhD, NCSP,** is a school psychologist with Newton Public Schools, in Newton, MA. Dr. Meigher has also worked as an Adjunct Professor, teaching classes in clinical practice related to working with secondary school students, in the William James College School Psychology Department. Dr. Meigher received her PhD in School Psychology from the University of Minnesota, Twin Cities. Specific areas of interest include student engagement and motivation to learn, dialectical behavioral therapy, and school safety.

**Barbara Miller, PhD, LEP, NCSP,** is an Assistant Professor in the School Psychology Department, William James College. She received her PhD in clinical psychology from McGill University and is a licensed school psychologist. Dr. Miller worked in the public schools for over 30 years and has taught in several of the School Psychology training programs in Massachusetts. Dr. Miller has been involved in the leadership of the Massachusetts School Psychologists Association; provides supervision to those seeking the licensed educational psychologist credential; and presents at conferences. Her research interests include social-emotional development and mental health services in schools.

**Craig Murphy, PhD, LEP, NCSP,** is an Associate Professor from the School Psychology Department at William James College, the Clinical Director of the Summit Therapeutic Middle and High School programs, and the owner of the Family and Educational Wellness Center (www.fewcenter.com). Dr. Murphy received his PhD in School Psychology from the Pennsylvania State University. His research interests include understanding and supporting students with emotional and behavioral challenges, school-based programming for at-risk students, and harnessing the power of social influence to improve schools. Dr. Murphy is a frequent presenter and well-respected clinical consultant to school districts throughout Massachusetts and Rhode Island.

**Tracey Borriello Murphy, PhD, LEP, NCSP,** is a school psychologist in the Newton, MA public schools. Dr. Murphy received her PhD in School Psychology from the Pennsylvania State University. In addition to working as a school-based practitioner, Dr. Murphy also supports families and school districts on a consultative basis through her private practice with the Family and Educational Wellness Center. Dr. Murphy's research interests include post-secondary transition, motivation, and teacher training.

**Nadja Reilly, PhD,** is the Associate Director of the Freedman Center for Child and Family Development at William James College. Dr. Reilly received her PhD in Clinical Psychology from the University of Miami. Prior to joining William James College, Dr. Reilly was at Boston Children's Hospital, where she worked in different settings, including inpatient medical, outpatient psychiatry, schools, and communities.

Dr. Reilly's interests include consultation around social-emotional learning, and treatment of pediatric anxiety and depression. She is the author of the book *Anxiety and Depression in the Classroom: A Teacher's Guide to Fostering Self-Regulation in Young Students.*

**Arlene Silva, PhD, LEP, NCSP,** is Chair of the William James College School Psychology Department, Director of the MA/CAGS Program, and an Associate Professor. Dr. Silva received her PhD in School Psychology from the University of Maryland, College Park. Prior to joining William James College, Dr. Silva garnered a broad range of professional experiences in public school, university, and clinical settings. Dr. Silva's research interests include consultation, supervision, and culturally responsive practice. She is a frequent presenter and author and has been involved in the leadership of the National Association of School Psychologists since 2006.

**Gemima St. Louis, PhD,** is an Associate Professor in the Clinical Psychology Department at William James College (WJC). She is the Co-Director of the Center for Multicultural & Global Mental Health and a faculty member in the Concentration on Children and Families of Adversity and Resilience at WJC. She is also the Director of the *PATHWAYS Program*, a school-based counseling initiative that provides trauma-focused, evidence-informed mental health services to urban youth in the Boston Public Schools. Her primary clinical and research focus is on culturally diverse children, adolescents, and families with histories of trauma, chronic diseases, and behavioral and psychosocial challenges.

**Elana Wolkoff, PhD, LEP,** is an Assistant Professor of School Psychology at William James College. Dr. Wolkoff earned her MEd at Harvard Graduate School of Education and her PhD at Northeastern University. Having begun her career as a special education teacher, Dr. Wolkoff has since worked as a school psychologist in both urban and suburban settings, working with children from preschool through grade 12 as well as with their parents and teachers. Dr. Wolkoff teaches classes on Special Education and School-Based Consultation. She presents on topics including School Refusal and Truancy, Increasing Resiliency, Having Difficult Conversations, and High-Quality Supervision.

# Foreword

*Stanley Berman*

*Vice President of Academic Affairs*
*William James College*

There are extraordinarily high demands placed on contemporary public schools. Parents, legislators, concerned citizens, and students have a long list of deliverables. These expectations include stellar training in critical thinking and analysis, fluid and cogent writing, mastery of mathematics and the sciences, as well as the humanities and foreign languages. We can add to this the ability to be a sophisticated and accomplished "test taker."

There are also many expectations beyond learning content, such as training students how to be good citizens and preparing them for effective participation in a democracy. These skills involve learning to respect cultures and approaches different from one's own, collaborating and working effectively on teams, learning to resolve differences and manage conflict, and recognizing and responding to bullying and harassment. This also means the capability to build a sense of confidence in oneself and to self-regulate behavior and affect, to learn how to problem solve in a complex and often ambiguous world, and to handle disappointment and challenging emotion in a constructive way. Finally, it is important our students learn how to be innovative and novel problem solvers, to "think outside the box" and to develop a sense of "ownership" in being a good steward for our world.

With this list, which is arguably not even fully described above, we all recognize the intense pressure on students and educators alike. The competing agendas at times appear to be too much to respond to. There are political and economic positions which inevitably value some goals over others, and high emotions prevail as we sort out the key goals of a solid primary and secondary education.

Into this arena enters the school psychologist. These professionals are in unique positions in many school settings. They bring their traditional, well-honed skills in educational and psychological assessment, as well as a solid understanding of learning differences and disabilities, developmental challenges and the impact of medical illness, stress and economic challenge, loss and trauma on students. They are skilled in consulting with teachers and administrators, in running groups, and in implementing individual interventions with children. They support concerned parents as they advocate for the needs of their children.

Most often, school psychologists are the first assessors and intervenors in child and adolescent mental health. They encounter children where they spend the majority of their days; school is a child's job. It is an invigorating and challenging profession which demands many well-developed competencies. This model of the school psychologist employing "empirically supported, data driven, and culturally competent services" which address children, families, and schools at both the student level and the systems level is, of course, the model for current practice (National Association of School Psychologists, 2010, pp. 1–2). While school psychologists certainly craft and deliver primary prevention and promote wellness, they are also agents of both secondary and tertiary prevention. They are indeed the front lines in serving the mental health and optimal functioning of children. Drawing on this broad range of training and expertise, this volume describes how best practices from the field of school psychology can be applied by those who care for and work with children and adolescents.

This is a unique book as it has been created by a single academic department. The editors, Ms. Gayle Macklem and Dr. Arlene Silva, faculty member and Department Chair respectively, invited their colleagues in the School Psychology Department at William James College to create a book which responds to many of the pressing issues facing parents and educators today. The book's three parts, I: Fostering Positive Mental Health and Social-Emotional Development, II: Supporting Academic Progress and Positive Behavior, and III: Proactive, Systemic Strategies in Schools, cover both classic topics within school psychology as well as areas that have become part of the expanded role of the school psychologist as the profession has continued to evolve. Part II contains strong chapters on reading, ADHD/executive functioning, autism, and learning disabilities. Parts I and III highlight the key role of healthy school culture and promoting vibrant child and adolescent development. Social and emotional learning skills are also highlighted; the pioneering work of Roger Weissberg and CASEL (https://casel.org/) has encouraged educators to re-balance the intense attention on testing achievement to include teaching well- functioning, confident, and curious life-long learners. In chapters as diverse as talking about race, crisis events, suicide prevention, managing challenging behavior, bullying, and home–school collaboration, topics are explained and practical tips are presented by seasoned academics and practitioners.

This is an important book because it draws from the evidence and practice in the field of school psychology to promote healthy development from an individual, school, family, and cultural framework. The editors and writers underscore the broad set of challenges and opportunities facing educators and parents today to ensure students benefit and thrive and school climate and culture are enhanced.

## Reference

National Association of School Psychologists. (2010). *Model for comprehensive and integrated school psychological services, NASP practice model overview* [Brochure]. Bethesda, MD: Author.

# Acknowledgments

We would like to acknowledge Dr. Stanley Berman and Dr. Nicholas Covino, Vice President of Academic Affairs and President of William James College, respectively, for their encouragement throughout this project. We would also like to give a special note of thanks to School Psychology Department Coordinator Ms. Malory Reynolds, who provided invaluable editorial and organizational support.

Finally, we would like to acknowledge our past, present, and future graduate students, from whom we continue to learn so much. Through our work at William James College, we are grateful for the opportunity to influence the next generation of school psychologists as they make significant differences in the lives of children and adolescents, and the functioning of schools.

# Part I

# Fostering Positive Mental Health and Social-Emotional Development

# 1 What Children Need to Understand About Emotions and How to Manage Them

*Gayle Macklem*

Emotional competency can be thought of as a set of skills that develop not only in childhood, but also throughout life (Lau & Wu, 2012). Emotionally competent children and adolescents tend to be well adjusted; they have friends and get along well with others. Emotionally competent students tend to pay attention in school and can negotiate this complex learning and social environment. All students need a developmentally appropriate level of emotional competency for mental health and for academic success.

Although there are many skills that need to be mastered in order to be emotionally competent, some skills are more basic and therefore more critical than others. Parents and teachers can facilitate the development and mastery of the most critical skills needed to accept, tolerate, and regulate emotions (Berking et al., 2008). Children need to be able to understand and label their own emotions and those of others. They need skills to tolerate and accept strong negative emotions in order to interpret what may have caused the way they are feeling, and to support themselves in upsetting situations. When children experience negative emotions too intensely, skills are needed to control and modify the emotion that caused the distress in order to problem solve. Although the skills that describe the ability to understand, accept, tolerate, modify, and regulate emotions may seem simple, they are actually a complex set of competencies that must be mastered to an adequate degree if children are going to function well.

## Notes from the Field

### *Jackson*

*Jackson's middle school teacher and his parents are worried about his behavior. He speaks out in class and is defensive when corrected. His teacher has tried to talk with him. She has treated him with kid gloves at times and alternatively has come down hard on him, which results in tearful anger. His teacher is at a loss to know what to try next.*

### *Jamal*

*Jamal is an intense teenager. He is loud when things are going well and is both angry and loud when things are not going well. His teachers feel that he is easily triggered, and they interact with him cautiously. The assistant principal confronted him in the corridor between classes and demanded to know where he was going. When Jamal didn't respond, the assistant principal raised his voice and stepped toward him. Jamal turned away and hit the wall with his fist. Now the principal has referred Jamal for a threat assessment.*

### *Camila*

*Camila's teacher complained to the school psychologist that this child does not often speak in class. No matter how much encouragement Camila is given to become involved in class, Camila remains shut down according to her teacher. She does not participate when children are working cooperatively, she never raises her hand to contribute to class, and when she is called on she doesn't respond with any confidence. Camila frequently asks to go to the nurse's office.*

### *Lucas*

*Lucas is well known to his peers at recess. He frequently disagrees with other kids about the rules of the game and how things are going. He is disruptive in games if he does not do well. He will argue, yell, demand that things go his way, and if he strikes out in a baseball game, he totally disrupts the game. In class, he isn't much better.*

These students seem to be very different one from the other but they all are having difficulty regulating their emotions. This chapter will address emotional competency and emotional regulation primarily during elementary and middle school. If emotional competency is addressed during these school years, teachers and parents will help children avoid emotional delay and difficulties later on.

## Why It Matters

There are strong associations between language competence and emotional competence. Children connect the labels for their feelings to their experiences. When asked to list as many emotion words as they can, elementary aged children do not tend to name very many different emotions (Beck, 2013). Although children can list a great many names for animals, they do not have the same proficiency listing emotion words (Beck, 2013, p. 89). Emotions are abstract, which may make them harder to learn. Knowing the words for emotions may depend on the extent to which families and teachers talk about emotions, and the extent to which children are read (or read) stories containing emotion words.

### *Emotions Have Names*

Emotional literacy is the ability to express feelings using *specific* words. Children need to recognize the emotions they and others experience and know that these emotions have names. This important skill arms children with resiliency and gives them an important strategy to regulate emotions. The ability to use emotion words is one of the critical skills of emotional competency (Beck, Kumschick, Eid, & Klann-Delius, 2011). A child's receptive vocabulary is closely related to emotion knowledge, the ability to recognize facial expressions, and awareness of more complex concepts such as mixed emotions. As children enter and progress through elementary and middle school, they experience significant growth in their emotional vocabulary. Putting feelings into words helps students regulate stressful experiences. Children who easily use emotion language are also more successful socially than their peers.

The simple act of labeling emotions causes emotions to decrease in intensity (Lieberman et al., 2007). When students at all ages are taught to label emotions correctly, it is much easier to teach them to deal with the negative emotions that drive their upset (Hannesdottir & Ollendick, 2007). When children are taught which emotions they are most likely to feel when they are going to be in particular environments or situations, they will be in a better position to use the emotion regulation strategies they know. This may protect them from being overcome with emotion and thereby unable to use the strategies they have learned.

### *There Are No "Bad" Emotions*

Negative thinking in general is likely to result in feelings of sadness, anger, shame, guilt, fear, and anxiety (Hannesdottir & Ollendick, 2007). Sadness, fear, and withdrawal can predict anxiety and depressive symptoms (Clifford, Lemery-Chalfant, & Goldsmith, 2015). Positive emotions, such as happiness, help children think flexibly when they are faced with problems (Davis, 2016). However, children must be able to regulate both positive and negative emotions in order to be emotionally healthy (Djambazova-Popordanoska, 2016). Negative emotions are not "bad," nor do they need to be avoided necessarily. At the same time, children need to know that emotions can be helpful, or they can cause trouble (Gross, 2015). Emotions can cause problems when they are expressed with the wrong intensity for the situation. They cause problems when they last too long, occur too often, or bias a student's thinking and behavior.

### *Emotions Are Not Forever*

Children need to understand that emotions are not permanent. Emotions may be intense, and come on quickly in reaction to stressful situations, people, and events, but they do not last forever. Emotions need to be accepted and tolerated. The fact that they are not permanent can encourage children and adolescents to learn to regulate them. Some children will benefit from being taught to react to physical signs of upset and use these as cues to use relaxation strategies (Hannesdottir & Ollendick, 2007). This is helpful in situations that are mildly upsetting. Regulation strategies help students get work done even though they may continue to feel somewhat stressed.

Some schools use a mindfulness strategy to help children develop emotion regulation. Mindfulness, or focusing on the immediate moment and letting one's feelings flow without reacting, has promise for helping children regulate emotions. Practicing mindfulness skills reduces the intensity of emotions, letting individuals recover from an intense emotional experience quickly, and helping the student to think beyond himself/herself, and focus on goals (Roemer, Williston, & Rollins, 2015).

Mindfulness is a skill (Grecucci, Pappaianni, Siugzdaite, Theuninck, & Job, 2015). Unfortunately, the success of mindfulness for emotion regulation depends on practice. Individuals who practice mindfulness can regulate emotions by accepting their emotions and attending to the moment. Children or beginners in developing mindfulness skills may be more successful using a reappraisal strategy (changing the way they are thinking about what is stressing them). Students who have mastered mindfulness, or the ability to control their attention and awareness of their body sensitivities, may find mindfulness very useful.

### *Emotions Have Functions*

Emotions occur quickly, and they trigger tendencies to behave in certain ways or not to act at all (Gross, 2015). Various emotions have specific triggers that result in specific behaviors (Clifford et al., 2015). When students experience specific emotions, they may wonder why they have to experience these emotions at all. Importantly, students need to know that emotions have specific jobs or functions. The function of sadness is to push students to withdraw and conserve energy when upset over a loss. Anger triggers children to act (Clifford et al., 2015). Fear's function is to trigger avoidance, which may protect a child from harm. However, in other situations, fear can trigger aggression when a student is cornered and cannot avoid a threatening situation, event, or person. Fear can instigate escape as well (Pekrun, Hall, Goetz, & Perry, 2014). Anger, anxiety, and boredom can generate irrelevant thinking. Anxiety has a negative effect on complex tasks that require thinking and concentration, although it does not have much impact on easier tasks. Curiosity, joy, hope, pride, and interest are important emotions to foster. These emotions help children focus on tasks and consider what they might do in order to learn more.

Pekrun and colleagues (2014) found some emotions increase energy or activate behavior, while other emotions decrease or deactivate activity. In regard to positive emotions, enjoyment is activating and may help engage students in tasks. Pride is an example of an activating emotion most likely related to intrinsic motivation. In contrast, relaxation and contentment are deactivating emotions. In regard to negative emotions, anger and frustration tend to activate behavior along with anxiety, shame, and anger. Boredom, sadness, disappointment, and certainly hopelessness are deactivating emotions and will most likely reduce a student's attention to learning. Negative emotions generally result in use of more rigid strategies to deal with emotions and lead to superficial processing of the information that a teacher is presenting.

### *We Can Learn to Control (i.e., Regulate) Emotions*

Children with better regulation of their emotions tend to do better in school, have better social skills, and are less likely to experience mental health difficulties (Davis, 2016). We would like all children to understand that they can be in the driver's seat, so to speak, and can learn to manage difficult emotions. Emotion regulation has to do with *which* emotions a child has, *when* the child has them, and *how* the child experiences or expresses these emotions (Gross, 2015). Children learn strategies by watching how their parents and teachers manage emotions, and they also learn from siblings and peers (Davis & Levine, 2013). Children may prefer to use some strategies more than they like to use other strategies, depending on their temperament or on physiological differences. Some children, for example, see the 'downside' of situations when they are stressed and tend to think negatively. This temperament is known as negative emotionality. Students with this temperament can lose control and exhibit misbehavior more readily than their classmates (Clifford et al., 2015). It may be harder for these children to learn to regulate emotions and they may need more support than their peers.

Children can use positive emotions as a strategy to regulate negative emotions. If a child can produce positive emotions after a stressful event, this will help the child recover and repair the effects of negative emotions (Hannesdottir & Ollendick, 2007). Children who have experienced an upsetting event can generate positive emotions by recalling how they successfully coped in the past, by recalling positive experiences, by thinking of something funny, or by engaging in an activity that is distracting or fun. Of course, children may need gentle reminding to use this strategy.

There are five groups of emotion regulation strategies. Each group has different short- and long-term consequences for how a child will feel, act, and think right after using a strategy. Keep in mind that, while use of one of these strategies can be helpful, sometimes it may not be in the student's best interest to use that particular strategy (Gross, 2015). The five families of strategies include:

1. Choosing the situations in which the child wants to participate;
2. Changing or modifying the situation so that it is more comfortable;
3. Controlling what the child pays attention to;
4. Changing one's thinking about the situation or event; and
5. Changing one's response to the distress.

Although a child may not have much power to change the situation in which she or he finds himself, adolescents may be successful in choosing or avoiding certain stressful situations. However, a child may be able to change a stressful situation by using a coping strategy. A child may learn to redirect his/her attention away from the situation or may use distraction. Distraction can decrease the intensity of the emotion the child experiences. Or, a student may use his or her thinking to relieve distress by deciding that the situation isn't important or may use self-talk to encourage problem solving.

The strategy that has the most success in regulating emotions has to do with thinking differently, or reappraisal. The reappraisal strategy helps children look at an event or situation as less important or less meaningful for them. Reappraisal helps children think about how things will get better (Davis, 2016). The reappraisal strategy influences emotions but also a child's thoughts, perceptions, and impressions (Davis, 2016, p. 1618). Use of this strategy results in decreased sadness, increased feelings of happiness, and better memory for details in class. This strategy tends to be successful for children up to a point; when a student's distress becomes very intense, distraction works better.

Distraction is an important strategy for dealing with difficult situations. A child can shift his or her attention to something neutral when upset (Hannesdottir & Ollendick, 2007). Teaching children to problem solve and teaching the strategy of thinking of other options when in difficulty can be very helpful, but keep in mind that it is extraordinarily difficult for children to do this when they are overwhelmed. Students who are overwhelmed need to decrease the intensity of their negative emotions first and then use an appropriate strategy. Having too few strategies, relying on one exclusively, or having difficulty switching from one strategy to another, can present problems for children. Children also need to be able to match the strategy they want to use, to the specific situation at hand. Developing the flexibility children need to successfully regulate emotions takes practice. This fact may urge school professionals to implement a social-emotional learning curriculum emphasizing emotion regulation.

### *Emotions Are Social or Interpersonal*

Emotions have to do with social interaction. Children need to learn to pay attention to how others feel in order to build relationships. Children with well-developed age-appropriate ability to regulate their emotions are able to engage with friends and classmates positively and are accepted by their peers (Blair et al., 2015). Emotion regulation provides a foundation for social competence. Proficient emotional regulation is related to good social skills, peer group acceptance, and friendship quality throughout development. Proficient emotion regulation predicts competent social skills at age seven years. More proficient social skills at age seven are connected to stronger emotion regulation at age 10 years. Emotional development and social development are interdependent and develop together over the period of childhood. Social skills acceptance and friendship quality remain stable over the elementary grades. This is true even with changing teachers and changing classmates as students move through the grades.

Recently, researchers are identifying interpersonal emotions and are studying interpersonal emotion regulation (Niven, Garcia, van der Löwe, Holman, & Mansell, 2015). Connecting with others is important and can result in many benefits, such as emotional support. Popularity or being well-liked by peers and accepted by classmates, along with participating in social groups and sports groups, is a goal for many children. Children must use emotion regulation strategies in new social situations and when they anticipate entering new social situations (Niven et al., 2015).

Additionally, we now know that children can get some help in regulating their emotions from others when interacting, and they can try to influence the way others feel as they interact in turn. Behavioral strategies such as communicating support to the other person, comforting a friend, and validating the other person's emotions are critical skills to master. These strategies are perceived by others as helpful and facilitate new relationships and popularity. Additional strategies that are helpful include listening, encouraging, making someone laugh to help them feel better, and providing distractions. Trying to change the way the other person is looking at a situation, however, is associated with negative popularity, especially in regard to online relationships (Niven et al., 2015).

### *Emotions Are Important for Learning*

Emotions are very important in regard to academic performance and learning in school (Pekrun et al., 2014). Children need to understand that their emotions go to school with them. Emotions influence children's attention, memory storage, memory retrieval, and problem solving. When children experience strong emotions in class, they focus on what is causing the intense emotion, and as a result there are fewer resources available for what students may be working on in class.

Students who have difficulty regulating their emotions at home tend to have difficulties at school as well. These students have difficulty learning and are less likely to complete their work or to complete it accurately. Children who are more successful regulating their emotions have a somewhat better relationship with their teachers. They are less likely to get in trouble in school. Children with age-appropriate emotional regulation do better on standardized early literacy and math achievement tests (Graziano, Reavis, Keane, & Calkins, 2007). Children who can regulate emotions are able to focus and maintain attention on what the teacher is saying and on school tasks.

Students need to control their emotions and their emotional reactions so that learning is not affected in the classroom (Kurki, Järvelä, Mykkänen, & Määttä, 2015). Unfortunately, children may have to deal with being criticized by teachers, rejected by peers, and with making academic or social mistakes. They may be faced with challenging and difficult tasks when at the same time the classroom is being disrupted or the tasks are boring. It is important that school professionals realize that negative behavior may be a strategy to fight boredom for some students, especially as they get older. Children may daydream or disrupt the class when bored (Kurki et al., 2015; Macklem, 2015). It may be practically impossible for some children to avoid negative emotions in school.

When upset, children pay attention to whatever is emotionally important to them and do not pay attention to other concerns, such as learning (Davis & Levine, 2013). Negative emotions can reduce working memory and make it less likely that students will make the effort to process information deeply (Fried, 2011). When frustrated, children use avoidance and distraction strategies. When disappointed, they may attempt to look at the situation in another way. Students may express emotions as a way to manage embarrassing situations when they make errors and when they want to maintain relationships.

### *What Works*

In schools, we can teach students healthy strategies to regulate emotion in the classroom. Importantly, there are several social and emotional curricula for the general education classroom that include developing an emotions vocabulary, such as the PATHS curriculum (Riggs, Greenberg, & Kusché, 2006), and the RULER Feeling Words curriculum (Brackett, Rivers, Reyes, & Salovey, 2012). Children at risk will need targeted interventions in small groups led by a school psychologist or another school-based mental health professional. Those children who are already showing signs and symptoms of emotion dysregulation will need evidence-based interventions with an emotion regulation component (Gross, 2015).

The good news is that training to improve children's understanding of emotion can be successful (Sprung, Münch, Harris, Ebesutani, &

Hofmann, 2015). Children can learn to: recognize emotions, appreciate that emotions have functions and are not bad, understand which emotions are triggered by which situations, learn to recognize and label one emotion from another, understand how to accept emotions because they do not last forever, and can learn how to use various emotion regulation strategies. As in all education interventions, children who have the most to learn benefit most from training.

## Practical Tools for School-Based Professionals

- Teachers can help by modeling strategies to manage emotions. They can discuss emotional experiences in the classroom and in stories read in class. Teachers can help by emotionally supporting students as the emotional climate of the classroom and the school is very important.
- Teaching an emotions vocabulary as part of the general education program is extremely important. It is a major way that teachers can help children learn to regulate their emotions. Children need a wide range of emotion words and need to be fluent when talking and writing about emotional experiences. Do not define words for students but rather explain what the emotion words mean using developmentally appropriate language. Give examples that make sense for children and then use the words frequently (Beck, McKeown, & Kucan, 2002). A broad emotions vocabulary is equally important for adolescents.
- Teachers and mental health professionals need to be aware of the child who spends too much time in the nurse's office. This child may complain of headaches, stomachaches, and feel jittery. A high frequency of these behaviors may reflect emotional distress and avoidance of anxiety-generating situations in class or with peers, when there is no physiological cause (Hughes, Lourea-Waddell, & Kendall, 2008).
- Children with poor emotion regulation skills and limited or rigid strategies for regulation gain the most from being taught strategies (Davis & Levine 2013). Teaching students specific strategies may facilitate academic achievement and memory for details, and improve both attention and behavior. Teaching children facing negative emotions in the classroom to think about how things could get better when things aren't going well is very helpful (reappraisal of outcomes). This strategy is particularly important for less regulated children who need to manage upset and turn their attention to schoolwork.
- There are now a number of evidence-based social and emotional learning (SEL) curricula from which to choose as well as whole-school models for supporting children's social and emotional competency. School staff must carefully match a strong curriculum or whole-school model to the needs of their own student and staff populations.

- School psychologists and other mental health professionals need to appreciate that some older children will need emotional literacy training before attempting a talking intervention such as cognitive behavioral training (CBT; Beck, 2011).

## Take Home Ideas for Parents

- When parents accept their children's emotions, and pay attention, showing interest when children are sharing distress, they help their children become aware of and accepting of their own emotions. When parents value their children's emotions, children learn how emotions direct their behavior and the behavior of others. This facilitates learning the skills children will need to control their emotions at home and in school. Attentive parent responses can support their child's ability to problem solve when under pressure (Rogers, Halberstadt, Castro, MacCormack, & Garrett-Peters, 2015).
- When children express negative emotions, parents can help by comforting their child, and encouraging their child to express and talk about the negative emotions (Rogers et al., 2015). This parenting practice, which involves emotion coaching, reduces children's distress. Parents can teach important strategies when children are upset by reinterpreting an emotionally difficult situation less negatively in order to calm their child. Children will learn from this approach to use the reappraisal strategy themselves and react less emotionally in the future (Rogers et al., 2015). It is especially important for mothers to support their child's expressions of sadness and for fathers to be supportive of their child's anger (Sanders, Zeman, Poon, & Miller, 2015). In each case, support and modeling of coping strategies is needed.
- As children reach middle childhood and are able to regulate their emotions consistent with their same-aged peers, it is important that parents reduce support when children are upset. This will allow their child to develop his/her own strategies to deal with distress (Rogers et al., 2015). Resist the urge to remove a child from a stressful situation. Let your child know she/he is trusted to deal positively with upsetting situations (Hannesdottir & Ollendick, 2007).
- The emotional climate of the family impacts a child's overall emotional development and the child's skills in regulating his or her emotions (Morris, Silk, Steinberg, Myers, & Robinson, 2007). The emotional climate of the family has to do with the qualities of relationships and the amount of positive and negative emotion shown to one another in the family. Positive emotionality and acceptance in the family helps children feel secure and free to express emotions. These children know that their emotional needs will be met.

## References

Beck, I. L., McKeown, M. G., & Kucan, L. (2002). *Bringing words to life: Robust vocabulary instruction*. New York, NY: Guilford Press.

Beck, J. S. (2011). *Cognitive behavior therapy: Basics and beyond* (2nd ed.). New York, NY: Guilford Press.

Beck, L. (2013). *What language tells us about emotional development in middle childhood*. (Doctoral dissertation). Berlin, Germany: Freien University.

Beck, L., Kumschick, I. R., Eid, M., & Klann-Delius, G. (2011). Relationship between language competence and emotional competence in middle childhood. *Emotion, 12*(3), 503–514. doi:10.1037/a0026320

Berking, M., Wupperman, P., Reichardt, A., Pejic, T., Dippel, A., & Znoj, H. (2008). Emotion-regulation skills as a treatment target in psychotherapy. *Behaviour Research and Therapy, 46*(11), 1230–1237. doi:10.1016/j.brat.2008.08.005

Blair, B. L., Perry, N. B., O'Brien, M., Calkins, S. D., Keane, S. P., & Shanaham, L. (2015). Identifying developmental cascades among differentiated dimensions of social competence and emotion regulation. *Developmental Psychology, 51*(8), 1062–1073. doi:10.1037/a0039472

Brackett, M. A., Rivers, S. E., Reyes, M. R., & Salovey, P. (2012). Enhancing academic performance and social and emotional competence with the RULER feeling words curriculum. *Learning and Individual Differences, 22*(2), 218–224. doi:10.1016/j.lindif.2010.10.002

Clifford, S., Lemery-Chalfant, K., & Goldsmith, H. H. (2015). The unique and shared genetic and environmental contributions to fear, anger, and sadness in childhood. *Child Development, 86*(5), 1538–1556. doi:10.1111/edev.12394

Davis, E. L. (2016). An age-related mechanism of emotion regulation: Regulating sadness promotes children's learning by broadening information processing. *Child Development, 87*(5), 1617–1626. doi:10.1111/edev.12552

Davis, E. L. & Levine, L. J. (2013). Emotion regulation strategies that promote learning: Reappraisal enhances children's memory for educational information. *Child Development, 84*(1), 361–374. doi:10.1111/j.1467-8624.2012.01836.x

Djambazova-Popordanoska, S. (2016). Implications of emotion regulation on young children's emotional wellbeing and educational achievement. *Educational Review, 68*(4), 497–515. doi:10.1080/00131911.2016.1144559

Fried, L. (2011). Teaching teachers about emotion regulation in the classroom. *Australian Journal of Teacher Education, 36*(3), 117–126. (Article 2). Retrieved from http://ro.ecu.edu.au/cgi/viewcontent.cgi?article=1543&context=ajte

Graziano, P. A., Reavis, R. D., Keane, S. P., & Calkins, S. D. (2007). The role of emotion regulation and children's early academic success. *Journal of School Psychology, 45*(1), 3–19. doi:10:1016/jsp. 2006.09.002

Grecucci, A., Pappaianni, E., Siugzdaite, R., Theuninck, A., & Job, R. (2015). Mindful emotion regulation: Exploring the neurocognitive mechanisms behind mindfulness. *BioMed Research International, 2015*. (Article ID 670724). doi:10.1155/2015/670724. Retrieved from www.hindawi.com/journals/bmri/2015/670724

Gross, J. J. (2015). Emotion regulation: Current status and future prospects. *Psychological Inquiry, 26*, 1–26. doi:10.1080/1047840X.2014.940781

Hannesdottir, D. K. & Ollendick, T. H. (2007). The role of emotion regulation in the treatment of child anxiety disorders. *Clinical Child and Family Psychology Review, 10*(3), 275–293. doi:10.1007/s10567-007-0024-6

Hughes, A. A., Lourea-Waddell, B., & Kendall, P. C. (2008). Somatic complaints in children with anxiety disorders and their unique prediction of poorer academic performance. *Child Psychiatry and Human Development, 39*(2), 211–220. doi:10.1007/s10578-007-0082-5

Kurki, K., Järvelä, S., Mykkänen, A., & Määttä, E. (2015). Investigating children's emotion regulation in socio-emotionally challenging classroom situations. *Early Child Development and Care, 185*(8), 1238–1254. doi:10.1080/03004430.2014.988710

Lau, P. S. Y. & Wu, F. K. Y. (2012). Emotional competence as a positive youth development construct: A conceptual review. *The Scientific World Journal, 2012.* (Article ID 975189). doi:10.1100/2012/975189

Lieberman, M. D., Eisenberger, N. I., Crockett. M. J., Tom, S. M., Pfeifer, J. H., & Way, B. M. (2007). Putting feelings into words: Affect labeling disrupts amygdala activity in response to affective stimuli. *Psychological Science, 18*(5), 421–428. doi:10.1111/j.1467-9280.2007.01916.x

Macklem, G. (2015). *Boredom in the classroom: Addressing student motivation, self-regulation, and engagement in learning.* New York, NY: Springer.

Morris, A. S., Silk, J. S., Steinberg, L., Myers, S. S., & Robinson, L. R. (2007). The role of the family context in the development of emotion regulation. *Social Development, 16*(2). 361–388. doi:10.1111/j.1467-9507.00389.x

Niven, K., Garcia, D., van der Löwe, L., Holman, D., & Mansell, W. (2015). Becoming popular: Interpersonal emotion regulation predicts relationship formation in real life social networks. *Frontiers in Psychology, 6*, 1452. doi:10.3389/fpsyg.2015.01452

Pekrun, R., Hall, N. C., Goetz, T., & Perry, R. P. (2014). Boredom and academic achievement: Testing a model of reciprocal causation. *Journal of Educational Psychology, 106*(3), 696–710. doi:10.1037/a0036006

Riggs, N. R., Greenberg, M. T., & Kusché, C. A. (2006). The mediational role of neurocognition in the behavioral outcomes of a social-emotional prevention program in elementary school students: Effects of the PATHS curriculum. *Prevention Science, 7*(1), 91–102. doi:10.1007/s11121-005-0022-1

Roemer, L., Williston, S. K., & Rollins, L. G. (2015). Mindfulness and emotion regulation. *Current Opinion in Psychology, 3*, 52–57. doi:10.1016/j.copsyc.2015.02.006

Rogers, M. L., Halberstadt, A. G., Castro, V. L., MacCormack, J. K., & Garrett-Peters, P. (2015). Maternal emotion socialization differentially predicts third-grade children's emotion regulation and lability. *Emotion, 16*(2), 280–291. doi:10.1037/emo0000142

Sanders, W., Zeman, J., Poon, J., & Miller, R. (2015). Child regulation of negative emotions and depressive symptoms: The moderating role of parental emotion socialization. *Journal of Child and Family Studies, 24*(2), 402–425. doi:10.1007/s10826-013-9850-y

Sprung, M., Münch, H. M., Harris, P. L., Ebesutani, C., & Hofmann, S. G. (2015). Children's emotion understanding; A meta-analysis of training studies. *Developmental Review, 37*, 41–65. doi:10.1016/j.dr.2015.05.001

# 2 Understanding Worry and Anxiety

## Tools for Teachers and Parents

*Nadja Reilly*

Experiencing some worry about school is quite common for children. For example, students might have worries about making new friends, tests, or about how to navigate a transition to a new school. Learning active coping skills can help children understand where their worried thoughts and behaviors are originating and how to manage them. Positive relationships with parents and teachers can also serve as sources of support for students. In this chapter, we will focus on how these positive relationships can be used to teach, model, and reinforce healthy coping strategies to help children successfully overcome their school-related worries.

Children as young as four to six years of age are able to provide self-reports about their worries (Carr & Szabó, 2015). Starting in first grade and continuing through fifth grade, the content of children's worries may focus on natural disasters, traumatic events, and separation. Also, at this time children may begin to worry about negative evaluation from others (Beesdo-Baum & Knappe, 2012). These worries are typically temporary. As children develop a growing sense of control and predictability over their environment, as well as develop more sophisticated ways to manage their emotions, the worries usually disappear, allowing successful adjustment to school and social routines (National Scientific Council on the Developing Child, 2010).

However, for some children, especially those that may be more sensitive, or for whom it may be more difficult to feel in control of their environments, reactions, and emotions, worries can persist. Persistent worries are associated with lower problem-solving ability, confidence, and perceived control, as well as self-depreciating thoughts (Lohbeck, Nitkowski, & Petermann, 2016; Parkinson & Creswell, 2011). Importantly, the worries are not directly related to skills deficits; that is, children may have the actual skills to solve problems, but lack the confidence and perceived ability to enact change (Lohbeck et al., 2016). Therefore, teaching children active ways to problem solve, cope with their worries, and build confidence and self-efficacy are essential in promoting emotional health and wellness.

## Notes from the Field

### *Sasha, Nine-Year-Old Girl*

*Sasha is a bright and sociable young girl who does well in school, has many friends, and enjoys engaging in many different activities. Her parents describe her as a sensitive soul who is very perceptive of how others feel, and of any changes in people or situations. She is always willing to lend a helping hand and prides herself in being a good friend. They also describe her as sensitive to her own emotions. Her feelings, when positive, can be, as they say very big and evident; or when negative, very low and impactful in the moment. Generally, when she experiences these big feelings, with some gentle reassurance and coaching, Sasha is able to bounce back and re-engage in normal activities.*

*One of Sasha's favorite activities is gymnastics, and she has been in classes for several years. Sasha consistently experiences some apprehension the day before gymnastic classes. She worries about what may happen if she feels sick, she worries about her coach not believing her if she is indeed sick, and she worries about what classes may be like in general. These worries occur in anticipation of the class, so car rides to class, as parents describe, can be difficult. But, once Sasha arrives in the class, she seems fine and enjoys being there.*

*Sasha is quite talented, and her coach has been increasingly giving her more advanced routines. Recently, she was invited to participate in a national competition for the first time. Sasha was thrilled to learn of this invitation and shared the happy news with parents while wearing a beautiful bright smile. However, the next day Sasha began to share worries about the competition. She asked her parents questions like "I've never been to the place before—what if I get lost? What if I don't understand what the judges are saying? What if I forget my routine? What if I can't reach you if I need you?" It seemed that each time she thought of some new aspect related to the competition, her worries compounded, and she felt more and more concerned. Her worries manifested not only in her thoughts, but also in her body. Sasha began to complain of stomachaches, headaches, and some nausea. Her already tenuous transition from school to gymnastic class became more difficult, with her worries and body symptoms now also appearing during the school day.*

As Sasha's story indicates, many children struggle with anticipatory worries; that is, worries about some event or situation that might or will come up. Often, this anticipation is linked with worries about not knowing exactly what the event or situation will be like. For children like Sasha, tolerating such uncertainty feels very difficult and may lead to feelings of being "stuck" or not knowing what to do.

***Bella, 11-Year-Old Girl***

*Bella is a kind and conscientious 11-year-old girl in the sixth grade. She has always been quite invested in her academic performance and takes great pride in completing all assignments on time, trying to get the highest grade possible, and not leaving homework until the last minute. Bella worries her teachers may not think she is a hard worker, so she goes out of her way to let her teachers know about all the work she is doing. At times, when Bella has found a new lesson or project difficult, she has asked her teachers many questions, worrying that she may be missing something or that she may not be able to successfully complete the project. With repeated instructions and reassurance from her teachers that she could indeed try something new, Bella was able to proceed with her work.*

*This academic year, Bella transitioned from a small elementary school into a larger middle school, where she began the sixth grade. While her transition has generally been positive, Bella is experiencing significant worries about her math class. She indicated that she was starting to have some of the same worries she had while in fourth grade. In fourth grade, Bella experienced some struggles with her timed math facts. She reported to teachers that she would get "stuck" sometimes and felt like she was forgetting her math facts. At that time, with support and finding strategies that worked for her, Bella was able to successfully complete her timed tests. While she reported that she still felt like her heart was beating faster before tests, she remembered her facts and felt successful.*

*Now that Bella is in middle school, her worries about math have returned. She describes the worries not so much as a fear of the test, but as intense worries that she will not be able to figure out what to do. She is worried that others will notice that she is not good at math and worries that her teacher may be disappointed with her performance.*

Worries about tests, or in a more severe form, test anxiety, are a serious problem for many students. With more frequent tests, standardized testing, and environments of high accountability, everyone in the school environment seems more vulnerable to the effects of test-related anxiety. Worries about tests have indeed become a growing concern among K-12 students, with research citing the onset as early as age seven (Yeo, Goh, & Liem, 2016).

Of particular note is that, in cases such as Bella's, the worry itself interferes with children's ability to recall and utilize learned skills. Upon feeling unable to recall the skills needed, children may in turn feel helpless, not smart, or unable to change their situation. Therefore, even though they indeed know the needed skills to perform in a test and are capable of problem solving, children may start to question their overall abilities and competence (Yeo et al., 2016).

***Logan, 14-Year-Old Boy***

*Logan is a bright, creative, and kind young man who is about to begin ninth grade at the high school. His parents describe Logan as a good student who is motivated to do well academically. He can be initially reserved and somewhat shy in new situations, but once he has had an opportunity to become familiar with the people and setting, he is able to participate and adjust well overall. At home, he has preferred routines for relaxing and doing his work. He has a very good relationship with his parents and seeks their input and help whenever he may feel worried or distressed.*

*Recently, Logan has been sharing with his mother some worries he has about ninth grade. He is feeling a bit uneasy about the move to the large school, wondering how he will find his way around and how he will be able to manage some classes that include students in different grade levels. Logan is also concerned about the different expectations that teachers will have and how he will keep all his work organized based on different teachers' expectations.*

*When his mom tried to reassure him that he would be fine in the ninth grade, Logan indicated that he was not really "worried, worried," but just trying to sort out new things that he would encounter at the high school and thinking about ways that he could manage them. In other words, Logan was trying to anticipate some areas that would be new and was also trying to come up with alternatives to deal with these new situations.*

As Logan's story indicates, some children report that worrying helps to solve problems, be organized, and figure out how to avoid problems in the future (O'Neal & Cotton, 2016). Therefore, it may be that, for some children, worries could be the beginning process of problem solving, where the difficult situations are identified and processed. The next step is not continued worry in terms of perseverating on the fearful or anxious aspects of the thoughts, but a progression to more active problem solving with a clear plan. As Carr and Szabó (2015) indicate, the emergence of such problem-solving aspects may be associated with the development of increasingly complex cognitive coping abilities between middle childhood and early adolescence (p. 130).

## Why It Matters

While the majority of research focuses on adult patterns of worry, a burgeoning field is investigating the developmental progression of worry for children and adolescents (Carr & Szabó, 2015). Generally, normal worrying involves attempts to cope or problem solve. However, the method by which children do this varies by age. For younger children, worry is more closely associated with a fear response, and the experience may involve avoidance and somatic responses of fear (e.g., rapid heartbeat, sweaty palms). Older children, around age nine or 10, as they develop a more complex thinking process, experience worries less as fears and more as thoughts (Carr & Szabó, 2015; Kertz & Woodruff-Borden, 2013). These thoughts, in turn, can lead to different problem-solving strategies. When worried thoughts lead to proactive coping, such as anticipating possible obstacles and figuring out different problem-solving strategies, then the worry has served a positive purpose. Worries may interfere with functioning when either the child is unable to tolerate uncertainty, is unable to control negative thoughts, and/or lacks confidence in his/her ability to solve problems (Carr & Szabó, 2015). Given this important distinction, it is important for parents, caretakers, and teachers to be intentional in understanding the nature of children's worries. Therefore, important interventions to help children develop emotional health and wellness include: (1) promoting an understanding of the thoughts behind the worries; (2) active problem-solving and coping skills; and (3) self-efficacy around effecting change.

There are two general categories of coping skills children may use when distressed: reappraisal and suppression. Reappraisal involves changing the way one thinks about a situation in order to change its emotional impact (Hughes, Gullone, Dudley, & Tonge, 2010). For example, prior to starting a spelling test, a third grader may worry that she will not do well. If she uses reappraisal, she may think "Sometimes I worry about how I will do with spelling, but I know that I studied and practiced my words all week, so I will know the words and will get a good grade on the test." By identifying her worry and changing the way she thought about the situation, this student is able to change her emotions so that they are more positive and calm, thereby allowing herself to focus her attention on the test.

In contrast to this example, children who struggle with worry characterized by high levels of fear or helplessness often use suppression as a coping strategy. Suppression is based on avoidance and involves hiding one's emotional response from others (Hughes et al., 2010). For example, another third-grade student in the same class is also very nervous about the spelling test and worries that she will not do well. She pretends she is fine and does not tell the teacher about her fear of failing. She tries to just ignore her worries. While this student's attempt to just put the worry out of her mind is an effort to decrease experiencing negative emotions, this approach actually increases symptoms of distress (Amstadter, 2008). The key distinction here is that the second child is not actively employing an action-based coping skill to manage her worries (e.g., identifying the fear and challenging negative thoughts) but is instead trying to avoid the emotion altogether. This more passive style of coping does not effectively get rid of the worries, as despite efforts to ignore it, the worries persist, and children are unable to shift their attention away from the fear and threat.

During normative development, starting at around age 9–10, children begin to weigh the short and long-term consequences of different emotion regulation strategies. Younger children typically try to stay away from negative situations in order to avoid negative feelings. Older children, however, consider that initially facing a negative situation may cause intense emotions, but engaging in that situation may lead to problem solving and therefore relief and positive emotion. The long-term positive consequences are viewed as important enough to tolerate the emotional distress in the short-term (Stegge & Terwogt, 2007). For example, while talking to some mutual friends, Lisa, a fifth grader, found out that her best friend Becky was mad at her. Lisa felt sad, confused, and worried about what might have upset Becky. Lisa decided that, although it might feel uncomfortable, she would approach Becky and ask her directly what happened. Lisa understood that, while the initial confrontation might be anxiety-provoking, she would likely find a reason for Becky's upset, and therefore find an opportunity to restore the friendship (Reilly, 2015).

Taken together, teaching children a proactive approach to understanding, tolerating, and managing worries is important for emotional health. Factors that promote emotional well-being include hope, gratitude, self-efficacy, belongingness, prosocial activities, school engagement, and strong relationships with adults (Bandura and Schunk, 1981; Howell, Keyes, & Passmore, 2013). These factors can be taught and practiced within multiple settings, including home and the classroom.

This focus on preventive interventions to promote resilience and positive mental health has highlighted a core group of activities that can help children feel more empowered and successful in their ability to understand and manage their worries (Guva & Hylander, 2012; Stallard et al., 2014). These interventions include:

- Relaxation: focusing on relaxing the body due to tension and sensitivities associated with worries and fears;
- Understanding worry: sharing information about worries and how they impact emotions, thoughts, and actions;
- Changing thoughts by recognizing thinking traps: identifying the negative thoughts that perpetuate worries and create a sense of helplessness;
- Using positive self-talk: changing thoughts to reflect increased possibilities and self-efficacy;
- Facing fears and being brave: encouraging the child to use active coping and confront worrisome situations rather than using avoidance as a primary coping skill; and
- Helping to tolerate ambiguity or uncertainty: helping children tolerate the momentary distress associated with uncertainty and find ways to use coping skills to find more control and efficacy.

When research on children's worries and research on the efficacy of active coping skills are understood in concert, it leads to a clear approach on how to best help children with worries. Rather than labeling all worries as indications of pathology or distress, and therefore trying to dismiss them as a way of managing them, adults should help to promote the aspect of worries that deal with problem-solving attempts. The next section of this chapter will share specific ideas for teachers and parents to help their children.

## Practical Tools for School-Based Professionals

Humans are social beings. There is very little, if any, development and learning that occurs in isolation, and therefore, the quality of relationships has an incredible impact on children's outcomes. In addition to the impact on academic achievement, the teacher–student relationship also has a significant impact on children's emotional development. As Diamond (2010) indicates, "teachers' expectations are part of the students' social world and have powerful effects and shape students' expectations for themselves" (p. 6). Therefore, when teachers are able to model, teach, and practice effective skills for managing worries, children are able to develop and internalize these skills within the context of a safe and nurturing relationship. The tools below may be used in the school setting to help children manage their worries.

- Introduce deep breathing and relaxation exercises to the whole class. This builds an expectation that relaxation is important and useful for all students. This is an example of a breathing exercise you may use, though there are many variations available.

  > Take a slow, deep breath through your nose and exhale out your mouth. Take another deep breath in, feeling your tummy expanding. Now exhale through your mouth, letting all the air out. Let's practice one more time. Deep breath in through your nose, feeling that tummy get large, and deep breath out your mouth, letting out all the air. Now, as you breathe in through your nose, think of a special calming word to yourself. It can be any word you want. As you breathe out your mouth, think of another calming word. It can be any word you like that makes you feel calm and safe. Let's practice the deep breathing again, this time with your special words. Ready? Deep breath in through your nose, think of your word, and breathe out your mouth, thinking of your other special word. Let's do this, two more times.
  >
  > (Reilly, 2015)

- Help students find ways to share the level of worries they are experiencing and create a list of positive ways they can manage those worries.

- Together with your student, create a scale to indicate the level of worry the child is feeling.
  With younger children, you can use symbols:

  ☺ 😐 ☹

  With older children, you can use numbers:

  0 = no worries 3 = some worries 5 = very worried
- Create a list of things the child can do to manage the worries at each level. For example, when the rating is 2 or 3, take three deep breaths and take a movement break. When the rating is at 4 or 5, take a break from the current activity/work and help the teacher with a particular task, or use positive self-statements. These should be written down on a card that the student can reference.

- Identify negative thoughts and use reappraisal and positive self-talk. Worry in children often leads to negative thoughts either about one's ability, about other people's feelings or expectations, or about the likelihood of adverse present or future events. For example, if a child is worried about a test, her negative thoughts may be "I don't think I can pass this test. I can never remember how the teacher taught me to solve these equations." These negative statements, in turn, lead the child to feel helpless and unable to problem solve or effect change. Given these negative thoughts and distressing feelings, the child's resulting behavior might include refusing to go to school, crying, or other actions that would lead to avoiding the test entirely (e.g., asking to go see the school nurse). Reappraisal is an activity where the child is encouraged to identify the negative thoughts that are causing distress and change them into positive self-talk statements. Negative thoughts are general and make the child feel helpless. In contrast, positive self-talk statements are specific, offer encouragement through reminders of self-efficacy, and include an action step. Using the example above, the identified negative thought, "I don't think I can pass this test. I can never remember how the teacher taught me to solve these equations," can be changed to a positive self-talk statement: "I studied really hard for this test and I know the material. If I read one problem at a time and I don't rush I will be able to do my work." The positive self-talk statement offers reminders of self-efficacy ("I studied hard for this test and I know the material") and includes a clear action step ("If I read one question at a time and I don't rush I will be able to do my work"). Teachers can coach their students through this process of reappraisal by following the two main steps of: (1) identifying negative thoughts, and (2) changing the negative thoughts to positive self-talk. More examples of positive self-talk statements can be found in Table 2.1.

*Table 2.1* Positive Self-Talk Statements

| *Negative thought* | *Positive self-talk* |
|---|---|
| "I don't want to work on that group project. Everyone will see that I don't know what I'm doing." | "I have worked on group projects before and I ended up enjoying working with my friends. If I have a question, I can ask my friend who's in the group, or I can ask the teacher." |
| "I have butterflies in my stomach and I'm sweaty—I don't know what's happening and I must be going crazy." | "I know that when I worry, my stomach feels a little upset and I can get sweaty. When I feel these things happening, I can take three deep breaths to relax." |
| "I'm not even going to try; things are going to go wrong anyway." | "If I try and I don't get it the first time, it's OK. That has happened to me before and it's been fine. I'll figure out what did not go well and try something different." |

- Help children learn organization and studying techniques. Often, children worry about things such as not knowing how to approach a project, not knowing how to organize their materials or work, what others may think, and not doing well and disappointing the teacher. Organization techniques such as timetables, schedules, breaking assignments into smaller components, and checking in with a project buddy can all be helpful tools to ameliorate worries. Additionally, it is helpful for teachers to address the social component of worries. Initiating conversations such as "Sometimes we might worry about what others will think about our projects. What could we do for ourselves if those worries come up? What can we do for each other?" will send the direct message to students that they will be supported should they experience those worries.
- Encourage time outside and connection with nature. Allow students time to play in a way that is not focused on sports or competitive play only, but instead focuses on cooperative play and imagination. Promote opportunities for students to interact with and explore nature. Research has found that simply going for a walk in the outdoors or adding plants to a classroom increases students' feelings of comfort, preference, and friendliness, and reduces absences for illness and records of misbehavior (Chawla, Keena, Pevec, & Stanley, 2014).

## Take Home Ideas for Parents

Positive emotions (e.g., hope, joy, pride) are associated with self-efficacy, or a child's perceived ability to produce a particular action regardless of actual abilities (i.e., "I can do it, if I try"; Bandura & Schunk, 1981).

Therefore, parents can play an important role in promoting a child's emotional health by fostering opportunities to develop self-efficacy, active coping, and positive emotions. The following ideas may help parents address worries in their children.

- Help your child name and understand his/her worry. Help your child reflect by asking questions such as

  > Is this the kind of worry that helps you think about a particular situation and how to figure it out, or is it the 'sticky thought' kind of worry that just stays in your head but doesn't help you figure out what to do?

- Validate your child's worries and follow that validation with ideas for problem solving. For example, instead of saying "Everything will be fine, just don't worry about it," you may want to say "It sounds like you're worrying about your science project. Tell me more about how your worries are getting in the way. How can we think about the science project, so it feels less scary?"
- Help your child understand how he/she likes to problem solve. Some children ask many questions in order to have information available to decrease their anxiety. Such a situation may arise when changing to a new school, for example. Help your child gather facts and decrease uncertainty by taking active steps such as visiting the school before he/she begins, meeting some of the teachers, and practicing what the morning routine might be like. If your child seems uncomfortable with some of these suggestions, do not insist upon them, but instead invite him or her to offer ideas for what would be helpful. If your child likes to problem solve by talking through a situation (and sometimes they may do this over and over again!), be an active listener. Do not try to solve the problem for him/her, but instead allow your child to talk through and process the possible solutions. You may want to ask questions like "How can I be helpful? Do you want me to share some ideas or just listen?"
- Help your child change negative thoughts to more positive self-talk statements (see Table 2.1). Changing negative thoughts to specific, action-driven positive self-talk statements can make children feel more empowered to confront difficult situations.
- Encourage bravery! When children are worried about a particular situation or event, they may wish to simply avoid it as a way of dealing with their distress. However, avoidance as a coping skill can lead to increased feelings of helplessness and distress. Instead of allowing your child to avoid the worrisome situation, encourage him/her to persist. It may feel difficult to watch your child feel distressed, but resist the temptation to remove all situations that may be temporarily distressing

for your child. Learning how to tolerate ambiguity and some discomfort is important in developing confidence and self-efficacy.

- When your child steps out of his/her comfort zone, approaches something new, or takes a good risk (e.g., approaching a new peer), highlight and praise the importance of that action later. Use language that focuses on the process rather than on evaluation or judgment of the end result. Focusing on the process highlights that *it is the trying itself* that connotes success, not just the end product. You may share observations such as:

  a. "You weren't sure what to do but you thought about it and made a decision."
  b. "You were worried you would not know anyone at the party, but you still went."
  c. "You tried different ways to finish that project—way to go!"

- Develop a nightly check-in routine. Help your child reflect on his/her day by asking questions such as

  > What was your day like? What were some good things that happened? What were some tough things? What mistakes did you make today? What did you learn from those mistakes? How were you brave today? What are you grateful for?

  This reflective practice helps children use emotion vocabulary, experience safety in sharing feelings and gratitude, and understand that making mistakes is helpful for learning.
- Communicate with your child's teachers often. Sharing home strategies with teachers helps with maintaining consistency for children and helps them practice their coping skills in multiple settings. If you notice that your child is struggling academically, or that his/her anxiety is preventing him from learning, communicate with your child's teacher and inquire about what services are available through the school setting.

Sometimes children may continue to do well academically, yet their worries or anxiety may interfere with other areas of functioning. If you notice increased apprehension in your child, fears about engaging in new or unfamiliar situations, or declines in social functioning, seek out an evaluation from a mental health clinician who works with children. Meeting with a clinician can help to clarify whether ongoing therapeutic services may be helpful, as well as what services and what frequency may be best for your child.

## References


Amstadter, A. (2008). Emotion regulation and anxiety disorders. *Anxiety Disorders, 22*, 211–221. doi:10.1016/j.janxdis.2007.02.004

Bandura, A. & Schunk, D. H. (1981). Cultivating competence, self-efficacy, and intrinsic interest through proximal self-motivation. *Journal of Personality and Social Psychology, 41*, 586–598. doi:10.1037/0022-3514.41.3.586

Beesdo-Baum, K. & Knappe, S. (2012). Developmental epidemiology of anxiety disorders. *Child and Adolescent Psychiatric Clinics of North America, 21*, 457–478. doi:10/1016/j.chc.2012.05.001

Carr, I. & Szabó, M. (2015). Worry in children: Changing associations with fear, thinking, and problem-solving. *Journal of Early Adolescence, 35*(1), 120–135. doi:10.1177/0272431614529366

Chawla, L., Keena, K., Pevec, I., & Stanley, E. (2014). Green schoolyards as havens from stress and resources for resilience in childhood and adolescence. *Health & Place, 28*, 1–13. doi:10.1016/j.healthplace.2014.03.001

Diamond, A. (2010). The evidence base for improving school outcomes by addressing the whole child and by addressing skills and attitudes, not just content. *Early Education Development, 21*(5), 780–793. doi:10/108010409289.2010.514522

Guva, G. & Hylander, I. (2012). Diverse perspectives on pupil health among professionals in school-based multi-professional teams. *School Psychology International, 33*(2), 135–150. doi:10.1177/0143034311415900

Howell, A. J., Keyes, C. L. M., & Passmore, H. A. (2013). Flourishing among children and adolescents: Structure and correlates of positive mental health, and interventions for its enhancement. In C. Proctor & P. A. Linley (Eds.), *Research, applications, and interventions for children and adolescents* (pp. 59–79). Dordrecht, Netherlands: Springer.

Hughes, E. K., Gullone, E., Dudley, A., & Tonge, B. (2010). A case-control study of emotional regulation and school refusal in children and adolescents. *Journal of Early Adolescence, 30*(5), 691–706. doi:10.1177/0272431609341049

Kertz, S. & Woodruff-Borden, J. (2013). The role of metacognition, intolerance of uncertainty, and negative problem orientation in children's worry. *Behavioural and Cognitive Psychotherapy, 41*, 243–248. doi:10.1017/S1352465812000641

Lohbeck, A., Nitkowski, D., & Petermann, F. (2016). A control-value theory approach: Relationships between academic self-concept, interest, and test anxiety in elementary school children. *Child Youth Care Forum, 45*, 887–904. doi:10.1007/s10566-016-9362-1

National Scientific Council on the Developing Child. (2010). *Persistent fear and anxiety can affect young children's learning and development: Working Paper 9*. Retrieved from http://developingchild.net

O'Neal, L. J. & Cotton, S. R. (2016). Promotive factors and psychosocial adjustment among urban youth. *Child Youth Care Forum, 45*, 947–961. doi:10.1007/s10566-016-9364-z

Parkinson, M. & Creswell, C. (2011). Worry and problem-solving skills and beliefs in primary school children. *British Journal of Clinical Psychology, 50*(1), 106–112. doi:10.1348/014466510X523887

Reilly, N. (2015). *Anxiety and depression in the classroom: A teacher's guide to fostering self-regulation in young students* (pp. 36–81; 182). New York, NY: W.W. Norton & Company.

Stallard, P., Skryabina, E., Taylor, G., Phillips, R., Daniels, H., Anderson, R., & Simpson, N. (2014). Classroom-based cognitive behaviour therapy (FRIENDS): A cluster randomised controlled trial to prevent anxiety in children through education in schools (PACES). *The Lancet Psychiatry, 1*(3), 185–192. doi:10.1016/S2215-0366(14)70244-5

Stegge, H. & Terwogt, M. M. (2007). Awareness and regulation of emotion in typical and atypical development. In J. J. Gross (Ed.), *Handbook of emotion regulation* (pp. 269–286). New York, NY: Guilford Press.

Yeo, L. S., Goh, V. G., & Liem, G. A. D. (2016). School based intervention for test anxiety. *Child Youth Care Forum, 45*, 1–17. doi:10.1007/s10566-015-9314-1

# 3 Fostering Social Development in Children

## Strategies for Parents and Teachers

*Barbara Miller and Margaret Hannah*

Children getting along with others, being respectful and polite, and considering the welfare of all with whom they interact are often considered the hallmarks of social development and interpersonal skills. Such skills are integral to many areas of success in life. How do children acquire these skills? Some people feel that such skills are part of "interpersonal intelligence," whereas others think that these skills can be taught through lessons. Whatever it is that mediates these skills for children, it is important to realize there are different ways to foster social development. Yet, in today's societal state of hurriedness, attachment to technology, and hyper focus on academic achievement, interpersonal skills are in peril. It is now more important than ever to make a concerted effort to pay direct attention to them. To this end, the authors offer a framework of "Instruct, Model, Facilitate" (Miller & Hannah, 2017) so that parents and teachers can support each other's efforts and, where appropriate, use play (the activity that comes so naturally to children) as a vehicle to build interpersonal skills.

### Notes from the Field

#### *The Williams*

*The Williams never imagined that parenting could be so difficult. Their life is very hectic as they usher their young children to athletic practice, accelerated math tutoring, and music lessons. They are following the lead of other competitive parents in their community who believe that in order to be successful one has to be accomplished in many ways. In addition, the entire family is totally caught up in technology. Family life is unrecognizable compared to the ones they grew up in.*

#### *Mr. White*

*Mr. White is having significant difficulties managing the behavior of his students in his urban school. He is exasperated with the fact that several students are not kind to each other, are disrespectful to him, and are disrupting learning in the classroom. He is upset that "the parents have not taught these kids how to behave." His style of good old-fashioned discipline is not working, and he is very worried that the principal will give him a poor evaluation due to inadequate class management.*

### *Ms. Smith*

*Ms. Smith is a fourth-grade teacher in a suburban middle-class town. Student academic achievement is very important in this town and when the annual state-wide accountability testing has been completed the results are published in the town paper and reported by each school so that the elementary schools can be compared. The teachers have come to feel more and more pressure to focus on academics and the outcome data of high-stakes testing. One way that Ms. Smith supports student learning is that, if students have not completed their classwork, or if they have not brought in their homework, she uses recess time to have them do the work. She says that many teachers do this because there are only so many hours in a school day and there is so much material to cover.*

These scenarios reflect the manner in which contemporary life is negatively affecting opportunities for social skill development in our children. Now consider the following scenario, where the commitment to the value of social development is front and center.

### *Jackie and Lisa*

*Jackie (mom of Alex, age five) invites Matthew (age four years, nine months) and his mom, Lisa, over for a playdate. As Lisa and Matthew arrive, Alex immediately greets them with a smile and takes Matthew's hand and leads him to the play area saying, "I have some new toys we can play with." Matthew hesitates a little, but Lisa encourages Matthew to join with Alex in play, and the two boys head to the play area of the living room. Soon Jackie and Lisa can hear Alex and Matthew talking in raised voices; one can hear Matthew saying, "I don't want to play with the train anymore" and Alex is saying clearly, "I want you to play with the train. Will you play a little longer with me and with the train and then we can play with what you want to play with?" Both mothers want to intervene yet hold themselves back hoping the boys will work it out. There is silence from the play area for what seems to be a long period of time but is actually only two minutes. Lisa and Jackie check in on the boys and observe two quiet boys sharing a game with the train. Jackie comments to both boys that she notices how nicely they are playing with the train and wonders out loud to Alex, "Alex, I wonder if Matthew would like to choose a new toy to play with now."*

This vignette could have gone very differently. The boys might have needed instruction on how to take turns, or they might have needed modeling to show how to share time and toys. The interaction could have gone completely awry and the boys may have needed to be separated. In this situation, the parents chose to not intervene and then intentionally reinforced and instructed appropriate social skills. Through modeling and facilitation of the environment, the adult promoted the formation of a relationship. As it played out, this interaction and potential friendship has the foundational underpinnings for success, and Alex and Matthew will likely continue to want to spend time together.

Fostering these skills requires being mindful of developmental stages and applying different emphasis on particular skills, all the while looking through a framework of *instructing, modeling, or facilitating*. An interaction with a child might include the flexible use of one or more of the components of this framework, which are defined as follows:

- Instruct. Teaching appropriate skills very explicitly, with more emphasis on the appropriate skill or behavior versus the undesirable one. For example, an adult teaching please and thank you explicitly says, "Billy, I am going to hand you a book and before I let go I will be expecting you to say the words thank you."
- Model. Intentionally modeling the interpersonal skills of value. Modeling appropriate interpersonal skills actually accomplishes two things: teaching a way to interact appropriately by "showing" and creating a healthy, respectful relationship which has direct benefit to the child. For example, "Billy, now please pass the book to me."
- Facilitate. Providing opportunities for children to display and practice their skills. When facilitating social skill and relationship building, the adult intentionally looks for ways to let the situation or environment work for the child and the skill lesson at hand. Again, using Billy as an example, an adult could bring Billy to a group of children and encourage him to use "please" as a way to enter the group.

## Why It Matters

Certain children and adults are described as "a pleasure to spend time with." What exactly underlies this description? It has to do with interpersonal skills, which are the skills that people use to interact with others successfully and appropriately; the skills that affect a person's relationships with other people.

### *Interpersonal Skills*

Interpersonal skills have been referred to as communication skills, social skills, soft skills, or people skills (National Research Council, 2011).

Interpersonal skills include many components, such as communication, listening, attitude, and composure. Possessing good interpersonal skills requires an understanding of which behaviors are typical and expected within the culture. Individuals with good interpersonal skills are tuned in to the reactions of the people with whom they interact and are flexible in adjusting their part of the interaction accordingly (Garcia-Winner, 2013).

Following an extensive review of the literature, a broad definition of the term social competence is offered by Huitt and Dawson (2011), who conclude that the six fundamental components include: being aware of emotions (both your own and others'); managing impulses and behavior; communicating effectively; forming healthy and meaningful relationships; working well with others; and resolving conflicts.

In the workplace, interpersonal skills are referred to as soft skills, which are a complement to hard skills (the employee's knowledge and occupational skills). Goleman, Boyatzis and McKee (2013), use the term "EQ" or "Emotional Intelligence Quotient," as opposed to "IQ" or "Intelligence Quotient," to describe the cluster of personality traits, social graces, communication, language, personal habits, friendliness, and optimism that characterize one's relationships with other people.

Individuals with a well-developed set of interpersonal skills have an easier time succeeding in their professional, personal, and academic lives (Carmeli, Brueller, & Dutton, 2009; National Association of School Psychologists, 2002). They get along better with peers, work better in groups, can lead well, are able to manage their emotions under pressure, can clearly express their thoughts and feelings, can persuade others in a thoughtful and diplomatic way, and so on. People with good interpersonal skills appear confident and have a positive perspective. Those who lack these abilities frequently experience failure and frustration when attempting to interact with others. Poor interpersonal skills are seen in the child who appears lonely and isolated from the other children on the playground; a professional colleague who consistently annoys others; or an overly meek or aggressive superior.

There are numerous benefits associated with social competence, including:

- Increased mental and physical health (e.g., Merrell & Gimpel, 2014; Semrud-Clikeman, 2007);
- Higher career and financial success (e.g., Semrud-Clikeman, 2007);
- Positive self-assessment in terms of self-esteem and self-confidence (Merrell & Gimpel, 2014); and
- Academic success (e.g., Malecki & Elliott, 2002; Merrell & Gimpel, 2014).

In a longitudinal analysis of the relationship between social behaviors and academic achievement, Malecki and Elliott (2002) reported that social skills were positively predictive of concurrent academic achievement. In fact, they were the best predictor of future academic functioning. An increase in social skills was commensurate with increases in academic learning. They concluded that it doesn't mean that social skills make you smarter; it means that these skills make you more amenable to learning. Caprara, Barbaranelli, Pastorelli, Bandura, and Zimbardo (2000) found that children's social competence in third grade predicted changes in achievement in eighth grade.

Interpersonal skills evolve throughout the course of development and become more sophisticated with time (Fisher & Roccotagliata, 2017). It is worth keeping in mind the above-mentioned expectations for adult social skills when raising and teaching children. After all, this is where they are headed. In addition, one must keep in mind that there is likely variability in the specific skills different adults most value.

The top 10 social skills children need to succeed in school, based on surveys of 8,000 elementary teachers and two decades of classroom research, are (Elliott & Gresham, 2007):

- Listen to others;
- Follow the steps;
- Follow the rules;
- Ignore distractions;
- Ask for help;
- Take turns when you talk;
- Get along with others;
- Stay calm with others;
- Be responsible for your behavior; and
- Do nice things for others.

These are fundamental behaviors for overall success in our socially conscious world. Children need to be more than just cooperative; it is important for them to advocate for themselves and care for others. Finally, according to this study, the social skills valued by teachers and children have remained remarkably consistent (i.e., unchanging from the years 1989–2006).

Students in middle school and high school have more complex social skills to learn, due to heightened peer pressure and other developmental tensions of adolescence (Windell, 1999). There is tension between growing independence and needing to belong to a peer group, between vying for independent decision making, and in worrying about being judged. Windell concluded that adolescents can learn to be more emotionally intelligent if they learn to:

- Set personal goals;
- Identify and change self-defeating behaviors;

- Be assertive about his or her needs;
- Have feelings for others;
- Handle anger constructively; and
- Resolve conflicts peacefully.

When presented with evidence that interpersonal skills are crucial, it is important for parents and teachers to intentionally address them—especially as the lure of technology continues to take children away from the experience of meaningful face-to-face human interaction.

### *Framework of "Instruct, Model, Facilitate" for Home*

#### *Instruct*

The very busy and highly scheduled Williams family has to make deliberate decisions about which of the many components of interpersonal skills they explicitly want to draw attention to. Interestingly, a perusal of some popular contemporary websites suggests that parents still value the importance of respect, consideration of others, and good manners (Markham, n.d.). Parents need to be clear and specific about what they want to see in their children's behavior.

Parents should also bear in mind that it is possible to shape social competence by how one describes situations to a child. Mize, Pettit, Laird, and Lindsey (1993) suggest that parents replace saying: "That kid is mean, he doesn't want to play with you" with, "Maybe he has other ideas about what he feels like doing" to teach the child an optimistic, resilient attitude toward social setbacks and to instill the belief that social situations can be improved with effort and positive behavior. This also addresses perspective taking and empathy.

For preteens and young adolescents, instruction may be more like coaching and role-playing. For example, using role-playing to handle interactions that feel awkward, or to demonstrate how to make a persuasive argument (Markham, n.d.).

#### *Model*

Modeling positive interpersonal skills might include showing confidence when we relate to others, being friendly to people we meet, offering to help others, and also treating our children with respect (Mize et al., 1993; Mize & Pettit, 2010). As we become more wed to our technology than ever, it is becoming increasingly imperative to model active listening. This is accomplished by making eye contact, removing distractions, and by acknowledging attention and interest by nodding and asking follow-up questions.

### *Facilitate*

The Williams must also make a conscious decision about how they will provide opportunities to practice social behaviors. Developing interpersonal skills is best done within social interaction (Zins, Payton, Weissberg, & O'Brien, 2007). Play provides a perfect opportunity to both learn and practice these skills. Children will learn crucial skills by simply playing with their parent(s). Children whose parents frequently play with them have more advanced social skills and get along better with their peers (Mize & Pettit, 2010). This is especially true if parents play with them on their level, following their lead and in a "peer-like" manner. Through such play, children can learn what more socially competent behavior looks like (as the parent models it). In addition, they have an opportunity to experience the fun in play, and to feel competent (Mize et al., 1993). So, in spite of the fact that parents have a million things to do, and in spite of the fact that they would probably prefer doing something of more interest to them, there is a great pay-off to playing with their child.

Children learn social skills from parents but also to a very large degree from their peers, so parents should make sure to encourage friendships and arrange playdates. Parents should also use each rich opportunity the way Jackie and Lisa did in the play scenario described previously. These parents made very conscious decisions about whether it was time to step in and instruct, or not, and to balance the degree to which the play was child-led or adult-directed. They kept in mind that undirected play allows children to learn how to work with others, to share, to negotiate, to resolve conflicts, and to learn self-advocacy skills (Smith & Lotyczewski, 2016).

## *Framework of "Instruct, Model, Facilitate" for School*

Since interpersonal skills have such high-stakes importance for lifetime personal and employment success, and even academic success, schools need to partner with parents in teaching interpersonal skills to students (Albright & Weissberg, 2010). Mr. White must first alter his conviction that teaching interpersonal skills is the sole responsibility of the parents. He can then consider the framework as a vehicle to implement change in his classroom.

### *Instruct*

Mr. White can build explicit instruction around some specific social behaviors he would like to see in the classroom. O'Connor, Strawhun, Hoff, and Peterson (2014) describe a number of published evidence-based curricula that address explicit instruction in various aspects of social skills. Additionally, Mr. White should give children positive feedback for engaging in healthy social interactions, and he might share information about how he is fostering social interaction with the family members of his students.

### *Model*

Mr. White might be reminded that, according to social cognitive theory, students develop many skills by watching other people perform those skills (Bandura, 1986). Teachers can serve as live models to teach social behaviors and positive communication skills. Thus, teachers as role models foster interpersonal skills by modeling positive social interactions and creating positive relationships.

Additional benefits accrue, because modeling contributes to caring and secure relationships between teachers and students. Students not only see the display of appropriate behavior but also benefit from the teacher–student relationship that is developed because of this respectful behavior. Rimm-Kaufman and Sandilos (2011) confirm that teacher–student relationships provide essential supports for learning by contributing to students' resiliency, reducing the prevalence of bullying, and improving peer relationships, and are the foundation for developing a safe and supportive classroom climate. Additionally, studies have demonstrated an association between teacher–student relationships and academic achievement (Rimm-Kaufman & Sandilos, 2011).

Mr. White might re-think his style of discipline and become more aware of his interaction style and its subtle influences on students. Students will note whether he shows warmth and respect toward them, to other students, and to adults at school. They will notice how he manages his emotions and just might model their own behavior after his (Jones, Bouffard, & Weissbourd, 2013).

### *Facilitate*

There are good examples provided from early education about the importance of how the physical and social environments can be arranged by teachers to facilitate social development (Lynch & Simpson, 2010):

- Offer materials that are motivating, novel, and culturally sensitive;
- Select materials that are relevant to students' needs, interests, and lives;
- Include materials and activities that promote social interaction;
- Give students ideas for using the materials or suggest ways to engage in an interactive activity;
- Provide visual cues in the environment that support and promote social interaction;
- Consider the impact of the social environment;
- Take students' characteristics into consideration when grouping children;
- Consider the number of students in each group or center to maximize social interaction;
- Pair socially competent students with shy or less socially skilled students;

- Give students with limited social skills many opportunities to interact with others;
- Replace a disciplinary style with one of facilitating more appropriate student interaction; and
- Use recess as an opportunity for learning and practicing interpersonal skills through play.

Growing evidence links recess to improved physical health, social skills, and cognitive development. Ms. Smith needs to know that the American Academy of Pediatrics (AAP) recommends that recess should never be withheld as a punishment, or minimized, because it serves as a fundamental component of development and social interaction that students may not receive in a more complex school environment (Ginsburg, 2007). A well-functioning and facilitated recess can foster supportive relationships among students and provide opportunities for social involvement, leadership, negotiation, conflict resolution, and other life skills (AAP, 2013). Principals report that after recess children listen better, are more focused, have better social development, and report better general well-being (Jarrett, 2013). Furthermore, there is no evidence that mandated standardized test scores are improved by keeping children in class longer without recess (Jarrett & Waite-Stupiansky, 2009). In fact, in one study, third graders who had more recess time behaved better and were also more responsive to academic instruction (Barros, Silver, & Stein, 2009). Play should not be an afterthought in the schools, and we must pay attention to the value it serves in social development (Miller & Almon, 2009).

## Practical Tools for School-Based Professionals

- Make the fostering of social skills a home–school collaborative effort.
- Embrace the idea that interpersonal skills are as important as academic skills. Keep in mind that these skills are really life skills, which are necessary both during childhood and throughout adulthood.
- Take a proactive stance on fostering interpersonal skills by discussing appropriate social skills and behavior with students and modeling positive interactions.
- Be proactive; do not wait for negative interactions to arise in the classroom.
- Do not take recess away as a punishment, and do not use recess time to accomplish schoolwork. Recess provides an important opportunity in the school day for social development. Taking away recess can have a negative effect on not only social skills but also cognitive development, physical health, and academic achievement.
- Develop a supervision plan for recess in such a way that it becomes a genuinely facilitated play opportunity to foster social development as well as a time to burn off energy. Recess provides opportunities to

practice skills such as conflict resolution and for learning from other children and from the adults who model and facilitate the interactions.

- Pay attention to each child's ability to handle interpersonal social situations that involve following directions, holding age-appropriate conversations, listening, managing transition times, dealing with teasing and bullying, showing empathy, or being able to maintain at least a couple of friendships.
- Remind yourself of the connection between interpersonal skills and both academic success and well-managed classrooms.
- Foster social development at teachable moments, looking through the lens of the "Instruct, Model, Facilitate" framework.

Assess yourself by asking:

- Which interpersonal skills do I really value or want to reinforce?
- Am I instructing the skills that contribute to interpersonal competence?
- Am I modeling good interpersonal skills with adults and children?
- Am I advocating for giving attention to the development of interpersonal skills, maintaining well-supervised recess, and providing opportunities for play, both self-directed and directed?
- How am I relating to students?
- Do I want to consider videotaping or audiotaping myself, devising a student questionnaire, or asking the school psychologist or another colleague to observe me?

## Take Home Ideas for Parents

The AAP recommends that all children should get ample, unscheduled, independent, non-screen time to be creative, to reflect, and to decompress. Additionally, AAP emphasizes the advantages of active play and discourages parents from the overuse of passive entertainment (e.g., television and computer games). It also recommends that, although parents should certainly monitor play for safety, a large proportion of play should be child-driven rather than adult-directed.

- Do not underestimate the value of play. Arrange playdates, play with your child, and provide time for your child to simply play alone. Monitor play, keeping in mind the framework of Instruct, Model, Facilitate.
- Avoid being too much of a helicopter parent; give your child an opportunity to practice resolving a conflict before stepping in.
- When you buy toys, consider the place of electronic toys in your plans for facilitating social development (Levin & Rosenquest, 2001). Make sure that as part of your child's toy collection there are plenty of toys that encourage creative, imaginative play.

Assess yourself by asking:

- Which interpersonal skills do I really value or want to reinforce?
- Am I instructing the skills that contribute to interpersonal competence?
- Am I modeling good interpersonal skills with adults and children?
- Am I advocating for school personnel to attend to the development of interpersonal skills, to maintain a well-supervised recess, and to provide opportunities for play, keeping in mind both self-directed and directed forms of play?
- Do I make it clear that interpersonal skills are as important as academic skills?
- Am I balancing extracurricular and structured activities with free time, and am I providing opportunities for my child to focus on friends?
- Do I have a family plan for how and when we will use technology? Have I created boundaries to prevent too much tech-time? Most importantly, am I concerned about technology hurting my children's interpersonal skills?
- How do I judge my child's ability to handle interpersonal social situations that involve following directions, holding an age-appropriate conversation, listening, managing transition times, teasing and bullying, showing empathy, or being able to maintain at least a couple of friendships? Does this issue require additional coaching?
- Do I know who to contact at the school, in addition to the teacher, if I have some concerns?

We can all foster social development by thinking about the different types of interpersonal skills, their subcomponents, and their application to the day-to-day activities in a child's life.

## References

Albright, M. I. & Weissberg, R. P. (2010). School-family partnerships to promote social and emotional learning. In S. L. Christenson & A. L. Reschly (Eds.), *Handbook of school-family partnerships* (pp. 246–265). New York, NY: Routledge.

American Academy of Pediatrics (2013, January). Policy statement: The crucial role of recess in school. *Pediatrics, 131*(1), 183–188. Retrieved from http://pediatrics.aappublications.org/content/131/1/183

Bandura, A. (1986). *Social foundations of thought and action: A social cognitive theory*. Englewood Cliffs, NJ: Prentice-Hall.

Barros, R. M., Silver, E. J., & Stein, R. E. K. (2009). School recess and group classroom behavior. *Pediatrics, 123*(2), 431–436. doi:10.1542/peds.2007-2825

Caprara, G. V., Barbaranelli, C., Pastorelli, C., Bandura, A., & Zimbardo, P. G. (2000). Prosocial foundations of children's academic achievement. *Association for Psychological Science, 11*(4), 302–306. doi:10.1111/1467-9280.00260.

Carmeli, A., Brueller, D., & Dutton, J. E. (2009). Learning behaviours in the workplace and the role of high quality interpersonal relationships and psychological safety. *Systems Research and Behavioural Science, 26*, 81–98. doi:10.1002/sres.932

Elliott, S. & Gresham, F. (2007). Top 10 social skills students need to succeed. Retrieved from https://news.vanderbilt.edu/2007/09/27/top-10-social-skills-students-need-to-succeed-58465/

Fisher, C. L. & Roccotagliata, T. (2017, February). Interpersonal communication across the life span. *Oxford Research Encyclopedia of Communication.* doi:10.1093/acrefore/9780190228613.013.201

Garcia-Winner, M. (2013). *Why teach social thinking?* Santa Clara, CA: Think Social Publishing, Inc.

Ginsburg, K. R. (2007, January). The importance of play in promoting healthy child development and maintaining strong parent-child bonds. *Pediatrics, 119*(1), 182–191. doi:10.1542/peds.2006-2697

Goleman, D., Boyatzis, R., & McKee, A. (2013). *Primal leadership: Unleashing the power of emotional intelligence.* Boston, MA: Harvard Business Review Press.

Huitt, W. G. & Dawson, C. (2011, April). Social development: Why it is important and how to impact it. *Educational Psychology Interactive.* Valdosta, GA: Valdosta State University. Retrieved from www.edpsycinteractive.org/papers/socdev.pdf

Jarrett, O. S. (2013, November). A research-based case for recess. Retrieved from www.allianceforchildhood.org/sites/allianceforchildhood.org/files/file/Recess_online.pdf

Jarrett, O. S. & Waite-Stupiansky, S. (2009, September). Recess—it's indispensable! *Young Children, 66–69.* Retrieved from www.elegantbrain.com/edu4/classes/readings/depository/294/recess_time.pdf

Jones, S. M., Bouffard, S. M., & Weissbourd, R. (2013). Educators' social and emotional skills vital to learning. *Kappan Magazine, 94*(8), 62–65. doi:10.1177/003172171309400815

Levin, D. E. & Rosenquest, B. (2001). The increasing role of electronic toys in the lives of infants and toddlers: Should we be concerned? *Contemporary Issues in Early Childhood, 2*(2), 242–247. doi:10.2304/ciec.2001.2.2.9

Lynch, S. A. & Simpson, C. G. (2010). Social skills: Laying the foundations for success. *Dimensions of Early Childhood, 38*(2), 3–12. Retrieved from www.southernearlychildhood.org/upload/pdf/Social_Skills_Laying_the_Foundation_for_Success_Sharon_A_Lynch_and_Cynthia_G_Simpson_Volume_38_Issue_2_1.pdf

Malecki, C. K. & Elliott, S. N. (2002). Children's social behaviors as predictors of academic achievement: A longitudinal analysis. *School Psychology Quarterly, 17*(1), 1–23. doi:10.1521/scpq.17.1.1.19902

Markham, Laura. (n.d.). How to raise a socially intelligent child. Retrieved from www.ahaparenting.com/parenting-tools/socially-intelligent

Merrell, K. W. & Gimpel, G. A. (2014) *Social skills of children and adolescents: Conceptualization, assessment, treatment.* New York, NY: Taylor and Francis.

Miller, B. & Hannah, M. (2017). *Fostering social development in children.* Manuscript in preparation.

Miller, E. & Almon, J. (2009). *Crisis in the kindergarten: Why children need to play in school.* College Park, MD: Alliance for Childhood. Retrieved from www.allianceforchildhood.org/sites/allianceforchildhood.org/files/file/kindergarten_report.pdf

Mize, J. & Pettit, G. S. (2010, December). The mother–child playgroup as socialization context: A short term longitudinal study of mother–child–peer relationship dynamics. *Early Child Development and Care, 180*(10), 1271–1284. doi:10.1080/03004430902981470

Mize, J., Pettit, G. S., Laird, R. D., & Lindsey, E. (1993, April). *Mothers' coaching of social skills and children's peer competence: Independent contributions of substance and style.* Paper presented at the biennial meeting of the Society for Research in Child Development, New Orleans, LA.

National Association of School Psychologists (2002). *Social skills: Promoting positive behavior, academic success, and school safety.* Bethesda, MD. Retrieved from www.naspcenter.org/factsheets/socialskills_fs.html

National Research Council (2011). *Assessing 21st century skills: Summary of a workshop.* Washington, DC: The National Academies Press. doi:10.17226/13215

O'Connor, A., Strawhun, J., Hoff, N., & Peterson, R. L. (2014, March). Examples of social skills curricula and programs. (*Resource Brief.*) Lincoln, NE: Student Engagement Project, University of Nebraska. Retrieved from http://k12 engagement.unl.edu/strategy-briefs/Resources%20for%20Social%20Skills%20 Curricula%209-22-2014_0.pdf

Rimm-Kaufman, S. & Sandilos, L. (2011). *Improving students' relationships with teachers to provide essential supports for learning: Positive relationships can also help a student develop socially.* Retrieved from www.apa.org/education/k12/ relationships.aspx

Semrud-Clikeman, M. (2007). *Social competence in children.* New York, NY: Springer. doi:10.1007/978-0-387-71366-3

Smith, L. & Lotyczewski, S. (2016). *Primary Project: 2015–2016 Rochester City School District (RCSD) program outcome summary.* Retrieved from www. childrensinstitute.net/sites/default/files/documents/primary-project_rcsd-program-outcome-summary.pdf

Windell, J. (1999). *Teaching social skills to your teen: Six steps to an emotionally intelligent teenager.* New York, NY: Wiley.

Zins, J. E., Payton, J. W., Weissberg, R. P., & O'Brien, M. U. (2007). Social and emotional learning for successful school performance. In G. Matthews, M. Zeidner, & R. D. Roberts (Eds.), *The science of emotional intelligence: Knowns and unknowns* (pp. 376–395). New York, NY: Oxford University Press.

# 4 Talking with Children About Race

*Elana Wolkoff, Ronda Goodale, and Gemima St. Louis*

Children often bring up the topic of race, frequently leaving parents and teachers uncomfortable and confused about how to respond, perhaps even avoiding the topic altogether. Children in white families are often in the majority in their communities; as a result, these topics may not arise naturally, making the occasional question or observation potentially awkward for parents and other caretakers. In contrast, due to experiences of racism and discrimination, these discussions occur frequently, even on a daily basis, in many families of color. Regardless of family makeup, parents, guardians, and teachers are in key positions to make these conversations productive and to set a framework for successful relationships in a diverse society. The practices that are shared in this chapter are intended to help white parents and educators, who may be less experienced or comfortable discussing race and privilege, to engage in these conversations more effectively with children of all races.

## Why It Matters

Conversations about race are critical for children and avoiding them comes at a high cost. Young people observe awkward, distant, or strained dynamics between people of different races. They need to have their perceptions validated and their understanding developed to become socially competent. If children are not given this opportunity, they are unable to move past their initial perceptions and biases. The lack of discussion breeds discomfort, which can turn into rejection of people who are different. For youths who struggle to develop a positive racial identity, this lack of opportunity further impacts them by resulting in the development of a negative self-concept which can impede healthy development.

Race is an integral part of the developmental experience in the United States, even when there is limited interaction, and conversations can be valuable tools for increasing understanding. Parents and educators share that these conversations are important; they also emphasize the numerous obstacles to having them. Practice makes these conversations easier and the discomforts less of an obstacle. As one educator said, "Everything about this conversation is hard, that's why no one wants to have them.... Doesn't change how important they are" (Wolkoff, Goodale, & St. Louis, 2017).

In U.S. society, race is inextricably linked to opportunity and privilege. It is important that children understand this relationship, so that they can accurately discern what underlies social and economic inequities. Many educators have advocated for a greater focus on race in the K-12 school curricula and suggest that providing students with an historical context of race relations and disproportionate access to opportunity in the United States makes these conversations more productive (Wolkoff et al., 2017).

In a recent survey (Wolkoff et al., 2017), educators expressed the importance of acknowledging the many ways that racism affects our daily interactions, including ways in which it is embedded in our school structures. They observe the frustration frequently experienced by students of color in regard to feeling they are not being heard or that listeners are unreceptive to a view that is different than their own. Students' reports of differential treatment in regard to school disciplinary practices are supported by Department of Education data (U.S. Department of Education Office for Civil Rights, 2014). However, students of color have reported being fearful to speak about their experiences and lacking trust that their perspectives would be taken seriously (Wolkoff et al., 2017).

### *Children's Developmental Understanding of Race*

Children of different ages have distinct abilities to understand race and conversations need to be developmentally appropriate. While younger children tend to focus on visible similarities and differences, older children can begin to understand the implications of race and how their personal experiences fit into the larger society. As one parent offered,

> I think starting young is great because it's good practice for making potentially difficult conversations easier ... treating race like anything else that is important ... we name body parts ... we name skin colors.... We read books about race and discuss it often.
>
> (Wolkoff et al., 2017)

#### *Preschoolers*

Preschoolers often focus on classifications and identifying who is "like me" and who is different. "We both have curly hair." "He has a penis, but I don't." They also learn colors and may apply those to the people around them. "She has light brown skin and mine is dark brown." Such comments rarely contain any judgment; rather, they are observations and represent children's efforts to understand how they fit in with those around them (Derman-Sparks, Higa, & Sparks, 1980). Preschoolers tend to notice shared qualities and children of color may be excited when they notice that someone's skin is a similar shade to their own.

Children at this age tend to think in very concrete terms and their reasoning is generally limited to what they can see. They may be confused about why people who look very different from each other may be categorized as alike; for example, people with light brown and dark brown skin may all be identified as being black. Because the range of skin tones that our society determines to be black and white are social constructs and are not intuitive, they can be confusing to young children who are just learning society's implicit rules.

Children often wonder how someone got their skin color or other physical characteristics and whether these characteristics will change over time. A child may ask, "Did Jennifer get white skin because she only drinks white milk?" Because they know that so much changes as they grow up, young children have a poor sense of which physical characteristics are permanent and which are transient (Biles, 1994) and may ask questions, such as, "Will Elijah have dark skin when he grows up like his daddy?" They expect that children will look like their parents and may become confused when they do not.

### *Elementary School*

In the early elementary grades, children become more social; they begin to develop multiple alliances and to enjoy learning about and connecting with people who are different from themselves. This is an excellent time to promote the development of a coherent community within the classroom. Even in a homogeneous setting, the early development of positive relationships with a broader group of children provides a foundation for future relationships in a multicultural society.

Children often repeat what is said to test it out, even if they anticipate it will not be well received. If adults are prepared, comments based on stereotypes or misinformation can be clarified. As they notice injustices within their own environment and become focused on fairness, children benefit from being exposed to developmentally appropriate examples of injustices in the larger community (Derman-Sparks et al., 1980). It is important to incorporate into these discussions the power of individuals to promote justice, whether in the classroom or in the larger community.

While children begin with the concrete perspective that things are only fair if everyone gets the same thing, with guidance they can develop a greater capacity to understand that people have distinct needs and require different resources in order to have equal access (Kuh, LeeKeenan, Given, & Beneke, 2016). This provides the foundation for an understanding of both equity and social justice.

Because of their greater awareness of racial differences, children of color are more likely to notice examples of unequal treatment and to wonder whether to attribute negative reactions to an individual's group identity. As they move through the elementary grades, all children can be helped to understand dynamics associated with racism, the fact that they are not inevitable, and the ability of individual people to promote change. If forums for discussion have been created, children are more likely to raise these issues, and are less likely to experience a sense of confusion and powerlessness.

### *Middle School*

As children progress toward middle school, frank and respectful discussions of current events and both classroom and community dynamics can provide the opportunity to clarify misconceptions. Children at this developmental level are eager for accurate information on human behavior. They should be taught about prejudice and stereotypes and prepared to recognize when they are present. They should also be taught to recognize commonalities in human experience. Most importantly, children need to feel that these subjects are "speakable" and that they have a forum for open and honest conversations to help them understand the complexities of human interactions in a diverse society.

### *High School*

As teenagers venture out with greater independence, their interactions are likely to expose them to examples of both explicit racism and implicit bias. It is important for young people to have their experiences and observations validated by adults, so that they trust their own perceptions and can think clearly about the most effective ways to respond. Being able to have these conversations with adults of different races builds interracial understanding.

### *Be Aware of your Cultural Lens*

Students of color often report being treated unfairly or having assumptions made about them because of their race (Wolkoff et al., 2017). While some of these negative experiences may be instigated by explicit racism, they also occur despite the belief of white adults that they are being fair and equitable. Culturally based norms of behavior and communication define expectations, causing people to have reactions without even being conscious of them. This is often called implicit bias. Let's consider this scenario on a Monday when Jared and his friend Alenzo, who are both black, are transitioning to math class:

*Jared and Alenzo haven't seen each other since Friday and are happy to reconnect. Jared yells to Alenzo when he sees him entering the room. Alenzo bumps into him playfully and Jared smacks him on the head, laughing. Jared backs up and bangs into the table behind him. Both boys are laughing. The teacher, Ms. Cooper, who is white, says, "Enough acting like wild animals; let's focus on math." Jared's mood changes. "Is she calling us wild animals? Would she have called us wild animals if we were white?" He becomes increasingly irritable as the class progresses. He keeps thinking about what he would like to say to Ms. Cooper and has trouble paying attention. Ms. Cooper takes note of his change in mood and thinks to herself how inconsistent he is, one minute happy and the next irritable. She had been thinking about which math class to recommend him for the following year. Although he sometimes gets good grades, his work is inconsistent. She worries that between his moodiness, which causes him to miss instruction, and the fact that there is nobody at home in the afternoons and evenings who can help him with higher level math work, that a lower level class may be better.*

Ms. Cooper's impatience with the boys' physicality may be a result of both her own culturally based interpersonal style and her natural desire to begin instruction. Most importantly, she is unaware of the impact of her words on her students. As adults, we must make every effort to be aware of our own culturally based expectations for behavior and performance and to work with young people to address negative interactions so that we do not create obstacles to their success.

## Notes from the Field

The authors recognize that there are multiple racial groups in the United States, each with their own experiences. Due to the unique history of black/white relations in this country, these scenarios were designed to focus primarily on dynamics related to this experience.

### *Adena*[1]

*Adena was a biracial girl born to a middle-class family, with a white mother and an African American father. She had two half siblings that were white. Her classmates often questioned her about whether she was adopted. She was never sure how to respond. After several years of struggling silently, Adena asked her mother if she was adopted. Her mother explained that she was not and added, "You look like your dad's mom. Let's look at the pictures." They revisited this conversation again and again.*

*Adena lived in a primarily white suburban district and attended local schools. Many of the students of color in her school attended as part of a voluntary desegregation program that brought children from a neighboring city. Adena reported experiencing painful responses from black students from urban areas, who often teased her. She felt that teachers and administrators anticipated that she would easily connect with the black students based on their common race. They seemed not to grasp different personalities, or the gap created when children of color from different socioeconomic backgrounds are placed together with the assumption that the fact that they are not white will connect them. Adena commented:*

> *I remember people saying I was adopted ... finding common ground with a Native American student because we were in classes together and we were the only students of color. I remember always thinking it was a race thing that I was in special education. I was so angry. I remember (being teased by the other kids). I would listen to music to tune them out, but teachers would say headphones weren't allowed, which meant I just had to endure their taunts.*

*It took years for Adena to share her experiences with adults. It surfaced in a conversation with her parents when she was in high school. Once they were aware of the situation, they were able to work with the school to support her more effectively. Adena's mother said:*

> *It is important for educators to understand potential isolation and provide options for students. Some rules like no headphones can make the difference between surviving in high school and feeling defeated. Providing a range of options for students is key, anticipating the potential roadblocks.*

### *Jason*

*Seven-year-old Jason was white, as were all of his family members. He lived in an urban area and attended a public school with a diverse population. Jason, his mother, and older cousin, Mark, were watching a TV program in which a talk show host was interviewing a racially diverse group of high school valedictorians. Mark commented, "Wow! Look at how many of them are black!" Jason turned, confused, and asked, "Why does it matter that they are black?"*

*Jason's mother knew that his comment was associated with a level of privilege. He was unaware of the disproportionate number of obstacles and access to opportunity for people of different races in the U.S. as well as a stereotype that suggests that academic success is reserved for people with white skin. She wanted to help Jason maintain his recognition that skin color should not matter, while expanding his understanding of why it continues to matter in contemporary American society.*

*After soliciting Mark's opinion, Jason's mother said:*

> *It is true that the color of someone's skin should not matter, but this country has a history that is complicated and sad. While things are*

*better than they were, this country is still not fair to people with brown and black skin in many ways. Some have less money than white people and fewer opportunities to get good jobs, live in safe neighborhoods, or attend good schools. Some white people don't give black and brown people a fair chance. So, while we want everyone to do well, we sometimes get especially excited when people with black and brown skin succeed, because they often have to work even harder than we do.*

### *Damonte*

*Damonte was an African American fourth grader who participated in a voluntary desegregation program that transported him daily from his neighborhood in an urban area to a local wealthier suburb that is primarily white. Damonte adored his fourth-grade teacher, Ms. Smith, who was white, and he generally got along with his classmates, most of whom were also white. Ms. Smith was warm and kind and smiled often. Damonte loved when she spent time alone with him, helping him with his writing or listening to him read. However, when the school bus arrived early, and he came to the classroom before school, she was often meeting with another student and told him to go downstairs until the bell rang. He noticed that many different students would meet with her before school and that she never asked him to do so. He became increasingly distraught about this, so that he began to feel resentful of the students that he saw in the room and began to talk back to Ms. Smith.*

*As the students were going to recess one day, Ms. Smith asked Damonte to stay back so they could talk. She asked him why he was acting disrespectfully toward her and if he was upset about something. Damonte started to cry and said, "You don't like me as much as the other kids because I have brown skin!"*

*Internally, Ms. Smith's first reaction was to become defensive and say that of course he was wrong. However, instead, she took a few deep breaths to calm down her emotional response, took a listening stance, and asked him why he thought that. Damonte explained that she never wanted to meet with him in the morning and only met with the white kids. Again, she took a deep breath and tried to understand how things looked through his eyes.*

*Ms. Smith was aware that there had been times when Damonte was not invited to join after school activities or his mother was not included in communications among parents. She also knew that when the boys in her class became rowdy, Damonte was often the first one disciplined by adults in the school.*

*Ms. Smith listened respectfully to Damonte's perceptions. She said that he was correct that sometimes people are treated differently because of their skin color and that people with brown skin are sometimes treated unfairly. She explained that every student in the class received the same amount of time to work on their reading and writing with her, but because his school bus arrived at unpredictable times, she always scheduled his times during the school day. Ms. Smith reminded Damonte that his parents were experts at having brown skin in a society that sometimes treats people unfairly and that whenever he had a question about whether something was done because of prejudice, he should discuss it with them. Ms. Smith later solicited Damonte's mother's thoughts on the interchange, as well as any suggestions that she had for supporting Damonte in the classroom.*

*Damonte was able to have an honest conversation with his teacher because they already had developed a level of trust. Ms. Smith's classroom was filled with books and posters that represented diverse lives and experiences. Ms. Smith had previously initiated conversations with her students about the complexities of race dynamics in American society. She had also previously communicated to Damonte her confidence in his abilities, commitment to his education, and genuine affection for him. It is this foundation that allowed Damonte to feel safe enough to engage in open and honest communication about such a sensitive topic.*

## Practical Tools for School-Based Professionals

- Establish trust. An established trusting relationship is a prerequisite for students to honestly engage in discussions about race. Students of color may be accustomed to discussing race with friends and family, but cautious with adults at school. With white educators, students of color are likely to need substantial evidence of sincerity and commitment, including examples of a willingness to discuss both explicit racism and implicit bias within our society and, even more importantly, within the school. White children are likely to have less experience thinking and talking about race, particularly in communities in which they are the majority. These students need multiple exposures to the historical context of race, the ways in which it is part of the fabric of our daily lives, and language that can be used to discuss these complex issues effectively.
- Create opportunities for discussion. Some teachers never find openings for conversations about race, while others find many. A more racially diverse setting is likely to elicit more racially related comments and questions. However, the amount of discussion on the topic of race is also a product of the classroom and school climate that has been created and the messages that students have received in regard to what should and should not be discussed at school.
- Ask students how they feel when they are in school, including which aspects feel supportive and which do not. Asking parents how their children feel being one of the only children of their race in a classroom or a different race from the teacher will often elicit

important information as well. Asking questions in a direct and genuine manner communicates that these topics are "speakable" and that teachers are prepared to support their students on multiple dimensions.

- Think about timing. Teachers are expected to cover large quantities of material at a steady pace and to address multiple academic, social, and emotional needs throughout the day. Comments related to race, ethnicity, religion, and socioeconomic differences are teaching opportunities that are easily missed if they are solely regarded as disruptions to academic work. It is often beneficial to return to the topic later when there is sufficient time to give the discussion the attention it deserves.
- Take a listening stance (Ryken, 2015). For many of us, our natural response to a comment that we perceive as offensive is to shut it down, whether to protect vulnerable students or in response to our own discomfort. This prevents discussion and growth and can lead to shame, which may be counter-productive. Following up with genuine curiosity, either immediately or at a later time, saying, "I was thinking about what you said... What makes you think that?" can lead to reflection and growth.
- Affirm students' experiences. As one teacher notes, when students of color share negative experiences, it is helpful to be:

> open and honest ... in affirming that racism does exist and is sometimes at play in the scenario they describe and then talking about what I can do to be supportive as well as giving them tools they need to combat stereotypes.
>
> (Wolkoff et al., 2017)

- Be aware of cultural norms. In order to be able to have such discussions in a genuine manner adults need to honestly reflect on their own perspectives and biases. Teachers must be aware of how their own assumptions, as well as those of the school, may differ from those of the students and their families. Dr. Kalise Wornum, a Boston area educational leader and teacher trainer, uses the term "cultural pause" to describe a period of time when a student enters a community with a different culture and needs to spend time learning the expectations and acclimating before they are able to fully access the curriculum. This transition can be smoother when cultural norms and expectations are discussed explicitly with parents and children.
- Determine what differences in verbal and nonverbal communication exist. Do parents give directions in the same manner as school personnel? Does one set of adults ask for consent to participate ("Are we ready to go to music now?"), while the other states expectations with authority ("We are now going to music. Put your things down and get in line")? Recognize the extra effort required when children have to translate from one communication style to another.

- Repair negative interactions. When a student of color reacts negatively or with discomfort to an interaction, the onus must be on the adults to non-defensively explore what elicited the reaction and to consider whether they may have said or done something that felt disrespectful or unfair. Students' inability to discuss these experiences in a frank manner can result in their distancing themselves from the school environment and an inability to be fully receptive to learning. Regardless of the intent of the educator, if the goal is maximizing learning, the focus must be on the meaning that the student made of the interaction, because this, of course, determines its impact.
- Tolerate discomfort. Conversations about race come more naturally with practice. Creating an environment in which students know that they can discuss these topics results in difficult experiences related to race having less of a negative impact.

### *Box 4.1* Additional Tips for Educators

- Make sure the visuals in your room illustrate your values about diversity and inclusion.
- To be able to speak in productive ways with our students about race, we need to have honest conversations with each other. Practice by using shared readings and having intentional discussions with friends and colleagues.
- Communicate to all of your students that you want to know who they are. Practice genuine interest and curiosity.
- Be explicit about your confidence in all children's ability to succeed.
- We cannot always protect students from being offended within our schools, but we can communicate our commitment to understanding their experience and working with them to reach their full potential.
- Provide explicit instruction on stereotyping and prepare students to recognize it when they see it.
- Teach all students to self-advocate in productive ways.
- Speak openly about the role of privilege and how it has affected your own development as a professional.
- Make expectations explicit, so that nobody is disadvantaged by being unaware of culturally based norms.
- Discuss current events and have students imagine how different groups of people may experience the same events differently.
- Be conscious of your feelings, because they will impact how you respond.

## Take Home Ideas for Parents

- Listen to children. Chang and Conrad (2008) discuss the importance of following children's lead in conversations about race and that adults must "be willing to use children's terminology, build on children's ideas, and try to understand their racial statements in the context of children's experiences" (p. 38). Questions such as, "What makes you think that?" can help children learn to be reflective about their own assumptions.
- Find opportunities. Opportunities for conversation arise when watching TV shows or the news. Ask children about their own reactions, but don't hesitate to share your own opinions and reflections about why you reacted as you did.
- Tolerate discomfort. Some of the obstacles parents have noted to successful conversations about race include their own discomfort with racial dynamics and a tendency to try to get too much into a single conversation. Remember that authentic conversations about difficult topics are not neatly wrapped up and can always be returned to at a later time.

### *Box 4.2* Additional Tips for Parents

- Kids are perceptive. If you are uncomfortable, admit it and discuss why you feel that way.
- Answer the question that is being asked: The answer to the question, "Why is Danny's skin darker than mine?" is: "Melanin is something in our skin; people with more melanin have darker skin."
- Although it is important to share the knowledge of your experiences, take care not to transfer guilt and resentment onto children.
- Don't be afraid to mention the color of somebody's skin; not mentioning it does not keep anyone from noticing it.
- Do not frame racism as an issue only for people of color; we all pay a high price when not everyone is able to reach their full potential in our society.
- It is OK (and sometimes best) to return to a conversation later after you have had a chance to think about it.
- We teach children our values by telling them what we believe; if we do not discuss something, they may not know what we believe.
- Reference your family's values and help your children to use their own values as a guide. Does this behavior or perspective match our values? If not, let's try to understand it better.
- Acknowledge that we don't have all the answers, but that we are willing to think about these complex topics with them.
- Be conscious of your feelings, because they will impact how you respond.

*Note:* Developed in collaboration with Dr. Kalise Wornum, a Boston area educational leader and teacher trainer.

## Note

1. This case story is included with permission. All other case examples are fictitious.

## References

Biles, B. (1994). Activities that promote racial and cultural awareness. In C. M. Todd (Ed.), *Family Child Care Connections, 4*(3), 1–4. Urbana Champaign, IL: University of Illinois Cooperative Extension Service. Retrieved from www.pbs.org/kcts/preciouschildren/diversity/read_activities.html

Chang, K. & Conrad, R. (2008). Following children's leads in conversations about race. In M. Polock (Ed.), *Everyday antiracism: Getting real about race in school* (pp. 34–38). New York, NY: The New Press.

Derman-Sparks, L., Higa, C. T., & Sparks, B. (1980). Children, race and racism: How race awareness develops. *Interracial Books for Children Bulletin, 11*(3 & 4), 3–9. Retrieved from www.intergroupresources.com/rc/children,race,and,racism.pdf

Kuh, L., LeeKeenan, D., Given, H., & Beneke, M. (2016, March). Moving beyond anti-bias activities: Supporting the development of anti-bias practices. *Young Children,* 58–65. Retrieved from www.naeyc.org/resources/pubs/yc

Ryken, A. (2015). Engaging children's spontaneous questions about social diversity. *Multicultural Perspectives,* 2, 99–105. doi:10.1080/15210960.2015.1022450

U.S. Department of Education Office for Civil Rights. (2014). *Civil rights data collection. Data snapshot: School discipline.* Washington, DC: U.S. Department of Education. Retrieved from https://ocrdata.ed.gov/downloads/crdc-school-discipline-snapshot.pdf

Wolkoff, E., Goodale, R., & St. Louis, G. (2017). *Talking with young people about race.* [Raw data from a survey of educators, parents, and recent high school graduates]. Department of School Psychology, William James College, Newton, MA.

# 5 Understanding the Needs of LGBTQ Youth

*Terry Bontrager and Ronda Goodale*

This chapter focuses on the major concerns of and controversies surrounding LGBTQ youth as well as the supports that translate into positive outcomes for them. The chapter addresses the following topics:

- The letters in the "alphabet soup" of LGBTQQIP2SAA … ad infinitum;
- How gender identity is distinct from sexual orientation;
- The concept of gender identity and sexual orientation existing within ranges; and
- Resources for creating further reading and for creating constructive dialogues around these topics with students, families, and fellow school professionals.

The overarching theme is that regardless of our personal beliefs, all children and adolescents should be able to learn in a positive, affirming environment.

## Why It Matters

It can be difficult to be comfortable when one does not readily identify with gender and/or sexual norms. Students may experience teasing and rejection if they are perceived as non-heterosexual or non-cisgender. Sexual stereotyping, even in toys, is still the rule rather than exception, despite the increasingly more open attitude in our society. Students who wrestle with their sexuality are more likely to abuse drugs, engage in unsafe sex practices, become depressed or suicidal, and in general feel more isolated, particularly in school (Haas et al., 2011). Surveys of LGBTQ youth reflect the negative impact their school experiences can have. In one study, 84% reported being verbally harassed, 40% physically harassed, and 18% physically assaulted in school (Kosciw, Greytak, Diaz, & Bartkiewicz, 2010). These students also skipped school more often. These elevated risk factors call for interventions that schools and parents need to adopt to promote and support mental health. Therefore, raising awareness and acceptance of diverse gender identity is critical.

### *Definitions—an "Alphabet Soup"*

There are many terms associated with gender and sexuality that are not exclusively binary (i.e., male–female or heterosexual–homosexual). The non-heterosexual community is often referred to as LGBTQ. That abbreviation refers to lesbian, gay, bisexual, transgender, and queer. Sometimes people append additional letters to that designation. The following definitions borrow heavily from Robert Hulshof-Schmidt's 2012 article, "What's in an acronym? Parsing the LGBTQQIP2SAA community":

- Lesbian refers to a female who is romantically and sexually attracted to another female.
- Gay is a general term used to define a homosexual person, that is, a person sexually or romantically attracted to someone of the same sex. It is more often used for males attracted to other males.
- Bisexual is an individual romantically and sexually attracted to the same or opposite sex.
- Transgender is an individual whose gender identity is opposite to their assigned gender (trans men and women).
- Queer is defined as individuals who reject traditional gender identities and seek a broader, less conformist definition of their sexuality.

There are also the following additional terms:

- Questioning is the category for those who feel uncertain about their gender or sexuality.
- Intersex refers to a person born with reproductive or sexual anatomy that does not conform to typical definitions of female or male. The Intersex Society of America considers the intersex condition to be a disorder of sexual development.
- Pansexual refers to those who describe their romantic attraction without regard to the sex or gender of the other individual. Their emotional attraction is open to people with all forms of gender and sexual identities, including transgender and intersex individuals (StopHomophobia.com, 2017).
- Two Spirit, a term that comes from Native American traditions, recognizes a third gender in which individuals fill both male and female roles. Two Spirit individuals were often healers and keepers of traditions—for instance, by relating stories of the creation.
- Asexual people do not feel sexual attraction to others nor do they find having sex to be interesting or important.

Underlying these definitions is the idea that sexuality and gender are totally different constructs. *Sexuality* has to do with romantic or emotional attraction. In contrast, *gender* refers to the intersection of three aspects of gender—biology (the birth sex), identity (the inner sense of being male, female, both, or neither), and expression (outward behaviors).

When we first think about sexuality, we often do not realize it is far broader. In his ground-breaking research in the 1940s and 1950s, Alfred Kinsey and others (Kinsey, Pomeroy, & Martin, 1998) found that only 10% of the population was clearly heterosexual or homosexual. This means that most of us fall some place in the continuum between the two end-points. Although the majority of us identify in just one way, the reality is that sexuality for most people is more fluid, with components of both kinds of sexuality. In a similar manner, gender is increasingly seen as being on a somewhat similar continuum with some individuals expressing themselves in the gender that corresponds to their anatomy (cisgender), others expressing themselves in another gender (transgender), and still others sensing fluidity within the gender designation. The importance of the concept of a continuum is its potential for promoting more acceptance of sexuality and gender expression at any level.

The dominant approach is far more restrictive, causing children and young adults to feel pressured to identify as solidly in one sexual place. Adolescent same-sex experiences are often seen as experimentation when an individual later identifies as heterosexual. In contrast, Kinsey's research implies that sexuality is on a continuum, and the same-sex experience may be part of an individual's total sexuality.

From a developmental perspective, infants and preschoolers already express preferences for gender-stereotyped toys (Todd, Barry, & Thommessen, 2016). Studies vary, but by age 11 gender identity is often clearly indicated, although it may not be solidified in total awareness until age 15 or 16. Before age 7, the assertion of a gender identity may not persist (Steensma, Biemond, de Boer, & Cohen-Kettenis, 2011). The important factors are that the persistence as well as consistency in how a person self-identifies translates into what might be the permanent identity (Steensma et al., 2011).

## Notes from the Field

### *Scenario 1: LaQuandra and Yesenia*

*LaQuandra and Yesenia meet in a social setting and discover they have similar concerns for their five-year-old sons. LaQuandra's son loves taking ballet lessons despite being the only boy in the class. He also prefers drawing to playing outside. In his Kindergarten class, he is often isolated from other boys who do not want him in their group. Many times, girls too exclude him, saying they want only girls in their playgroups. The other mother related how a classmate corrected her son for liking pink, informing him that pink is for girls. Yesenia wondered why it is socially acceptable for girls to be tomboys—to show interest in stereotypically male topics—whereas boys risk being teased, made fun of, and ostracized for varying from that same range of interests.*

*Both parents are comfortable with whatever choices their sons make. But they are at a loss for how to handle the peer responses to their sons' choices. What action might these parents take? What should the school response be?*

### *Scenario 2: Marcel*

*Over the summer, Marcel, age 13, started what his parents called "crazy talk." First, he said he was a girl. He asked that his parents, siblings, and friends call him Chase and refer to him as she or her. But as the school year approached, the child began to vacillate between Marcel and Chase. Some mornings began with the announcement "I am Marcel today." Other mornings started with, "Today I am Chase." Once the academic year began, the child announced both at school and at home, "You can call me Marcel, but please refer to me as they/them/their."*

*Marcel's parents do not know what to make of this. They want their child to be happy and well-adjusted, but using they/them/their instead of he/him/his just seems strange. Marcel's seventh-grade teachers have expressed the same puzzlement and frustration. The school already has a policy on bathroom use, but this seems to be a new challenge. Should the family comply with Marcel's wishes? Should the school?*

### *Scenario 3: Masako*

*The referring concern was social anxiety for Masako's weekly sessions with the school psychologist. Over the past five sessions, Masako has come out to the school psychologist as lesbian. Now the issue of social anxiety has morphed into concerns about whether Masako can feel safe coming out to friends and family. The faculty and staff at this high school have worked hard to develop a culture of caring and support. Furthermore, Masako's parents have impressed the school psychologist as being loving and supportive. Should the school psychologist encourage Masako to come out to her friends? To her family?*

## Practical Tools for School-Based Professionals

### *Response 1: LaQuandra and Yesenia*

- Lead discussions about the qualities of being good citizens and positive team members.
- Create groups based upon students' mutual interests or for a problem-solving task. This promotes students seeing how they are similar to each other in a variety of respects.

- Pair students so they build relationships on shared strengths.
- Model acceptance as a means of promoting self-acceptance and toleration for a range of differences.
- Choose books and toy materials that offer a range of experiences as well as allowing for exploration and growth.
- Let students know your classroom or office is a "Safe Space"; consider putting up a "Safe Space" sign. "Safe Space" kits can be ordered from: www.glsen.org/safespace

### *Response 2: Marcel*

- Ensure the student's safety in the educational environment. School professionals can do this by modeling acceptance and respect (NASP, 2014).
- Respond quickly and decisively to bullying and harassment (NASP, 2014).
- Encourage the student to join social or support groups for gender-diverse students (NASP, 2014).
- Educate the school community about gender expression and issues relating to LGBTQ youth (NASP, 2014).
- Let students know your classroom or office is a "Safe Space"; consider putting up a "Safe Space" sign. "Safe Space" kits can be ordered from: www.glsen.org/safespace

### *Response 3: Masako*

Joe Kort's (2003) adaptation of Vivienne Cass's (1979) Developmental Model of Gay and Lesbian Identity Formation conceptualizes coming out as a process with multiple steps. It emphasizes the fluid nature of progressing through the stages—that an individual may advance, regress, then advance again, only to regress once more. This implies that an individual should not come out publicly until fully prepared to do so. The model details that coming out to friends and family comes toward the end of the entire process; it is stage five of the six-stage model. Misunderstanding the readiness of the individual as well as the supportive nature of the environment can have severe consequences. In a similar vein, Rivers and D'Augelli (2001) caution that coming out to family can put individuals at risk for emotional and physical abuse, as well as homelessness.

- The school psychologist in the scenario would do better to ensure the student carry out the tasks of each developmental stage rather than suggesting coming out prematurely. Following the model will help the student forge a strong identity as well as personal resources for confronting challenges along the way. The student can come out to family and friends when she feels ready.

- School personnel should be sure to include issues of sexual orientation and gender identity into discussions and curricula about human diversity (NASP, 2011).
- School personnel can also support and/or sponsor a Gay Straight Alliance (GSA). Toomey, Ryan, Diaz, and Russell's (2011) research found that having a GSA in a middle or high school did much to increase LGBTQ students' attendance, increase their feelings of safety and belonging, and decrease harassment.
- School mental health professionals should be informed about community resources that foster and support healthy LGBTQ development. They can then share those resources with students and their families (NASP, 2011). Let students know the classroom or office is a "Safe Space"; consider putting up a "Safe Space" sign. "Safe Space" kits can be ordered from: www.glsen.org/safespace

## Take Home Ideas for Parents

### *Response 1: LaQuandra and Yesenia*

- Model and promote self-acceptance and tolerance for a range of differences.
- Let their child know they are loved just as they are.
- Speak to teachers or the administration raising concerns about social isolation and suggesting problem-solving approaches to create more inclusive classroom experiences.
- Use literature to explore topics of inclusion. The sources listed in Table 5.1 treat this topic with sensitivity.

### *Response 2: Marcel*

- Immediate family members may experience a developmental process of their own as they confront Marcel's gender nonconformity.
    - They may feel embarrassed for their child as well as concerned about community and extended family criticism if they do not inhibit this gender expression.
    - The father may question his efficacy as a male role model for his son.
    - The parents want their child to be happy and well adjusted.
    - They want to protect their child from ridicule, harassment, and danger.
- The most positive outcome for the child is for the parents to ensure that the home is a safe and supportive place. Brill and Pepper (2008) recommend that parents:
    - Make their love for their child apparent; and
    - Require others to respect their child.

*Table 5.1* Resources from Literature

| *Title* | *Brief description and notes*<br>*Bibliographic information* |
|---|---|
| *Ferdinand* | The classic tale of a bull that prefers to smell flowers than fight in the ring. It is beautifully illustrated. |
| | Leaf, M. (2011). *Ferdinand*. New York, NY: Viking Juvenile. [ISBN 9780670674251] |
| *Jacob's New Dress* | A young boy first wants to wear a dress and be a princess during dress-up time in school. Later he wants to wear a dress to school as his regular outfit. Despite being teased, he finds support in his parents, teacher, and a friend. Jacob's mom tells him, "There are all sorts of ways to be a boy." |
| | Hoffman, S. and Hoffman, I. (2014). *Jacob's new dress*. Park Ridge, IL: Albert Whitman. [ISBN 9780807563731] |
| *My Princess Boy* | An extended poem from a parent to a gender-nonconforming child. |
| | Kilodavis, C. (2010). *My princess boy*. New York, NY: Aladdin. [ISBN 9781442429888] |
| *Pugdog* | Upon learning that Pugdog is biologically female, the owner tried to "feminize" Pugdog with a grooming makeover, adorning the pooch with ribbons in lieu of a spiked collar. But things don't work out quite as planned. This book may be out of print, but it is worth seeking out in a library. |
| | U'ren, A. (2001). *Pugdog*. New York, NY: Farrar, Straus, Giroux. [ISBN 9780374361495] |

### *Response 3: Masako*

- Model and promote self-acceptance and tolerance for a range of differences.
- Be available for discussions of a wide variety of topics.
- Let their child know they are loved just as they are.

## References

Brill, S. & Pepper, R. (2008). *The transgender child: A handbook for families and professionals*. San Francisco, CA: Cleis Press.

Haas, A. P., Eliason, M., Mays V. M., Mathy R. M., Cochran, S. D., D'Augelli, A. R., … Clayton, P. J. (2011). Suicide and suicide risk in lesbian, gay, bisexual, and transgender populations: Review and recommendations. *Journal of Homosexuality, 58*(1), 10–51. doi:10.1080/00918369.2011.534038

Hulshof-Schmidt, R. (2012). *What's in an acronym? Parsing the LGBTQQIP2SAA community*. Retrieved from https://hulshofschmidt.wordpress.com/2012/07/11/whats-in-an-acronym-parsing-the-lgbtqqip2saa-community/

Kinsey, A. C., Pomeroy, W. B., & Martin, C. E. (1998). *Sexual behavior in the human male*. Bloomington, IN: Indiana University Press.
Kort, J. (2003). *Cass model of gay and lesbian identity formation*. Retrieved from https://web.archive.org/web/20081002073940/www.joekort.com/PDF/cassmodelofidentityformation2.pdf
Kosciw, J. G., Greytak, E. A., Diaz, E. M., & Bartkiewicz, M. J. (2010). *The 2009 National School Climate Survey: The experiences of lesbian, gay, bisexual, and transgender youth in our nation's school*. New York, NY: GLSEN.
NASP. (2011). *NASP position statement: Lesbian, gay, bisexual, transgender, and questioning youth*. Bethesda, MD: National Association of School Psychologists. Retrieved from www.nasponline.org/x26826.xml
NASP. (2014). *Safe schools for transgender and gender diverse students*. Bethesda, MD: National Association of School Psychologists. Retrieved from www.nasponline.org/x26835.xml
Rivers, I. & D'Augelli, A. (2001). The victimization of lesbian, gay, and bisexual youths. In A. D'Augelli & C. Patterson (Eds.), *Lesbian, gay and bisexual identities and youth: Psychological perspectives* (pp. 199–223). New York, NY: Oxford University Press.
Steensma, T. D., Biemond, R., de Boer, F., & Cohen-Kettenis, P. T. (2011). Desisting and persisting gender dysphoria after childhood: A qualitative follow-up study. *Clinical Child Psychology and Psychiatry, 16*, 498–516. doi:10.1177/1359104510378303
StopHomophobia.com (2017). Retrieved from www.stop-homophobia.com/pansexuality.htm
Todd, B., Barry, J., & Thommessen, S. (2016). Preferences for "gender-typed" toys in boys and girls aged 9 to 32 months. *Infant and Child Development, 26*. doi:10.1002/icd.1986
Toomey, R. B., Ryan, C., Diaz, R. M., & Russell, S. T. (2011). High school Gay–Straight Alliances (GSAs) and young adult well-being: An examination of GSA presence, participation, and perceived effectiveness. *Applied Developmental Science, 15*, 175–185. doi:10.1080/10888691.2011.607378

## Web Resources

GLAAD—Gay and Lesbian Alliance Against Defamation: www.glaad.org/
GLSEN—Gay, Lesbian and Straight Educators Network: www.glsen.org/
Massachusetts Department of Elementary and Secondary Education *Guidance for Massachusetts public schools creating a safe and supportive school environment: Nondiscrimination on the basis of gender identity*: www.doe.mass.edu/sfs/lgbtq/GenderIdentity.html
National Association of School Psychologists (NASP): Policy documents on transgender youth: www.nasponline.org/resources-and-publications/resources/diversity/lgbtq-youth/transgender-youth
Schools in transition: A guide to supporting transgender students in K-12 schools: www.genderspectrum.org/staging/wp-content/uploads/2015/08/Schools-in-Transition-2015.pdf
*Teaching Tolerance* magazine and www.tolerance.org/

# 6 When Bad Things Happen

## How to Talk to Children and Adolescents About Crisis Events

*Arlene Silva*

When crises occur, adults can influence how children and adolescents process the events and help them cope effectively. Schools, classrooms, and homes that foster safe and supportive climates are ideal environments for discussing and responding to crises that occur in our communities and world and providing children and adolescents with the comfort of routines and social support. School-based professionals and parents can *prepare, communicate,* and *act* by finding the right time to engage in conversation, responding to children in factual and developmentally appropriate ways, modeling honest and healthy responses to the crisis, promoting resilience, and knowing when to seek professional support for themselves or their children.

### Why It Matters

The news is reporting another car accident, cancer death, hurricane, or mass shooting. Crisis events are a given in our modern society, and when they happen, adults often wonder how to respond to children and adolescents. They may ask, "Should I mention it or ignore it?" "How will I know if my child or adolescent is coping in a healthy way?" And, "Should I hide my own emotions, or is it better to be honest about how I am feeling?"

Before considering these questions, it is helpful to understand the three characteristics of crisis events, which are: "(a) extremely negative, (b) uncontrollable, and (c) unpredictable" (Brock et al., 2016, p. 15). As such, they have the potential to cause substantial physical and/or emotional pain. The following factors are associated with a more traumatic crisis experience (Brock et al., 2016):

- Having a more negative perception of the crisis event;
- Feeling less control over the crisis event;
- Experiencing a human-caused event (vs. a natural disaster);
- Having a longer or more intense exposure to the crisis event; and
- Experiencing devastating consequences (e.g., multiple fatalities) as a result of the crisis.

The scope of this chapter does not include responding to children and adolescents who are in a crisis state or have been personally traumatized as a result of the factors listed above. (See Brock et al., 2016, for information on implementing the PREPaRE crisis response model in schools, which includes mental health interventions for students who are directly impacted.) Instead, this chapter aims to address a more commonly occurring situation: that of knowing what to say and do around children and adolescents who have heard about a crisis that has occurred within their community or world, but who were not in physical danger as a result of the crisis.

## *The Importance of Context*

In 2013, the National Association of School Psychologists, together with five key educational and mental health professional associations, developed a policy framework which describes best practices associated with safe, successful schools (Cowan, Vaillancourt, Rossen, & Pollitt, 2013). The framework highlights the importance of developing a positive school climate, and building trusting relationships amongst staff, students, and families to enhance psychological safety. Schools that implement multi-tiered systems of academic, behavioral, and social-emotional supports will be in a better position to develop positive school climates, and therefore better prepared to talk with students about crisis events when they occur.

In addition, it almost goes without saying that the quality of the bond between parents and their children is of utmost importance; the effect of the parent–child relationship on social-emotional and physical well-being has been well documented (e.g., Andersson, 2016). Parents who have been able to develop respectful, trusting relationships with their children, while still setting developmentally appropriate behavioral limits, will have an easier time talking to their children about crisis events.

## *Prepare*

As with many situations in life, preparation can be helpful before engaging in a conversation about a crisis with children and adolescents. This type of conversation has the potential to either alleviate or aggravate feelings of anxiety and sadness and should be initiated thoughtfully. First and foremost, it is important for the adult to be aware of how they are feeling in response to the crisis. If adults are emotionally overwhelmed or feeling anxious about having the conversation with their children or students, adults should care for themselves first before engaging. Research suggests that children as young as one year old are attuned to their caregiver's emotional states and exhibit negative physiological changes in response to their mother's stress (e.g., Waters, West, & Berry Mendes, 2014). Adults should approach the conversation from a calm state, so they can be responsive to the needs of their children or students. Mindfulness techniques, including meditation and deep breathing, are free and easy to access, and have been linked to many positive benefits, such as stress reduction, increased focus, and decreased emotional reactivity (e.g., Davis & Hayes, 2012).

Next, an appropriate time and place for the conversation should be identified. In schools that emphasize social-emotional learning, structures for having difficult conversations are typically already in place, such as via a morning check-in at the elementary school level, or regularly scheduled "homeroom" time with a teacher at the secondary level. At home, parents should deliberately plan the conversation for a time and location where their child or adolescent feels comfortable and is most likely to engage, such as during nighttime snuggles with a younger child, or hanging out at home on a late weekend morning with a teenager.

### *Communicate*

Once a proper time for the conversation has been identified and the adult is feeling relaxed and ready to proceed, it's time for the conversation to begin. The American Psychological Association (APA, 2015), National Association of School Psychologists (NASP, 2015a, 2015b), and Substance Abuse and Mental Health Services Administration (2007, 2013) offer the following tips for talking to children and adolescents about crisis events:

- Model calmness and control, without appearing anxious or scared. Adult behavior sets the emotional tone within homes, classrooms, and schools.
- Ask the child or adolescent what they know. A straightforward way to start is to simply say, "What have you heard about this?" or "What have you seen on TV/the internet?"[1]
- Listen actively and nonjudgmentally to their response, even if it is unexpected.
- Be honest and straightforward about the crisis event. Provide factual information, without embellishment or speculation, and without dwelling on the magnitude of the crisis or graphic imagery. The younger the child, the briefer and more concrete the information can be. Upper elementary and early middle school children may need help separating fantasy from reality, and secondary school students may have opinions about the crisis event and may need help identifying credible sources of information.
- Validate their feelings and acknowledge the range of possible reactions by saying things like,

> Sometimes kids feel sad, angry, worried or confused. It's also okay to feel happy in general, even though you may feel sad about what has happened. It's okay to feel however you are feeling, even if it's different from how your friend is feeling.

- Acknowledge your own feelings about the crisis event, and model appropriate coping skills and self-care (including taking media breaks and seeking out additional support, if needed). When discussing a terrorist attack that has occurred elsewhere in the country, for instance, an adult might say,

> This is something that really upsets me, and I know I'm going to be feeling sad and scared more often than usual during the next several weeks. So, I'm setting aside time now to make sure I go for a run every other day, since exercise really helps me feel better.[2]

- Encourage questions, and provide honest, developmentally appropriate responses. Be willing to admit when you do not know the answers to their questions with a simple "I don't know."
- Reassure children and adolescents they are safe right now (assuming this is true), and discuss the steps the family, school, or community is taking to continue to help people feel safe. For instance, "Our house has working fire detectors that will wake us up in the middle of the night if there is ever a fire," and "The city has employed a special team of detectives to find the people who are responsible for this."
- Steer the conversation away from making stereotypes or generalizations about people involved with a violent crisis event. Frame crimes in the context of seeking justice for breaking the law, rather than seeking vengeance.
- Point out all helpers in the community who are making a difference for others, such as emergency workers, firefighters, police, and doctors. Focus on the acts of heroism, kindness, and generosity that typically occur in the aftermath of a crisis event.
- Allow the opportunity for children and adolescents to bring up fears and worries about unrelated issues, as these conversations can provide an opportunity for additional reassurance and support.
- Encourage children and adolescents to reach out and talk about the crisis event in the future, as other questions or concerns arise. Remind them they are valued and loved members of the family/school community, and that within a community, it is important for members to support each other.

Adults sometimes may feel uncomfortable discussing a crisis event with children. However, even young children can read their caregiver's reactions and know something bad has happened. Young children will benefit from having accurate information, and it can be more alarming for them if they feel their caregivers are too scared to talk about what has occurred. In addition, it is better for all children to hear factual information from their parents and teachers, instead of relying on rumors, social media, or television for information.

### *A Note on Death*

Crisis events often involve death, so talking to kids about crisis events usually involves talking about death. A mature conceptualization of death includes understanding four key components: *irreversibility, nonfunctionality, inevitability,* and *universality* (Hunter & Smith, 2008, pp. 143–144). In other words, the deceased will remain deceased and will no longer be able to function like a living physical body, all living beings eventually die, and there is nothing that can be done to avoid this eventual outcome. Research suggests that children as young as six years old are able to understand these concepts (Hunter & Smith, 2008). Therefore, it is important for adults to find out what the child or adolescent thinks and feels about death and tailor the conversation appropriately (Poland, Samuel-Barrett, & Waguespack, 2014). Euphemisms such as "He went to sleep" should also be avoided, as they can create confusion.

If a death has occurred within the school community, teachers and school-based professionals can help by educating students about the grief process, allowing students to express their grief and/or reminisce about the deceased (verbally, in writing, or through art), and coaching students to seek support from others if they experience strong grief feelings (Poland et al., 2014). In most cases, it will be important for teachers to acknowledge a death has occurred, and temporarily adjust academic expectations for students who may need additional time to grieve.

### *Act*

Once school-based professionals and parents have spoken with their students and children about the crisis event, they have taken meaningful steps toward supporting those in their care. However, the work does not end with this first conversation, as adults should make themselves available for follow-up conversations, and remain vigilant to ensure continued well-being. Adults should also monitor and limit media exposure for their students and children, as increased viewing of television in the aftermath of a crisis has been linked to post-traumatic stress symptoms and can sometimes be a sign of further distress (e.g., Pfefferbaum et al., 2001).

It is also important for typical routines to be followed at home and in school, as these routines provide built-in social support, comfort, and reassurance for all involved. However, flexibility may be needed for children and adolescents experiencing difficulty coping following a crisis event. According to NASP (2015b) and Poland et al. (2014), individuals may be at greater risk and in need of mental health support following a crisis event if they have: (a) a personal connection to the crisis event; (b) a history of trauma and/or recent losses; (c) a history of mental illness (e.g., anxiety, depression, and substance abuse); and (d) special needs. Parents and teachers should keep an eye out for each other, and for children and adolescents who exhibit persistent physical, behavioral, or emotional problems, or changes in sleep or behavior patterns, as these may be signs that additional help is needed.

Finally, parents, teachers, and school-based professionals can organize constructive responses to the crisis and encourage students' desires to help those who have been affected (e.g., NASP 2015a). Examples include writing thank you letters to first responders, making get well cards, participating in blood drives, updating family disaster plans, participating in community service, and attending community meetings.

### *Knowing When to Seek Professional Help*

In general, the rule of thumb around seeking mental health care following a crisis event is that it should be considered for anyone whose feelings are interfering with their daily functioning for an extended period of time. Children and adolescents spend the majority of their time in schools, so teachers and school-based professionals are in ideal positions to monitor student well-being and notify parents if concerns arise. According to NASP (2015b), the following signs can indicate the need for a referral to a mental health professional:

- Physical complaints in the absence of illness;
- Difficulty with peer and/or family relationships;
- Lack of interest in activities that were previously enjoyable;
- New difficulties with school performance or engagement;
- Difficulty sleeping and/or eating;
- Increased negative emotions;
- Behavioral regression (e.g., bedwetting or becoming clingy); and
- Turning to drugs and alcohol or other unhealthy coping mechanisms.

Parents who have concerns about their child's behavior following a crisis event are encouraged to seek guidance from their school's mental health professionals, which typically include school psychologists, school social workers or adjustment counselors, and school counselors.

### *Promoting Resilience*

The aftermath of a crisis event is a good time to teach and promote resilience, or the ability to adapt in the face of adversity (e.g., Poland et al., 2014). This can be done by identifying and encouraging strong personal relationships with adults and peers, helping others, setting realistic goals and achieving mastery, maintaining daily routines that include self-care (e.g., mindfulness, proper nutrition, exercise, and sleep), nurturing a positive self-concept, and maintaining optimism (Poland et al., 2014). Adults would do well to reflect on their own engagement with each of these factors, and make changes as needed so they can serve as role models for children and adolescents. Sharing a personal story about how an adult made changes in one of these areas in order to improve their own resilience can be a powerful example for children and adolescents.

## Notes from the Field

*A popular student at a large high school dies over the weekend in a car accident. He was alone in the car and was rumored to have been driving over the speed limit when he lost control and crashed into a tree not far from the high school. Alcohol and drugs do not appear to have been a factor. Since his death, hundreds of grieving students have visited the tree where the accident occurred and created a makeshift memorial, leaving cards, flowers, candles, and other mementos. A wake is planned for Monday night, and even students who didn't know the deceased personally are planning to attend with their friends to show support for his family. You are a high school honors English teacher, and you will be meeting with four classes of juniors on Monday. You didn't know the deceased student personally but taught his older brother and know his parents. Over the weekend, you lit a candle in the student's memory, and made a point to attend your yoga class in order to feel centered and prepared for Monday.*

*When you arrive at school on Monday morning, you notice students standing in small groups, many of them crying and hugging. The morning bell rings, and your first class of students enters. Instead of the usual energetic chatter, the tone is hushed and somber. Your lesson plan today called for a literary analysis of Charles Dickens' A Tale of Two Cities, to help prepare students for the upcoming Advanced Placement exam, but one look at your students tells you it will not be possible to follow the curriculum as intended today. Instead, you ask the students to rearrange their seats to form a circle, and you say, "Good morning, everyone. By now you've probably all heard that one of our seniors, Peter Santoro, died in a car accident over the weekend." The students are silent, staring at you. A couple of students are crying softly, and you feel a tear begin to form in the corner of your eye.*

> *Peter had lots of friends here at Windbrook High School, and some of you may be feeling really, really sad right now. I didn't know Peter personally, but I know his family, and I cried for them when I heard the news.*

*Your tear falls, and you don't hide the fact that you need to reach up and wipe your face with a tissue.*

> *I know this is going to be a hard week for me, and for the Windbrook High School community. So today, I'd like us all to have some time to*

*journal about our feelings about what has happened. I know writing can help me feel better, and I will be writing a journal entry too. I will read your entries and correct your grammar and writing mechanics, but not your content. Before we begin, I'd like to answer any questions you may have.*

*A student raises her hand and says she heard the accident happened because Peter was texting on his phone. Another student replies angrily, "No, that's not what happened. He hit a puddle of water and hydroplaned." You reply,*

*I don't know exactly what happened to cause the accident. Sometimes, accidents happen, and no one is at fault. I do know that drugs and alcohol have been ruled out as a cause of the accident. I also know that in general, it's important for all of us to drive safely by not texting while we're driving, and by not driving too fast.*

*There is a brief period of silence, followed by a question from a student who wants to go to the wake to support the family. She has never been to a wake and is worried because she has heard Peter's deceased body will be on display, and she doesn't think she can handle seeing it. You reply,*

*It's natural to have concerns about the wake, and wonder about what to do to show your support. In fact, any feeling any of you has right now is okay. Some of you will want to go to the wake. It's true that sometimes at wakes, caskets are open. I don't know if the casket will be open at this wake. It's also okay for you to decide not to attend the wake. You can also show your support by writing a sympathy card to the family or giving Peter's friends a hug if they are sad. As long as we are supporting one another and respecting each other's feelings, there is no one right way to react or to behave.*

*The students do not have any other questions and appear ready to move on to journaling. You hand out the composition books and spend the next 30 minutes in silence, allowing students to put their emotions on paper. You repeat this process for the remaining three classes of the day, answering questions matter-of-factly and acknowledging that a tragedy has occurred, and that it has affected you too. That evening, after a relaxing bath, you read the journals, which are rich with a range of emotions and expressions. As promised, you correct the writing, but not the content.*

*One journal entry catches your eye, as the student has indicated he is not upset about Peter's death because he "doesn't see the point of living anyway." The next morning, you ask to speak to the student after class, and ask him about his journal entry. The student responds in a flat voice, saying he's not upset because Peter is "better off dead." Your gut tells you this is a student who should be referred to a member of the school's mental health team. You thank the student for his honesty, tell him you care about him, and tell him you'd like to go with him to the school counselor or psychologist to talk more about how he's feeling. You wonder if the student may be having suicidal feelings, and while you don't feel comfortable engaging further in the conversation, you know that someone should follow up. Thankfully, the student accepts your offer to go with him to the school counselor. If he hadn't, you probably would have needed to tell him that you were concerned about him, and that as a teacher part of your job is to make sure all students have the support they need. To protect this student, you might have needed to tell your school mental health team about him even if he didn't want you to, so you are glad things worked out this way instead.*

## Practical Tools for School-Based Professionals

Teachers and school-based professionals can take steps to create safe and supportive school climates before a crisis event even occurs. Teaching social-emotional skills (e.g., interpersonal skills, problem-solving skills, and self-awareness) and implementing group communication structures make classrooms more conducive to conversations about crisis events. The following social-emotional learning web resources may be helpful:

- The Collaborative for Academic, Social, and Emotional Learning: www.casel.org/resources
- Second Step: www.cfchildren.org/second-step
- Responsive Classroom: www.responsiveclassroom.org

These additional resources provide information about responding to specific crisis events in school settings and can be found in our eResource at www.routledge.com/9781138293571:

- The National Association of School Psychologists' School Safety and Crisis Resources, which includes handouts in multiple languages.
- The American School Counselor Association's School Crisis Resources.
- The National Child Traumatic Stress Network's School Crisis Resources.

Finally, Common Sense Media lists a range of student-friendly news sources by age, such as TIME for Kids (ages eight and up) and NPR News (ages 13 and up).

## Take Home Ideas for Parents

Parents need to calm their own anxieties and fears before talking to their children about crisis events. Web resources to help parents practice mindfulness can assist parents as they prepare for conversations about crisis events with their children. These can be found in our eResource at www.routledge.com/9781138293571.

## Notes

1. This excerpt is adapted with permission from American Psychological Association (2015). *How to talk to children about difficult news* (Psychology Help Center). Washington, DC: Author. Retrieved from www.apa.org/helpcenter/talking-to-children.aspx. Copyright © 2015 American Psychological Association. Any further use requires written permission from the APA.
2. This excerpt is adapted with permission from American Psychological Association (2015). *How to talk to children about difficult news* (Psychology Help Center). Washington, DC: Author. Retrieved from www.apa.org/helpcenter/talking-to-children.aspx. Copyright © 2015 American Psychological Association. Any further use requires written permission from the APA.

## References

American Psychological Association (2015). *How to talk to children about difficult news* (Psychology Help Center). Washington, DC: Author. Retrieved from www.apa.org/helpcenter/talking-to-children.aspx

Andersson, M. A. (2016). Chronic disease at midlife. *Journal of Health and Social Behavior, 57*(3), 373–389. doi:10.1177/0022146516661596

Brock, S. E., Nickerson, A. B., Louvar Reeves, M. A., Conolly, C., Jimerson, S. R., Pesce, R. C., & Lazzaro, B. (2016). *School crisis prevention and intervention: The PREPaRE model,* 2nd ed. Bethesda, MD: National Association of School Psychologists.

Cowan, K. C., Vaillancourt, K., Rossen, E., & Pollitt, K. (2013). *A framework for safe and successful schools* [Brief]. Bethesda, MD: National Association of School Psychologists. Retrieved from www.nasponline.org/resources-and-publications/resources/school-safety-and-crisis/a-framework-for-safe-and-successful-schools

Davis, D. M. & Hayes, J. A. (2012, July/August). What are the benefits of mindfulness? *Monitor on Psychology, 43*(7), 64–70. Retrieved from www.apa.org/monitor/2012/07-08/ce-corner.aspx

Hunter, S. B. & Smith, D. E. (2008). Predictors of children's understandings of death: Age, cognitive ability, death experience, and maternal communicative competence. *Omega, 57*, 143–162. doi:10.2190/OM.57.2.b

National Association of School Psychologists (2015a). *Helping children cope with terrorism: Tips for families and educators* (School Safety and Crisis Resources). Bethesda, MD: Author. Retrieved from www.nasponline.org/resources-and-publications/resources/school-safety-and-crisis/war-and-terrorism/helping-children-cope-with-terrorism

National Association of School Psychologists (2015b). *Trauma* (School Safety and Crisis Resources). Bethesda, MD: Author. Retrieved from www.nasponline.org/resources-and-publications/resources/school-safety-and-crisis/trauma

Pfefferbaum, B., Nixon, S. J., Tivis, R. D., Doughty, D. E., Pynoos, R. S., Gurwitch, R. H., & Foy, D. W. (2001). Television exposure in children after a terrorist incident. *Psychiatry: Interpersonal and Biological Processes, 64*(3), 202–211. doi:10.1521/psyc.64.3.202.18462

Poland, S., Samuel-Barrett, C., & Waguespack, A. (2014). Best practices for responding to death in the school community. In P. L. Harrison & A. Thomas (Eds.), *Best practices in school psychology: Systems-level services* (pp. 303–320). Bethesda, MD: National Association of School Psychologists.

Substance Abuse and Mental Health Services Administration (2007). *Tips for talking to children and youth after traumatic events* (HHS Publication No. KEN-01–0091/KEN-01–0093). Rockville, MD: Author. Retrieved from www.samhsa.gov/sites/default/files/tips-talking-to-children-after-traumatic-event.pdf

Substance Abuse and Mental Health Services Administration (2013). *Tips for talking with and helping children and youth cope after a disaster or traumatic event: A guide for parents, caregivers, and teachers* (HHS Publication No. SMA-12–4732). Rockville, MD: Author. Retrieved from http://store.samhsa.gov/product/Tips-for-Talking-With-and-Helping-Children-and-Youth-Cope-After-a-Disaster-or-Traumatic-Event-A-Guide-for-Parents-Caregivers-and-Teachers/SMA12-4732

Waters, S. F., West, T. V., & Berry Mendes, W. (2014). Stress contagion: Physiological covariation between mothers and infants. *Psychological Science, 25*(4) 934–942 doi:10.1177/0956797613518352

# Part II

# Supporting Academic Progress and Positive Behavior

# 7 Addressing Reading Problems

## It's Complicated

*Joan Axelrod*

Reading difficulties often have a significant impact on a student's school experience and sense of well-being. Many students who have reading difficulty in third grade exhibit persistent academic difficulties for the remainder of their academic career (Francis, Shaywitz, Stuebing, Shaywitz, & Fletcher, 1996). It is essential for school personnel to recognize the signposts of reading difficulty and to advocate for effective and continuing intervention when necessary.

Research over the past two decades has helped us to identify students at risk for reading problems and has guided the development of interventions that are effective for many students struggling to learn to read. However, not all students benefit from these interventions and some students have persistent reading problems despite early intervention. School teams—school psychologists, teachers, reading specialists, and administrators—need to recognize students who are not responding to standard protocols and collaborate to individualize interventions for those students.

### Notes from the Field

In this author's experience as a psychoeducational consultant, there have been several recurrent themes in the cases for which parents or schools seek consultation about a child's reading difficulty. Parents will describe a child who labors over every word. With amazement, they explain, "We read with her every night and she may struggle to read a word in one line and when the same word appears two lines later, it is as if she never saw it before." Other parents will describe a child who was a little slow to get started with reading but then progressed through the expected levels of the school's reading program, but "he hates to read." These parents will often recount their frustrated efforts to find books which interest their child and their nightly struggles to get the student to complete reading assignments. School personnel, too, will seek consultations, often when a student has received extensive individualized, standard protocol interventions, like systematic phonetic decoding, yet is still exhibiting significant reading difficulty. Sometimes these students have had three or four years of intervention and are still reading at primary grade level.

How does the existing reading literature and clinical experience help us understand these cases, and how might it guide our intervention efforts? While it would be nice to have a clear answer to each of these inquiries, the answer is often: it's complicated.

## Why It Matters

In the late 1990s, the National Institute of Child Health and Human Development (NICHD) commissioned a panel of researchers around the country to review the scientific evidence on reading and approaches to teaching children to read. After an exhaustive review of literature as well as meetings with parents, teachers, and administrators, the National Reading Panel issued a report which identified five major areas of instructional need (National Reading Panel, 2000). At the earliest stages, children must develop *phonological awareness*, an understanding that words are made up of sounds which can be isolated, rhymed, and manipulated to make new words. Shortly thereafter, they learn the *alphabetic principle (or phonics)*, that each of those sounds can be represented by letters or groups of letters and that there are rules for combining letters to make specific sounds. They begin to recognize recurrent letter combinations that represent word parts and whole words (*orthographic units*) that they recognize automatically, by "sight." As they master those letter–sound correspondences and recognizable orthographic units, children develop *fluency* and begin reading continuous texts with ease. Reading, in turn, increases their accumulating base of *vocabulary* and knowledge. When all of these skills come together, children develop *comprehension* skills and strategies to understand texts. Deficient or underdeveloped skills in any of these areas impede reading development and lead to reading difficulty (Lyon, 1998).

Armed with the National Reading Panel (2000) summary of research and recommended intervention strategies, educators were faced with a mandate to prevent reading difficulty. Rather than waiting for children to fail, schools have increasingly developed early interventions to identify and address reading problems. Some of these efforts have yielded substantial gains for children who might have been at risk for reading difficulty (e.g., Al Otaiba & Fuchs, 2006; Fuchs & Vaughn, 2012) and many schools now regularly monitor students' early reading development to insure they are making progress. Yet, a significant portion of children who benefit from these early interventions still go on to have difficulties with reading comprehension in the upper elementary grades (Compton, Miller, Elleman, & Steacy, 2014; Fuchs & Fuchs, 2015) and in middle school (Solis, Miciak, Vaughn, & Fletcher, 2014).

Reading development is, to some extent, cumulative, and students who show deficits in some of the earliest building blocks—even when those weaknesses are relatively subtle—are at greater risk to exhibit later reading problems. Ideally, for each type of struggling student we see in the field, it would be useful to be able to identify exactly why their reading development faltered and then to target interventions accordingly. Unfortunately, it is not always that simple. Even for students with similar presentations, there may be multiple possible etiologies and multiple factors that influence whether an intervention will be effective. Reading research can offer considerable insight into what works at each stage of the reading process, but clinical experience, particularly with students for whom the obvious research-based strategies are not working, can also enhance our ability to address their reading challenges.

## Practical Tools for School-Based Professionals

### *Phonemic Awareness and the Alphabetic Principle*

Conventional wisdom often assumes that if a child can identify letters and can identify the sound associated with each letter, that child is ready to read. That is not the case for many children. In order to read a word like "bat," one must first recognize that there are distinct, separable sounds in the word. Only then does it make sense that letters represent each of those sounds or to expect that a word that rhymes with "bat," like "cat," might have a similar sequence of letters (Torgesen, J.K. & Mathes, P.G. 1998). Children at risk for reading problems often have difficulty discerning or "pulling apart" those sounds or blending them (O'Connor, 2011). A child may hear or read the word "dog" and a teacher or parent will ask "What is the middle sound?" The child will stare blankly, unaware that there is a sequence of three sounds in the word. Until one appreciates how sounds and sound sequences are connected to letters and letter sequences, each printed word remains an isolated "picture" to be memorized.

Clinical experience suggests that some students have persistent difficulty with phonemic awareness and letter–sound associations. Sometimes, these students have just not had enough active practice with phonemic awareness activities to develop automaticity. Even when a child has participated in small groups explicitly geared to teach phonemic awareness at their instructional level, he or she may have limited opportunity to practice the skills either because other group members respond more quickly than the target child or because some members distract teacher attention. It may also be that the teacher has not delivered the intervention with fidelity (Al Otaiba & Fuchs, 2006). Moreover, there is evidence that attention deficits or other behavioral variables can be significant predictors of non-response to early reading interventions (Al Otaiba & Fuchs, 2002). Even under the best instructional circumstances, some students seem to have greater difficulty "getting" phonemic awareness and the alphabetic principle, possibly due to more general speech or language liabilities. Any, or all, of these factors may also interact to impede progress.

### *What Works?*

The literature on reading intervention suggests that explicit instruction in phonemic awareness has a significant effect on word recognition and total reading skills (O'Connor, 2011; Suggate, 2016). Specifically:

- Provide explicit practice in recognizing rhyming words, identifying beginning and ending sounds, and changing or deleting individual sounds in words (particularly during the preschool and Kindergarten years).
- Teach sounds in conjunction with associated letters.
- Monitor progress in order to identify those students who are not mastering these very early phonemic awareness skills.

For students who are not responding to these generic strategies by segmenting words and discovering letter–sound associations, additional suggestions include:

- Provide targeted practice sessions of 15- or 20-minute sessions three times a week for 10 to 20 weeks (Al Otaiba & Fuchs, 2006) to see if additional practice in discerning sounds and making sound-to-letter correspondences improves performance.
- Begin by working on a very limited number of phonemes—for example, sorting objects into those that begin with /t/ and those that begin with /m/. Once the child has finally been able to distinguish between two initial sounds, he or she may then learn others more quickly.
- Use pictures which illustrate the unique position of the mouth and tongue for each phoneme, to enhance the ability to distinguish individual phonemes (Ehri, 2014).
- Provide more opportunities to actively manipulate and sequence sounds. Active manipulation might include moving letter tiles or using a white board to represent changing sequences of sounds in a word (e.g., Make PAT, now make it TAP, now TIP), gradually increasing the speed and automaticity with which they are expected to change the letters. Even second- or third-grade students seem to benefit and delight in this type of active manipulation of letters and sounds.
- If, after intensive practice, a child has not been able to make gains in identifying or sequencing all of the letter–sound correspondences in a word, focus on just *onsets* (first sounds) and *rimes* (the rest of a word) and a reading program that is based on word "families," or what Ehri (2005) called "reading by analogy."

### *Phonics*

Once a student has begun to appreciate the basic alphabet principle, sound (phoneme)-to-symbol (grapheme) relationships, the task then becomes decoding the letter–sound sequences in words with some level of proficiency. Systematic instruction in this process of decoding letter–sound sequences (i.e., phonics) is beneficial and results in better overall reading skills than incidental exposure or no phonics instruction (Kilpatrick, 2015). Efficient phonetic decoding requires recognizing that letters can have multiple sounds depending on the letters surrounding them. For example, the letter *E* has a different sound in the word "be" than in the word "bed" or the *C* in "chair" has a different sound than either of the *Cs* in circus. Students gradually infer, or are taught, basic phonetic patterns that help predict how a letter or group of letters will sound in a given word.

#### *What Works?*

- Intervene early: Phonetic instruction and systematic practice are particularly effective in Kindergarten or first grade (Juel & Minden-Cupp, 2000; National Reading Panel, 2000; Slavin, Lake, Davis, & Madden, 2011).
- Older students with decoding deficits may require individual or small group sessions at the instructional level four to five times a week, often for 45 to 60 minutes (Gersten et al., 2009).
- Try programs that focus on teaching and practice with phonetic rules (e.g., Orton-Gillingham, Wilson Reading©, and Lindamood Bell-LIPS©). There is not a lot of evidence that one program is preferable to another.
- Pair intensive practice in decoding with extensive opportunity to read connected texts *aloud*; the specific balance of time committed to phonetic instruction versus text reading may not be as important as the sheer amount of time committed to remedial instruction (Torgesen et al., 2001; Vaughn et al., 2010).
- There is no clear evidence about whether it is better to have students reading phonetically-controlled texts versus general trade books (Vaughn et al., 2010), although individual students seem to progress more quickly with controlled texts, whereas others are more engaged when they read generic trade books.
- For students who have difficulty mastering sound-by-sound analysis due to limited cognitive ability, limited *working memory*, or limited patience for laborious decoding, try a "word family" approach; practice reading words and passages that teach one rime pattern at a time with a lot of repetition (e.g., CAT, MAT, FAT and then CAN, MAN, FAN). Even students with cognitive limitations benefit from exposure to systematic phonetic instruction (Allor, Mathes, Roberts, Cheatham, & Al Otaiba, 2014).

### *Orthographic Coding*

Although learning to decode words phonetically is important, if not essential, for reading development, this type of decoding is laborious. By matching letter sequences with their associated sounds, students begin to recognize commonly occurring clusters of letters automatically, by "sight." These *orthographic units* become stored in memory as bonds which trigger their phonological pronunciation as well as their meaning (Ehri, 2005). As students accumulate words or letter sequences they recognize as familiar units, they can begin to build on these by analogy, quickly recognizing, for example, that the *ame* sequence in *name* is the same letter sequence as in *fame*, so they can just add the onset (first sound) rather than pronouncing it as */f// //m/* . The more attuned to how the letter sequences are representing the sounds, the more quickly and accurately one can make these connections and build up new words in their sight word memory. It is also important for students to be attuned to the specific context in which orthographic units occur, in terms of both the surrounding letters and the meaning they are carrying (Compton et al., 2014). A student needs to infer (or be taught) rules such as a *C* followed by *I* or *E* is pronounced as /s/ whereas if it is followed by another letter, it may be pronounced as /k/. Similarly, one must intuit that, even though we pronounce *ED* in *danced* as a /t/, it is written *ED* to mark a past tense verb. For most students, this is an intuitive, flexible, and self-teaching process (Compton et al., 2014; Share, 2008). For others, it is not.

There are two distinct, though intimately connected, neurological pathways for reading: one that supports sound-by-sound analysis and one that supports this process of recognizing orthographic units (Boros et al., 2016; Shaywitz, 2003). Typical readers can often learn an orthographic unit in one to four exposures, whereas students with reading difficulties often need many more exposures to learn a new word (Ehri, 2014; O'Brien, Wolf, Miller, Lovett, & Morris, 2011). These students may see a word they have decoded in a line or on a page or two previously and do not recognize it when they see it again. This may be because they have made only partial or inexact bonds between the sounds and letters in a word (Ehri, 2005). Other students with orthographic weaknesses exhibit competent phonological awareness skills but may have relatively slow symbol processing speed. They recognize whole words when they read but, when they spell, it is clear they have not accurately learned the exact sequence of letters in some words. Finally, some students have difficulty detecting the distinct morphological (meaning) role of specific orthographic units. For example, they will not recognize that the letter sequence *CIAN* is used to mark a person.

*What Works?*

- Have the child scan a text before reading it to find and highlight all of the words which contain a target orthographic unit (e.g., all of the words with "ight"); seeing the highlighted words as they read may cue them to recall the correct pronunciation.
- When reading orally, encourage the student to pause as necessary to decode unfamiliar words but then immediately ask them to reread the same sentence.
- Provide extensive practice spelling words sound-by-sound but also help students to correct errors as they spell; spelling is the "glue that bonds letters in written words to their pronunciations in memory along with meanings" (Ehri, 2005, p. 6).

### Fluency

Recognizing whole words and familiar orthographic units automatically is essential to fluent reading, and fluent reading is strongly associated with comprehension (Fuchs, Fuchs, Hosp, & Jenkins, 2001). Reading fluency is a function of both the accuracy of word recognition and the speed with which words are recognized. Students who labor through texts in a word-by-word fashion, even if they ultimately decode them correctly, are not likely to comprehend and retain what they read because they are expending too much cognitive effort deciphering the words. Not only does this decrease their willingness to read, it also reduces their total amount of text exposure, which further compromises their ability to develop automaticity.

In recent years, schools have been devoting more attention to reading fluency and many schools collect data on children's fluency several times a year to monitor their reading progress, at least in the primary grades. Early, focused, small group interventions for fluency can significantly decrease the number of children who have persistent reading difficulty (Fuchs & Vaughn, 2012; Gilbert et al., 2013). However, not all students respond to these interventions, and research has indicated that students' growth in word recognition fluency over the course of first grade is often a robust marker for how their reading fluency and comprehension will progress in subsequent years (Fuchs et al., 2012; Gilbert et al., 2013). We also know that even after intensive remediation has improved accuracy of word recognition, students with reading difficulty will often show improved, but persistently slower-than-average, fluency rates (Torgesen et al., 2001).

Reading fluency depends on the reciprocal coordination of multiple skills. One must be able to recognize many words automatically, as whole orthographic units, and quickly decode less familiar words by recognizing and combining familiar orthographic units. However, the word recognition process is also facilitated by the breadth of vocabulary knowledge, such that a reader can anticipate a word based on the preceding words in a sentence but also use phonetic information to cross-check that the anticipated word is phonetically logical. When a student with tentative decoding skills reads a phrase like, "The leaves whispered ..." and pauses momentarily, it is often a sign that he or she is cross-checking phonics and meaning, because we don't generally think of leaves as whispering.

While the increased attention to fluency in recent years has been useful in identifying and supporting students at risk for reading difficulty, students—and school personnel—often become so focused on fluency rates that they lose attention to the goal of reading: comprehension. Students will sometimes barrel through fluency assessments to demonstrate their reading prowess without necessarily focusing on the content of what they have read. It is important to remember that, even with remediation, some students may never reach "average" fluency for their grade level. What is more important is that their reading is sufficiently automatic and accurate that they can read comfortably enough to comprehend what they read. Nevertheless, some students expend so much cognitive effort to read a text accurately that is depletes the resources they have to comprehend the text. These students need fluency training.

*What Works?*

- Provide extensive opportunity for *oral* reading with *corrective feedback*; providing opportunities to read silently does not seem to improve reading skills (Hudson, 2011; National Reading Panel, 2000; Therrien, 2004).
- Some students benefit when corrective feedback is provided at the end of a paragraph or passage (Hudson, 2011) but others benefit when the student is asked to re-read the dysfluent sentence more fluently. This method seems to help "lock in" the orthographic features of the missed words.
- Practice repeated reading of a text to a criterion level of speed and accuracy (Hudson, 2011; Therrien, 2004; Vaughn et al., 2010).
- Select reading texts at a student's *instructional* level, i.e., where he or she can recognize around 95% of the words. This is more likely to yield gains than practice with text that is more difficult (Hudson, 2011).
- To increase transfer from practiced to unpracticed texts, there should be overlap in the words used in the two texts (Hudson, 2011); as such, read whole books written by one author because the vocabulary, characters, and sentence structure will have greater redundancy. Even at very easy reading levels, there are whole books that students find engaging (e.g., Tom and Ricky Mystery series; Wright, 2011).

### *Vocabulary and Comprehension*

Comprehension is, of course, the goal of reading intervention. It is a complex, bottom-up, and top-down process. The fluency with which a student recognizes words and reads a text will increase the likelihood of understanding that text and mastering any new vocabulary in the text. At the same time, the breadth of a student's vocabulary, understanding of morphology (word parts), and oral language skills will facilitate the ease with which he or she reads and understands the text (Carlisle & Rice, 2002). Comprehension is an active process in which the student analyzes and "makes meaning" of the text. Students who do not decode well may skip words they cannot decode easily or expend too much cognitive effort decoding the text to remember or interpret what they have read. However, some students who can read a text quite fluently nevertheless have difficulty understanding what they have read (Compton et al., 2014). Some may not infer the meaning of words based on relationships to other, morphologically related words (Nagy, Carlisle, & Goodwin,, 2013) (e.g., the relationship between "transit" and "transport" and "intransigent".) Some may have difficulty understanding how word order can affect meaning (e.g., "He painted the house white" vs. "He painted the white house") (Carlisle & Rice, 2002). Still others have trouble recognizing the organizational structure of a text or extracting the main ideas. These students may have subtle, but critical, language weaknesses which may or may not impede early reading acquisition but which continue to plague students in the upper grades (Solis et al., 2014; Spencer, Quinn, & Wagner, 2014).

Students need to see reading as an active conversation between themselves and the text. They need to be engaged in opportunities to question and ask questions and connect with the text. As with other aspects of remediation, students with comprehension deficits may need much more practice with facilitated, collaborative reading activities than their more able peers.

#### *What Works?*

- Provide activities in which students actively engage with a text.
- Ask students to act out a scene or conversational exchange they have just read. For example, "Show me what Molly looked like when she was alarmed by the spider."
- For expository texts, have students generate a brief "newspaper headline" which captures the point of each paragraph.
- Ask students to read a text and generate sample "test" questions about a text.
- Ask students to read a text and gather words or passages that other students might find hard to understand; then have them paraphrase these passages.

- Use the same graphic organizers repeatedly when mapping texts so that students begin to internalize their structure (e.g., use the same "cause and effect" graphic organizer each time students read a passage about historical events).
- Rather than merely explaining the meaning of a new vocabulary word, coach students to infer its meaning from the context and morphological clues.
- Offer students extensive immersion and exposure about one topic and multiple readings around the topic so they become "experts"; this may increase deeper comprehension (Compton et al., 2014).

## Take Home Ideas for Parents

In the end, there are no easy answers. It is complicated to identify all of the factors that may be interacting to inhibit reading progress for a given child. However, there are some general questions parents might ask to help facilitate better progress.

- Is there ongoing monitoring of reading fluency progress?
- Is there small group directed instruction that addresses the specific skills the student is struggling with?
- If the student is not progressing, who is responsible for analyzing and adapting the intervention?
- Is the student getting *active* practice applying the skills he or she is not mastering?
- Is the student getting sufficient repetition and opportunity to practice the target skills so they become automatic and fluent?
- Are there language or other specific liabilities, such as working memory, processing speed, or attentional challenges, which might necessitate more intensive or persistent intervention?
- Is the student's emotional reaction to his or her reading difficulties undermining progress and, if so, is a change of program or instructor or venue necessary?

## References

Al Otaiba, S., & Fuchs, D. (2002). Characteristics of children who are unresponsive to early literacy intervention. *Remedial & Special Education, 23*(5), 300–316. doi:10.1177/07419325020230050501

Al Otaiba, S., & Fuchs, D. (2006). Who are the young children for whom best practices in reading are ineffective? An experimental and longitudinal study. *Journal of Learning Disabilities, 39*(5), 414–431. doi:10.1177/00222194060390050401

Allor, J. H., Mathes, P. G., Roberts, J. K., Cheatham, J. P., & Al Otaiba, S. (2014). Is scientifically based reading instruction effective for students with below-average IQs? *Exceptional Children, 80*(3), 287–306. doi:10.1177/001440291 4522208

Boros, M., Anton, J. L., Pech-Georgel, C., Grainger, J., Szwed, M., & Ziegler, J. C. (2016). Orthographic processing deficits in developmental dyslexia: Beyond the ventral visual stream. *NeuroImage, 128*, 316–327. doi:10.1016/j.neuroimage.2016.01.014

Carlisle, J. F. & Rice, M. F. (2002). *Improving reading comprehension*. London: York Press.

Compton, D. L., Miller, A. C., Elleman, A. M., & Steacy, L. M. (2014). Have we forsaken reading theory in the name of "quick fix" interventions for children with reading disability? *Scientific Studies of Reading, 18*(1), 55–73. doi:10.1080/10888438.2013.836200

Ehri, L. C. (2005). Learning to read words: Theory, findings, and issues. *Scientific Studies of Reading, 9*(2), 178–188. doi:10.1207/s1532799xssr0902_4

Ehri, L. C. (2014). Orthographic mapping in the acquisition of sight word reading, Spelling memory, and vocabulary learning. *Scientific Studies of Reading, 18*(1), 5–21. doi:10.1080/10888438.2013.819356

Francis, D. J., Shaywitz, S. E., Stuebing, K. K., Shaywitz, B. A., & Fletcher, J. M. (1996). Developmental lag versus deficit models of reading disability: A longitudinal, individual growth curves analysis. *Journal of Educational Psychology, 88*(1), 3–17. doi:10.1037/0022-0663.88.1.3

Fuchs, D., Compton, D. L., Fuchs, L. S., Bryant, V. J., Hamlett, C. L., & Lambert, W. (2012). First-grade cognitive abilities as long-term predictors of reading comprehension and disability status. *Journal of Learning Disabilities, 45*(3), 217–231. doi:10.1177/0022219412442154

Fuchs, D. & Fuchs, L. S. (2015). Rethinking service delivery for students with significant learning problems: Developing and implementing intensive instruction. *Remedial and Special Education, 36*(2), 105–111. doi:10.1177/0741932514558337

Fuchs, L. S., Fuchs, D., Hosp, M. K., & Jenkins, J. R. (2001). Oral reading fluency as an indicator of reading competence: A theoretical, empirical, and historical analysis. *Scientific Studies of Reading, 5*(3), 241–256. doi:10.1207/S1532799XSSR0503_3

Fuchs, L. S. & Vaughn, S. (2012). Responsiveness-to-intervention: A decade later. *Journal of Learning Disabilities, 45*(3), 195–203. doi:10.1177/0022219412442150

Gersten, R., Compton, D., Connor, C. M., Dimino, J., Santoro, L., Linan-Thompson, S., & Tilly, W. D. (2009). Assisting students struggling with reading : Response to intervention (RtI) and multi-tier intervention in the primary grades. *National Center for Education Evaluation and Regional Assistance, 190*(1–3), 883–890. Retrieved from https://ies.ed.gov/ncee/wwc/Docs/PracticeGuide/rti_reading_pg_021809.pdf

Gilbert, J. K., Compton, D. L., Fuchs, D., Fuchs, L. S., Bouton, B., Barquero, L. A., & Cho, E. (2013). Efficacy of a first-grade responsiveness-to-intervention prevention model for struggling readers. *Reading Research Quarterly, 48*(2), 135–154. doi:10.1002/rrq.45

Hudson, R. (2011). Fluency problems. In R. E. O'Connor & P. F. Vadasy (Eds.), *Handbook of reading interventions* (pp. 169–197). New York, NY: Guilford Press.

Juel, C. & Minden-Cupp, C. (2000). Learning to read words: Linguistic units and strategies. *Reading Research Quarterley, 35*(4), 458–492. doi:10.1598/RRQ.35.4.2

Kilpatrick, D. A. (2015). *Assessing, preventing and overcoming reading difficulties*. Hoboken, NJ: Wiley.

Lyon, G. R. (1998). Why reading is not a natural process. *Educational Leadership, 55*, 14–18. Retrieved from http://educationalleader.com/subtopicintro/read/ASCD/ASCD_326_1.pdf

Nagy, W. E., Carlisle, J. F., & Goodwin, A. P. (2013). Morphological knowledge and literacy acquisition. *Journal of Learning Disabilities, 47*(1), 3–12. doi:10.1177/0022219413509967

National Reading Panel (U.S.) (2000). *Report of the National Reading Panel. Teaching children to read: An evidence-based assessment of the scientific research literature on reading and its implications for reading instruction*. Washington, DC. Retrieved from www.nichd.nih.gov/publications/pubs/nrp/documents/report.pdf

O'Brien, B. A., Wolf, M., Miller, L. T., Lovett, M. W., & Morris, R., (2011). Orthographic processing efficiency in developmental dyslexia: An investigation of age and treatment factors at the sublexical level. *Annals of Dyslexia, 61*(1), 111–135. doi:10.1007/s11881-010-0050-9

O'Connor, R. E. (2011). Phonemic awareness and the alphabetic principle. In R. E. O'Connor & P. F. Vadasy (Eds.), *Handbook of reading interventions* (pp. 9–26). New York, NY: Guilford Press.

Share, D. L. (2008). Orthographic learning, phonological recoding and self teaching. *Advances in Child Development and Behavior, 36*, 31–75. doi:10.1016/S0065-2407(08)00002-5

Shaywitz, S. E. (2003). *Overcoming dyslexia: A new and complete science-based program for reading problems at any level*. New York, NY: Knopf.

Slavin, R. E., Lake, C., Davis, S., & Madden, N. (2011). Effective programs for struggling readers: A best-evidence synthesis. *Educational Research Review, 6*(1), 1–26. doi:10.1016/j.edurev.2010.07.002

Solis, M., Miciak, J., Vaughn, S., & Fletcher, J. M. (2014). Why intensive interventions matter: Longitudinal studies of adolescents with reading disabilities and poor reading comprehension. *Learning Disabilities, 37*(4), 218–229. doi:10.1177/0731948714528806

Spencer, M., Quinn, J. M., & Wagner, R. K. (2014). Specific reading comprehension disability: Major problem, myth, or misnomer? *Learning Disabilities Research and Practice, 29*(1), 3–9. doi:10.1111/ldrp.12024

Suggate, S. P. (2016). A meta-analysis of the long-term effects of phonemic awareness, phonics, fluency, and reading comprehension interventions. *Journal of Learning Disabilities, 49*(1), 77–96. doi:10.1177/0022219414528540

Therrien, W. J. (2004). Fluency and comprehension gains as a result of repeated reading: A meta-analysis. *Remedial and Special Education, 25*(4), 252–261. doi:10.1177/07419325040250040801

Torgesen, J. K., Alexander, A. W., Wagner, R. K., Rashotte, C., Voeller, K. S., & Conway, T. (2001). Intensive remedial instruction for children with severe reading disabilities: Immediate and long-term outcomes from two instructional approaches. *Journal of Learning Disabilities, 34*(1), 33–58. doi:10.1177/002221940103400104

Torgesen, J. K. & Mathes, P. G. (1998). *What every teacher should know about phonological awareness*. Florida Department of Education, Division of Schools and Community Education, Bureau of Instructional Support and Community Services.

Vaughn, S., Fletcher, J. M., Francis, D. J., Denton, C. A., Wanzek, J., Wexler, J., ... Romain, M. A. (2010). Response to intervention for middle school students with reading difficulties: Effects of a primary and secondary intervention. *School Psychology Review, 39*(1), 3–21. doi:10.1177/0022219412442157

Wright, B. (2011). *Tom and Ricky mysteries.* Novato CA: High Noon/Academic Therapy Publications.

# 8 Teaching Children to Self-Regulate

*Elana Wolkoff*

Like most children, two-year-old Jessica was easily frustrated when she could not have her needs immediately met. As she grew up, she presented as bright and curious. However, while her peers developed skills for planning, organization, self-monitoring, and response inhibition, Jessica lagged in these areas. She called out in class, had difficulty completing assignments, was easily frustrated, and frequently engaged in behavior that she knew was inappropriate.

Self-regulation is comprised of both stopping behavior that is undesirable and organizing oneself to intentionally engage in behavior which is desirable (Bodrova & Leong, 2008). Children who can effectively self-regulate can delay gratification, manage negative emotions, suppress impulses, make a plan for appropriate behavior, follow through, and self-correct as they proceed. Without these abilities, people are unable to fully demonstrate their knowledge and meet their potential. While for most children, these skills appear to develop naturally, many children require explicit instruction, scaffolded supports, guided practice, and reinforcement to gain mastery in these areas (Dawson & Guare, 2009).

Difficulties with self-regulation, such as inattention, impulsivity, and over-activity, are core characteristics of attention deficit hyperactivity disorder (ADHD) and are often understood in this context (DuPaul & Stoner, 2015). The ability to sustain focused attention and resist impulses are also fundamental elements of what are called the *executive functions* (Center on the Developing Child at Harvard University, 2011), or the brain's ability to oversee and manage the activities of the brain. Whether a child's behavior meets the diagnostic criteria for ADHD, whether he/she is experiencing difficulties as a result of broader weaknesses in executive functioning, or whether the child struggles to self-regulate for other reasons related to development, anxiety, or stress, the need for developmentally appropriate support and explicit teaching of strategies is essential.

## Why It Matters

Children begin to develop self-regulation skills from infancy. Prenatally, infants are completely dependent on mothers for physiological regulation. A healthy full-term infant is prepared to self-regulate physiological responses, such as breathing, sleep/wake cycles, and body temperature. However, an infant who is born premature or with low birthweight may be less able to do so and may need external support for these functions until further development takes place. Similarly, if the prenatal environment was overly stressed, the infant may take longer after birth to develop this level of independence. Such difficulties may be evident in difficulties with feeding, sleeping, and self-soothing (Shonkoff & Phillips, 2000).

As they grow, children continue to develop the capacity to self-regulate physiologically (toileting skills, lasting longer between meals), behaviorally (not necessarily acting on impulses), and emotionally (managing emotional reactions in a constructive manner). Children go from being extreme in their emotional responses, exhibiting only great happiness or significant distress, to exhibiting more nuanced responses. Parents initially act as extensions of their children's internal regulatory systems with frequent reminders and then gradually wean them off this support, shifting the responsibility of regulation to their children. Preschoolers sometimes begin to demonstrate higher levels of self-regulation when they have negative experiences at school and only burst into tears once they are with their parents or guardians. These early years often also include the development of the ability to adjust responses based on the reactions of others (Shonkoff & Phillips, 2000).

While the growth of self-regulation is related to the developmental trajectory and neural development, the rate of development varies, even between typically developing children. Despite this, both society and schools impose arbitrary time lines in regard to the amount of internal regulation that is expected and, subsequently, the amount of external support that is provided. At school, children are expected to follow rules, interact appropriately, attend to directions and instruction (even if they are uninterested), participate in activities on demand, resist impulses to pursue their own interests, refrain from disrupting the learning and activities of others, and maintain a generally positive attitude. No wonder that so many children struggle with these expectations!

Note that difficulties may exist in *regulating* attention, rather than in *paying* attention. It may be surprising when children who are often inattentive are sometimes able to pay very close attention to something for a long period of time, particularly TV, video games, or construction activities. Children with weaknesses in regulation of attention may struggle to attend during class instruction or when reading; however, they can focus easily when an activity engages them, or in response to stimuli that are exciting and attention grabbing. Unfortunately, the more challenging the task, the greater the demand for self-regulation.

Notably, when under physiological or emotional stress, the ability to self-regulate deteriorates. This is true for children and adults regardless of their abilities. When we are stressed or tired, we are all more likely to lose our tempers and to have greater difficulty attending to complex information. Research has found that when humans experience stress, their brains release stress hormones, which can cause a fight, flight, or freeze response and less efficient planning and problem solving (Center on the Developing Child at Harvard University, 2011). Given this, it is not surprising that people under stress often act without thinking. For this reason, an important aspect of helping children to self-regulate more effectively is minimizing their levels of stress and anxiety.

While we cannot (and should not) entirely protect children from stress, we can help to teach them coping strategies, such as mindfulness, deep breathing, listening to music, and removing themselves from stressful situations. This is particularly important with children who experience chronic stress because of violence or fear in their families or communities. In addition, for students who struggle with academic performance, school often increases stress and anxiety. The greater vulnerability of these children makes them more likely to have difficulty with self-regulation and to be more in need of coping strategies.

As many parents know, children are born with an enduring temperament, which can impact their ability to self-regulate (Center on the Developing Child at Harvard University, 2011). Some children are shy and cautious, while others are exuberant and fearless. Temperament will impact the level of effort that is required to regulate behavior. An exuberant child may need to develop a higher level of self-regulation to manage his/her behavior within an identical context compared to that of a child who is naturally more inhibited.

In addition, families have different norms based on the temperaments of parents and their cultural background. Some families are loud and emotive, tending to speak their minds and interrupt each other, while others tend to be more reserved and less expressive about their opinions, deferring to each other in discussions. A child's ability to self-regulate is judged based on the expectations of the environment, whether at home or at school.

Self-regulation includes modulation of emotional reactions, attention, behavior, and effort. By teaching specific strategies in the context of supportive relationships, we can help children to internalize these essential skills.

## Notes from the Field

### *Jonah's Regulation of Behavior*

*Jonah was a first grader with a lot of energy and personality. He was adorable until he was frustrated, which happened daily with his peers during recess. Although his classmates were always eager to play with him at the beginning, their games inevitably resulted in Jonah feeling that something was unfair: either he got tagged when he shouldn't have, he didn't get tagged when he should have, someone touched him too hard or too lightly to notice, etc. The result was inevitably Jonah yelling at his peers, often supplemented by pushing or shoving, and then being required to miss recess as a consequence.*

*Jonah and his classmates were taught to use a strategy of* walk it out, talk it out, or rock it out *(adapted from Bossenmeyer, 1989). More specifically, they were told that each time they had a disagreement with a friend, they had three choices: they could walk away and choose to do something else; they could talk about it and compromise; or they could use a classic childhood game of rock, paper, scissors. Importantly, each of these solutions was modeled and students had opportunities for practice, so that they were clear about expectations. Finally, they were given clear rules to follow and got to ask clarifying questions. For example, in regard to rock, paper, scissors, they were told that the rule is "one and done" unless they both use the same sign, in which case they get to do it again. They were also told in advance that they should expect to sometimes win and sometimes lose. The clarity of these directions and expectations enabled the children to be well prepared for all contingencies.*

*Jonah latched onto the option of rock, paper, scissors and quickly became a leader in social negotiation. Each time he found himself in a conflict with peers, Jonah quickly interrupted it by saying, "Let's do rock, paper, scissors!" Remarkably, Jonah was eager to accept the results and move on, so that they could return to the game. Using this tool, Jonah now knew what to do in such moments and was no longer overwhelmed by the situation.*

### *Janelle's Regulation of Effort*

*Janelle was a bright ninth grader who enjoyed class discussions. When teachers presented new material, she appeared to understand it with relative ease. However, once she got home she took out her homework and stared at it. Sometimes she started an assignment, but often she began at a random point and became frustrated. The computer was always nearby, and she generally ended up watching a video on YouTube, which then became multiple videos, so that before she knew it, several hours had passed. It always seemed to her that she had completed more work than she had and was surprised the next day when she only had two assignments started and none completed.*

*Although some of Janelle's teachers initially perceived her lack of productivity as being a result of laziness, they agreed to work with the school psychologist to develop her ability to initiate a task and sustain independent effort. Teachers agreed to start with homework for one subject and then gradually add others. They chose to begin with English, as this was Janelle's strongest subject. While her other teachers were not happy about temporarily removing the expectation that Janelle do homework for their classes, they understood that she had not been completing it anyway and were hopeful about the intervention. Janelle's English teacher instructed her to come to her for 15 minutes after school to begin her assignment. The teacher helped her break down the task into smaller parts and identify a starting point and sequence for completion. Teachers worked with her to anticipate obstacles and strategize about what she should do when she got stuck, such as when she had trouble focusing on the reading or couldn't think of what to write next in an essay. These strategies were written down for Janelle to reference later. By initiating assignments at school and preparing for contingencies, Janelle was able to go home and complete the assignment independently. Each assignment successfully completed increased her confidence and ability to sustain independent effort. Within two weeks, Janelle was completing her English homework and it was decided to add math. She required less support from her English teacher and added time with her math teacher before going home.*

### *Joey's Regulation of Emotions*

*Joey was a fourth grader with significant difficulty seeing other people's perspectives and regulating his emotions. He had strong feelings about a lot of things and, when someone expressed a different view, he felt it as an assault and became enraged. He subsequently yelled or became physically aggressive. However, after the incident had passed, Joey always expressed regret. In discussions with the school psychologist, he railed against himself and often expressed a desire for self-harm.*

*Joey worked with the school psychologist to recognize the physical sensations that he had when he was about to have a negative reaction. He was instructed to put his hands in his pockets as soon as he started to feel these sensations, then turn his body, and walk away. Joey was given opportunities to role-play with an adult, so that he could practice hearing an opinion which was aggravating, and then practice the physical response of putting his hands in his pockets, turning, and walking away.*

*Initially, Joey checked in with the school psychologist twice daily to review whether he had successfully used this strategy. This kept the intervention in the forefront of his mind. Joey and the school psychologist kept track of his successes, so that when there was an incident in which he was not able to be successful he did not begin to think that the strategy was a failure. Initially, Joey did not notice the physical indicators until he already had his hands on someone else. He was told that this was not too late. He was given a script, to say, "Ah, never mind," and then walk away. It was important that this script allowed him to both save face in the moment and remove himself as quickly as possible. After one week, check-ins decreased to once per day, and soon thereafter to a couple of check-ins per week. While not totally eliminated, Joey's outbursts decreased from once or more daily to less than once per week.*

## Practical Tools for School-Based Professionals

- Help children recognize when they begin to become dysregulated. After becoming distraught, the sequence of events can feel like a blur. Children most commonly struggle with emotional regulation when they are frustrated, angry, or disappointed, but sometimes we can see it when children get overexcited as well. They may get stuck in a certain emotional response and lack the ability to self-calm and mentally move on. An individual's regulation of behavior and emotions must begin with an awareness of the internal indicators that he/she is about to react. Children benefit from being explicitly taught to identify their physical sensations before, during, and after their reaction, so that they can more effectively regulate their responses. Using an outline of a human figure or their own bodies, they can consider what they feel in their body immediately before they react in a manner that is inappropriate. Responses may include: *My head feels like it is going to explode*; *my arms get tight and my hands turn into fists*; or *my heart starts pounding*.
- In addition to noticing physical sensations associated with dysregulation, children will also benefit from being aware of the thoughts and feelings they have when they are about to react. To do this, it may be helpful to use a comic strip with speech and thought bubbles (see Figure 8.1). Although the goal is for them to be able to identify their feelings and thoughts *prior* to their reaction, most children are not

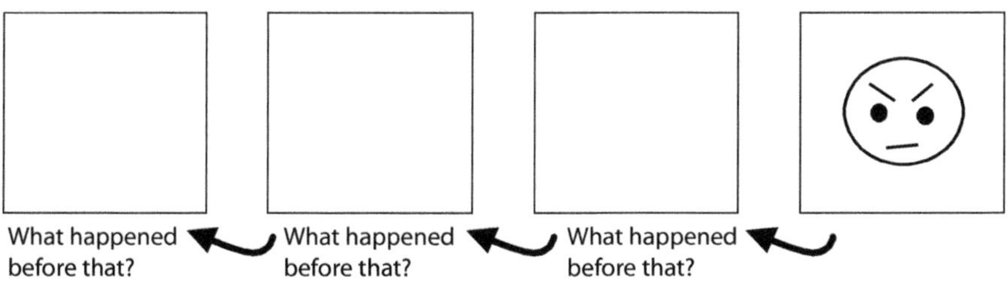


*Figure 8.1* Comic Strip for Increasing Self-Awareness.

initially able to do this. It can be helpful to begin the comic strip at the end of the incident (which will be most easily recalled), and then moving backwards, asking, "What happened before that?" and then again, "What happened before that?" Identified thoughts for each comic illustration may include: *I always get blamed for everything!* Or, *This is so boring!*

- Develop replacement behaviors. Once children have identified one or more indicators that they are about to react, they are able to learn a replacement behavior. Replacing a behavior is always easier than eliminating it. Replacement behaviors can be designed to self-calm, such as counting to 10 or breathing deeply, or they can be designed for avoidance, such as walking away, getting a drink of water, or putting hands in pockets. Most essentially, they must require action and be difficult to do at the same time as identified inappropriate behaviors. Other replacement behaviors can include writing down an idea instead of blurting it out, playing with a rubber band placed around your wrist instead of fidgeting with inappropriate objects, or either touching a smooth stone in a pocket or placing hands behind one's back instead of touching other people (see Table 8.1).
- Provide opportunities for practice. Once a child agrees to a certain replacement behavior, role-play so that he/she can experience how the alternative to reactivity will feel. Encourage the child to try to use the new behavior or action when experiencing the identified physical or mental indicators. Most children begin by remembering the replacement behavior after the fact. This is an excellent first step, even though they are still reactive! The subsequent steps involve thinking of it a few minutes earlier, and then a few minutes earlier, etc. Noticing their behavior (and recalling the replacement behavior) after the fact is a precursor to noticing the behavior as it is occurring, which is a precursor to noticing the urge for the behavior and responding effectively to it in advance. Remind children that even if it is after they have started to react, they should still engage in the alternative behavior (e.g., there is no such thing as "too late").
- Anticipate challenging moments. Replacement strategies are most easily applied when an adult can initially help the child or teen to anticipate challenging situations and to both plan and practice how to

*Table 8.1* Replacement Behaviors

| *Possible replacement behaviors* | *In place of ...* |
|---|---|
| Playing with a small object | Touching people or things |
| Writing thought down | Calling out |
| Holding your breath | Shouting/swearing |
| Hands in pockets | Hitting or shoving |

respond. This allows for mental preparation so that when the situation occurs, the person will avoid being caught off guard. It is important that such preparation and rehearsal not be tinged with judgment or criticism and that the tone be kept neutral. Sometimes adults hesitate to raise their concerns about behavior before it has presented itself in a given situation, because they believe it suggests lack of confidence in the child. To the contrary, if it is raised as a possibility based on previous experience, and without judgment, children tend to appreciate the collaborative problem solving.

- Make expectations explicit to improve accurate work production. In order to help children self-monitor and evaluate their own work, it is essential that they be sufficiently prepared for a task or activity. This involves previewing expectations, anticipating obstacles, and problem solving about how challenges will be addressed. Students should be shown models for "A" level work and "B" level work, or for "strong effort" and "poor effort" on a given task. What are the expectations in regard to both quantity and quality? Students should be given an opportunity to practice identifying work samples that fit into each category before being asked to complete the assignment independently. When they are done, they can compare their work to the standards or models before submitting.
- Break larger assignments into smaller parts to prevent students from becoming overwhelmed and shutting down. Work with them to predict how long each part will take. Have them pause after each part, check the accuracy of their prediction, and receive positive feedback from an adult for completion. This approach increases both productivity and an accurate sense of time.
- Getting started is often the hardest part. Initiating a task requires planning, regulation of attention to focus on one detail of the task and disregard all others, retrieval of the expectations for a specific task, and the confidence that the task can be completed. Children with difficulties in this area can be extremely frustrating for adults, because they may have all of the prerequisite skills, but be unable to engage in a task from start to finish. This is because someone who is capable of engaging in grade level work can still struggle with initiation. By providing support for how to approach and begin assignments, teachers can help students to move past this obstacle and successfully complete their work.
- Help to undo old habits. Note that older students who have not completed homework for years may require an additional, temporary modification. For these students, provide support for initiation and then begin by only requiring that one assignment be completed. The number of assignments can be increased over time. Such an approach enables the student to build up the "muscles" for sustained effort and to avoid feeling overwhelmed.

- Teach self-monitoring. After a task or activity is completed, students should be explicitly taught how to review their performance. Routinely being asked to reflect on what went well, what they think could have gone better, and what they could do differently to make that happen teaches students to internalize this skill. Again, while it must be externally directed at first, if students are given tools and frequent opportunities for practice, they will ultimately internalize the process and be able to use it independently (DuPaul & Stoner, 2015).
- Adults should work to monitor their own frustration. The danger in working with children who struggle to regulate productivity and effort is that their behavior often looks like laziness or obstinance, which can infuriate adults. However, these students are often enraged with themselves for their failure to perform up to their own standards and, once scaffolding and supports are put in place, they can thrive.
- Teach students to reset after losing focus. While students cannot necessarily prevent themselves from becoming distracted, they can benefit from being taught strategies to reorient themselves when they realize they have briefly tuned out, such as looking at the board or seeing what others are doing. Teachers can use cue words, such as "directions," or ring a bell to alert students to attend. Information should be presented visually as well as verbally so that students can refer to it as needed throughout the lesson to get back on track more efficiently. In addition to decreasing time off task, such strategies prevent students from becoming anxious, which can exacerbate their inattention.
- Use self-directive talk as a tool to help regulate behavior and thoughts. When we think through a complex problem or need to exert a large amount of mental energy, we often naturally use self-talk to guide ourselves. For simpler tasks, the self-directed talk is silent; for more complex tasks, it may be aloud (especially if nobody else is present). It can help us complete difficult tasks or follow through on multi-step directions and it allows for mental rehearsal (Bodrova & Leong, 2007). We can coach ourselves: "OK, take a breath. You can do this," and we can redirect ourselves: "Stop. Think. This is not right." We can also run through what we are about to say or do in advance so that we are better prepared when the time comes. Often, people use negative self-talk, which is counterproductive—for example, responding to frustration with, "I am so stupid!" or "I will never understand this!" Explicit instruction and practice can help children learn to use self-talk more productively.
- When teaching students to engage in self-directive talk, develop short, clear phrases that can be easily memorized. For example, "Stop, breath, listen" or, if children become anxious by what was missed after becoming inattentive in class, "Breathe, board, buddy," to remind them to take a breath to calm down, look at the board, and see what a buddy is doing as ways to reorient. The phonetic consistency

(beginning with the same letter, rhyming, etc.) makes these phrases easier to remember. Taking a few deep breaths enables children to move forward more effectively. Self-directive messages can also be written down in a place that can be seen as a reminder. Teaching self-talk will be most effective if children are given the opportunity to practice both what should be said and the actions which follow, so that they feel more natural in the moment. Initial use of this strategy will also be enhanced if adults can support children in anticipating situations in which they will be needed.

- Maximize motivation. Students who consistently fail to self-regulate have weaknesses which make these practices more difficult for them, but this does not mean that motivation does not play a role. While we all do what comes easily to us with minimal motivation, we require higher levels of motivation to do what is hard for us. With less motivation, we are all likely to give up on difficult tasks. So, as we ask our students to use new strategies to manage their areas of weakness, we must first make sure they are sufficiently motivated to take on the challenge.
- Provide external motivators when necessary. Maximizing motivation includes both decreasing the level of difficulty (or level of exertion required) and increasing external reinforcement until internal reinforcement develops. Because we believe children *should* be internally motivated, we tend to maintain the expectation that they *will* be. Unfortunately, internal motivation cannot be created upon demand and the expectation that it will do so tends to increase frustration in both adults and children. External motivators can include verbal praise, a token or point system, opportunities to engage in preferred activities, or small tangible items (see Table 8.2). A consistent system of external reinforcers that are based on specific behaviors can help to increase both self-awareness and motivation.

*Table 8.2* Nonmonetary Rewards to Increase Motivation

| *Rewards for home* | *Rewards for school* |
|---|---|
| • Stickers<br>• Verbal praise (Fantastic! Nice work using your strategies!)<br>• Nonverbal praise (high five, thumbs up, secret signal)<br>• Tangibles (extra dessert, small gadget, stickers)<br>• Time (extra screen time, later bedtime, extra time outside)<br>• Extra privilege<br>• Points (see end of chapter) | • Stickers<br>• Verbal praise (Fantastic! Nice work using your strategies!)<br>• Nonverbal praise ((high five, thumbs up, secret signal)<br>• Tangibles (pens, small gadgets)<br>• Time (homework pass, free time, computer time)<br>• Other intangibles (extra privileges, classroom jobs, helping younger children) |

## Take Home Ideas for Parents

- Recognize differences in temperament and response style. Parenting a child whose temperament and response style is similar to our own is significantly easier than parenting a child who requires more structure and predictability than we do. Parenting a child with a very different temperament precludes an intuitive style and makes daily activities more effortful. Clarity in expectations, support in anticipating obstacles, and use of strategies using a neutral nonjudgmental tone can help to minimize these difficulties.
- Maximize structure and predictability. As unexpected as children's responses are for those around them, they can be equally unexpected for the children, themselves. This can be anxiety-producing, particularly in novel situations. Unfortunately, anxiety can further increase dysregulation. For this reason, children with poor self-regulation benefit significantly from predictable routines and schedules.
- Plan for novel situations. When faced with a novel activity or setting, it is helpful to anticipate what will occur, how your child is expected to react, potential obstacles that may trigger reactivity, and how such difficulties should be handled. Children will be more invested in a plan if they are part of the problem solving. Provide gentle reminders to use planned strategies and understand that, initially, your child may only recall what should have been done after the fact. While this may be frustrating, it is an important first step in that he/she will be better prepared to recall the strategy at earlier and earlier points over time.
- Join your child in problem solving. Children often feel alone in their failure to self-regulate sufficiently to meet adult expectations. Let your child know that you will strategize together and that he/she is not "in it alone." Together, you will solve the problem and help him/her to be more successful. Most importantly, problem solving must occur in advance and when everyone is calm. There is a tendency to avoid conversations about problems in calm moments, because of the

*Box 8.1* **Increasing success by adequately preparing for work or activities**

- Provide clear and explicit expectations (what is expected and how should it look if it is done well?).
- Break it down into small steps.
- Anticipate obstacles.
- Provide strategies to overcome anticipated obstacles.
- Provide praise for completion at each transition.
- Jointly evaluate performance.

fear of instigating a reaction and destroying the (sometimes rare) peace. While every child is different, such conversations generally pay off if information is presented calmly, collaboratively, and without judgment.

- Keep track of triggers that you witness. This information will make it easier for you to help your child anticipate moments of vulnerability. Children often react when an adult says "no," their feelings are hurt, or they feel misunderstood. Cuing your child in advance and reminding him/her to use taught strategies will increase success.
- Use a point system to address specific behaviors that you want your child to change (see Tables 8.3 and 8.4). Instead of getting annoyed each time there is an infraction, quietly say, "Remember your points." At the end of the day, take some quiet moments to review the points chart together and give feedback on what was earned. This is most effective when there is at least one item which is easy for the child to earn. Any items which are not earned, should be acknowledged with, "That's OK. You will try again tomorrow."
- Five positive comments for every negative one. Children who struggle with self-regulation are accustomed to receiving negative responses

*Table 8.3* Sample Reinforcement System Using Points: Positive Behaviors and Points Earned

| *Points earned* | *Demonstrated positive behavior* |
|---|---|
| 1 point | Stopping when someone says to stop |
| 1 point | Being ready to leave the house on time in the morning |
| 2 points | Doing what you are asked to do the first time |
| 1 point | Doing what you are asked to do with one reminder |
| 1 point | Taking "no" for an answer right away |
| 1 point | Getting help for a problem without raising your voice |
| 1 point | Cleaning up without complaint |
| 2 points | Not talking back to adults all day |

*Table 8.4* Sample Reinforcement System Using Points: Ways to Spend Earned Points

| *Cost* | *Privilege* |
|---|---|
| 15 points | Extra dessert |
| 20 points | Treat at the corner store |
| 20 points | 15 extra minutes "cozy time" in bed at night |
| 25 points | 10 extra minutes being read to at night |
| 30 points | One dollar |
| 15 points | Read for 15 minutes longer at night |
| 35 points | Stay up one half hour later |
| 50 points | TV/computer time |
| 70 points | Trip to a movie or somewhere else special |

from adults, to the point at which they anticipate such responses before they even occur. For this reason, it is important to engage with children with warmth and affection, so that they feel safe and motivated to put forth effort even when their behavior has been problematic.

## References

Bodrova, E. & Leong, D. (2007). *Tools of the mind: The Vygotskian approach to early childhood education*. Upper Saddle River, NJ: Pearson.

Bodrova, E. & Leong, D. (2008). Developing self-regulation in kindergarten: Can we keep all the crickets in the basket? *Beyond the Journal: Young Children on the Web, 63*(2), 56–58. Retrieved from: www.researchgate.net/publication/237121551_Developing_Self-Regulation_in_Kindergarten_Can_We_Keep_All_the_Crickets_in_the_Basket

Bossenmeyer, M. (1989). *Peaceful playgrounds: An elementary teachers' guide to recess games and markings*. Byron, CA: Author.

Center on the Developing Child at Harvard University (2011). *Building the brain's "air traffic control" system: How early experiences shape the development of executive function*. (Working Paper No. 11). Retrieved from https://developingchild.harvard.edu/wp-content/uploads/2011/05/How-Early-Experiences-Shape-the-Development-of-Executive-Function.pdf

Dawson, P. & Guare, R. (2009). *Smart but scattered*. New York, NY: Guilford Press.

DuPaul, G. J. & Stoner, G. (2015). *ADHD in the schools: Assessment and intervention strategies*. New York, NY: Guilford Press.

Shonkoff, J. & Phillips, D. (2000). *From neurons to neighborhoods: The science of early child development*. Washington, DC: National Academy of Sciences. doi:10.17226/9824

# 9 The Concept of Independence in Autism Treatment

## Are We Speaking the Same Language?

*Ronald Lee*

The dramatic increase in the prevalence of autism spectrum disorders (ASD) over the past three decades has resulted in a corresponding demand for interventions that can effectively address the wide range of needs these individuals have. ASD is diagnostically defined by difficulties in two broad behavioral areas: (a) deficits in social skills and communication; and (b) a restricted range of behavior and preferences sometimes resulting in a strict adherence to routines or repetitive behavior (American Psychiatric Association, 2013). Although there are numerous theories on the fundamental deficit in ASD (e.g., Baron-Cohen, Leslie, & Frith, 1985; Frith & Hill, 2003; Levy, 2007; Rimland, 1964), there is one common element that underlies the behavioral characteristics shared by people with ASD. Arguably, most, if not all, behavioral concerns can be conceptualized as a deficit in independent, appropriate, or socially adaptive behavior. Although there can be many reasons for the lack of independence, educational and therapeutic approaches are typically geared toward improving the learner with ASD's ability to engage in independent adaptive behavior. It is important that educators and parents agree about their expectations of independence and understand the variety of factors that can influence the occurrence of independent behavior.

## Notes from the Field

### *"My Child Is Independent in That"*

*Bobby is a 12-year-old child with ASD being screened for educational placement in a new school that may be better equipped to address his needs. School administrators and educators conduct intake interviews to get an overview of his strengths and needs across a variety of areas. One area is Bobby's ability to engage in self-care daily-living activities that would be observed during the school day. These include putting away his belongings, putting on and taking off a jacket, feeding himself, and completing bathroom and toileting routines. His parents report that he is independent and does not need further intervention to address these areas.*

*Bobby is subsequently accepted into the program. On Bobby's first day, he is taken to the bathroom during a scheduled class bathroom trip and waits at the entrance of the bathroom until it is his turn. After being instructed that it is his turn, the teacher notices that Bobby does not seem to know what to do next and the teacher asks him if he has to go to the bathroom. After some questioning, Bobby enters a stall and uses the toilet. Noticing that Bobby is taking longer than seems necessary, the teacher instructs him to pull up his pants and come out. On his way out, the teacher reminds him to flush the toilet. As he starts walking out of the bathroom, the teacher also reminds him to wash and dry his hands. The teacher makes a mental note to contact Bobby's parents to discuss the lack of independence and the possible need to incorporate a goal to increase independence with bathroom and toileting routines.*

Is Bobby independent with his toileting behavior? The answer can differ depending on one's perspective. From the parents' perspective, Bobby might independently engage in different parts of completing a bathroom routine. That is, he might urinate without assistance, flush the toilet without assistance, and/or wash and dry his hands without assistance. Because he does not require assistance, such as hand-over-hand guidance, and will follow instructions to perform these responses, he is deemed independent. Thus, when looking at individual responses in isolation, his parents' judgment of independence is a fair one. His teacher, however, argues that Bobby does not engage in the various parts of the bathroom routine *unless* he is given instructions at each step. From the teacher's perspective, Bobby is dependent on verbal instructions or reminders. Because of this, the teacher argues that Bobby is in fact *prompt dependent* (i.e., reminder dependent) in completing a bathroom routine. Although it might seem counter-intuitive that independent performance and dependent performance can exist concurrently, this example illustrates that the judgment is heavily based on the perspective of the observer.

### James Knows How to Ask for What He Wants. Why Doesn't He?

*James is a six-year-old with ASD who is verbal, but typically only speaks when spoken to. He has recently started receiving services during his school day to address much needed skill deficits, and to reduce problems with tolerating frustration. His educational team quickly comes to a consensus that he would function better in his environment if he were able to communicate more effectively. They implement an intensive teaching procedure to teach James to engage in independent requests. They identify foods that James likes to eat and items with which he likes to play. Next, they operationally (i.e., specifically) define the desired response. James is verbal and so the team decides it would be appropriate to teach James to ask for desired items using sentences such as, "I want an apple" or "Can I have an apple?" A speech therapist carries out the teaching protocols by (a) holding up a preferred item (e.g., an apple) and (b) asking, "What do you want?" First, James is taught to imitate modeled requests with a variety of items and foods. The speech therapist models the correct response, which James imitates. After imitating the model, James is given a reward. Gradually, the speech therapist's model is eliminated. As the sessions progress, James quickly learns to ask for a variety of items and foods without the need for models from the speech therapist. The speech therapist is pleased with James's progress and reports the observed increase in independent communication to James's teacher and parents. Over time, the speech therapist begins to notice that, although James consistently requests items within the training sessions, he rarely does so outside of the training session. His classroom teacher and parents verify this by reporting little to no independent communication in other situations. The educational team plans to reconvene to consider what went wrong.*

Similar to Bobby's case, James will only engage in an independent request under a set of specific circumstances. In contrast to Bobby's case, however, the judgment of independence is not based on the perspective of the observer. Instead, all observers agree that James is engaging in an independent response under one circumstance but not under others. For example, he has learned to request the item that is shown to him during a structured teaching session and after being asked, "What do you want?" but does not engage in independent requests throughout the school day, at home, or in other situations. This problem can be conceptualized as a lack of generalization of the learned skill. That is, what is learned in one setting or context does not transfer to different settings or contexts. Many learners with ASD do not demonstrate generalization of learned skills without specific strategies to promote generalization. Although often considered characteristic of ASD, it is more helpful to consider how the techniques used during teaching can enhance or inhibit generalization of a skill. In James's case, he is doing precisely what he has been taught to do.

### *Sarah Can Be Independent—But Isn't*

*Sarah is a 14-year-old with ASD in an inclusive classroom setting. She is described as "easy to get along with" and cooperative but is considered aloof and uninterested in much of her surroundings. Her teachers have consistently reported that obstacles to her success are that she seems to lose focus quickly, is easily distracted, and does not appear motivated to work. Her educational team has prioritized resolving these issues particularly because she will be entering the transition-to-adulthood stage where educational priorities begin to shift from academics toward functional life skills. The first part of their strategy is to implement a token economy. Token economies are motivational systems that are commonly used to reward desired behavior and can be used in different settings, such as in classrooms (McLaughlin & Williams, 1988) and at home (Christophersen, Arnold, Hill, & Quilitch, 1972). Additionally, the educational team agrees that a token economy will have educational value in teaching Sarah skills related to money management, such as earning and saving tokens that can be used to purchase rewards and commodities. Most importantly, token economies have been demonstrated to be effective at improving student performance across domains, such as academics, vocational skills, and social behavior (Matson & Boisjoli, 2009). The team hopes that by implementing this evidence-based technique, a dramatic increase in Sarah's independence will be observed across activities and settings.*

*The token system is implemented and, shortly after, Sarah's teacher reports an improvement in Sarah's consistency and independence. Her teacher indicates that Sarah seems to be interested in the tokens, is on-task more frequently, and is generally more responsive than before the token economy. Over the next few weeks, however, progress with the token economy seems to stall. Sarah's interest in them wanes, and her motivation to work reverts to pre-token levels. Instructors suggest that Sarah may not fully understand how the token economy works. They support this with observations that Sarah needs reminders to earn tokens to get other items and that she often accumulate tokens, but has little interest in exchanging them. Despite having constant practice in using tokens, she fails to show any independence or initiative in using tokens. The team has attempted reducing the number of tokens needed before trading for another item and introducing different tokens, such as coins, check marks, or stickers. Except for brief changes in performance, nothing works consistently.*

## Why It Matters

The first and most obvious culprit to address when faced with a lack of independence is whether the learner knows what to do. The appropriate intervention is to provide instruction in the skill that is needed. Bobby's, James's, and Sarah's case examples, however, represent deficits in independence that are not due to a lack of knowledge. In Bobby's case, he did not engage in a toileting routine without reminders, although he could complete individual parts of the routine without assistance. In James's case, he did not independently communicate outside of highly structured therapy sessions, despite showing a great deal of independence within therapy sessions. In Sarah's case, she was likely capable of much more independence, but would only demonstrate this when interested or motivated. For each of these cases, the key factor affecting independent performance involved factors within the environment. In addition, the relevant factor for each case is different, illustrating that different issues can influence independence to varying degrees and may therefore require individualized intervention approaches. Thus, recognizing and understanding how various issues can affect independence is crucial for maximizing treatment and educational resources.

### *Defining the Target Response (Sequence)*

Perhaps the simplest case is Bobby's. In resolving the disagreement over whether his behavior is independent, the teacher and parents need only come to an agreement about what is meant by independence. In doing so, they will more clearly state their expectations for independent toileting. Ultimately, they must refine and agree on their definition of independent toileting. A definition of the desired behavior should be an objective description of a phenomenon in clear terms, so educators agree when a particular behavior has occurred (Cooper, Heron, & Heward, 2007). Operationally defining behavior is a best practice in scientific disciplines such as medicine and has a good fit with educational and therapeutic approaches. Taking the time to clearly state and agree on the expected performance can avoid many problems that occur later stemming from a lack of clearly stated expectations. Despite being considered a critical step in forming goals (Hawkins, 1979) as well as being important in facilitating the implementation of high-quality intervention (Fiske, 2008), it is a step that doesn't always happen. This step may be taken for granted or overlooked by practitioners, educators, and parents.

In defining Bobby's behavior, it is important to note that any behavior, such as reaching to a faucet to turn on water, can be considered:

- The desired response in and of itself;
- One of a larger set of desired responses, such as in washing one's hands; or
- The product of a sequence of separate smaller responses, such as (a) raising one hand, (b) extending raised hand to faucet, (c) grasping the faucet handle, and (d) turning the faucet handle.

The importance of clarifying which of the above is the expected outcome will heavily influence parent and teacher judgment of Bobby's level of independence.

### *Teaching Procedures and Generalized Independence*

James's case illustrates a deficit in independence that is largely attributable to the teaching procedures. That is, although James learned to request preferred foods and items, he was taught to do so only under a specific set of circumstances. Those circumstances entailed components that were conspicuously present in the teaching procedures, such as (a) being shown a desired item (and perhaps specifically by an adult) and/or (b) being asked,

"What do you want?" With ongoing training, either component, or the combination of the two, may become an indication to James that he is expected to request the item he sees. As a result, these components become essential to James's requesting. Thus, requests will not occur in any situation in which these components are not present. In other words, James will not request desired items unless they are presented before him and he is asked, "What do you want?" This type of selective attention and responding is commonly reported in people with ASD (Lovaas, Koegel, & Schreibman, 1979: Lovaas, Schreibman, Koegel, & Rehm, 1971; Reed, Stahmer, Suhrheinrich, & Schreibman, 2013).

Although clearly stating the circumstances under which requesting should occur would be helpful, the most appropriate solution to the problem does not stem directly from adding to the definition of the response, as in Bobby's case. Instead, the lack of (generalized) independence is a product of teaching procedures that promote control by cues that do not represent the full range of circumstances under which requesting is expected. For example, although we may ask for preferred items when we see them (e.g., from a menu or a store display) or when we are asked, "What do you want?" from people in our environment, these are not the only situations in which we do so. Additionally, requests often occur in the absence of any prompting from others and appear to be "spontaneous." Such examples include saying, "I would love a nap" when feeling tired, or "I want to find something to eat" when feeling hungry. Thus, the training protocol described for James is, at best, incomplete and needs to include teaching to request items that one wants or needs irrespective of whether you see that item.

Great strides have been made in establishing and refining procedures used to teach requesting behavior. These include a variety of techniques used to teach different requests such as requests for attention (Wacker, Harding, & Berg, 2008), for escape or breaks from work (Geiger, Carr, & LeBlanc, 2010), for tangible items and materials (Hagopian, Wilson, & Wilder, 2001), for information (Taylor & Harris, 1995), and for assistance with difficult tasks (Rodriguez, Levesque, Cohrs, & Niemeier, 2017). Other refinements have addressed characteristics of requesting behavior itself, such as increasing spontaneity of requesting (Charlop-Christy, Carpenter, Le, LeBlanc, & Kellet 2002) and increasing variety of requests (Betz, Higbee, Kelley, Sellers, & Pollard, 2011).

### *Independence and Motivation*

Sarah's is a case example of a student who has the skill to exhibit a greater level of independence than she typically does because she lacks the motivation to engage in independent behavior at a consistent level. Learners like Sarah are often reported to be capable of much more than they actually demonstrate. Inconsistent motivation that results in inconsistent performance can be confused with incomplete learning of desired skills or of prerequisite skills. This can lead to educational time and resources devoted to activities such as providing additional lessons, practice, and exposure to targeted tasks. These additional learning opportunities can be helpful under certain circumstances but, at best, would be an indirect resolution to Sarah's inconsistency. Enhancing motivation is the most direct means of resolving this problem. Although motivational or reward systems can produce positive outcomes, long-term benefits are more likely when the factors that influence motivation and performance are understood.

The lack of consistent motivation is likely to be familiar to parents and educators. Numerous examples of motivational strategies can be found in forums, workshops, tutorials, news articles, blogs, parent groups, magazines, journals, and so on. At the time of this writing, an internet search using the phrase *increase student motivation* returned over four million results. The volume of available resources speaks to the commonality of this problem, but also implies that the problem persists despite no difficulty in obtaining advice on increasing motivation. Part of the issue is illustrated in the attitude that learners should learn for its own sake. This perspective suggests that gratification from learning is a choice made by the learner. Rather than waiting for learners to come to the decision that learning is worthwhile, however, it is more productive to approach motivation as something that can be influenced externally. For example, learners with ASD often require external rewards to encourage participation and engagement. Unfortunately, it is also common for people with ASD to show little interest in social interaction. Thus, many people with ASD may not respond to social praise and other rewards commonly used with same-aged, typically developing peers. As a result, greater effort and creativity are needed to effectively plan and structure motivational systems for a learner with few consistent reinforcers. The common approach of introducing materials, rules, or systems may have positive effects, but those effects may be temporary if attention is not given to how those supplements are supported. For example, Sarah's tokens were only as motivating as the rewards that could be purchased. If Sarah was generally unmotivated by rewards in her environment, the tokens would have no greater value (and hence, motivational effect) than those rewards.

Unfortunately, there are few solutions to address problems with motivation besides finding or developing effective motivators. There are, however, numerous tools and approaches that can be helpful. For example, a variety of assessments have been developed to facilitate the identification of potential reinforcers (see Tullis et al., 2011 for a review). Additionally, studies using these assessments have investigated a wide variety of potential motivators, such as edible items (Fleming et al., 2010), leisure activities (Hanley, Iwata, Lindberg, & Conners, 2003), olfactory stimuli (Wilder et al., 2008), and social-interaction style (Smaby, MacDonald, Ahearn, & Dube, 2007). Methods for developing new motivators have also been investigated and include teaching learners to respond to music and approval (Dorow, 1975), vocal sounds (Yoon & Bennett, 2000), praise (Dozier, Iwata, Thomason-Sassi, Worsdell, & Wilson, 2012), and tokens (Becraft & Rolider, 2015) as reinforcers. None of these techniques in isolation may be sufficient for addressing pervasive and persistent motivational problems but, along with other avenues of intervention, such as curricular and teaching modifications, they make up a powerful set of tools that increase the likelihood of success.

## Practical Tools for School-Based Professionals

Does the lack of independence represent a difference in judgment of independence among observers?

- Meet and discuss with parents and educational team members to come to a consensus about the desired level of performance.
- Specify short-term goals, long-term goals, and their respective time frames.
- Clearly specify the context in which the desired behavior should occur.
- Ensure relevant members of the educational team are aware of the level of performance that is expected.
- Clarify and agree on procedures that should be followed when different levels of independence are observed.

Is the lack of independence due to a lack of generalization of the skill?

- Determine how the degree of desired generalization differs from the manner in which the behavior was taught.
- Teach the desired behavior in the desired context.
- Teach the desired behavior in a variety of desired contexts.
- Include parts of the natural environment into the teaching environment.

Is the lack of independence better conceptualized as a lack of motivation?

- Identify additional incentives; include the student whenever possible.
- Include a higher level of incentives or rewards for consistent independence.
- Offer choices; allow the student a degree of control in the incentive system.
- Gradually reducing the use of supplemental incentives may be more effective than eliminating them quickly.
- Increase the use of praise and positive attention to facilitate the removal of supplemental incentives.

## Take Home Ideas for Parents

- Be aware that the factors that influence independence at school may be different from those that influence independence at home!
- Use the school-based team as a resource for how to translate activities and procedures to the home.
- Practice desired skills at home and in the community to the extent possible.
- Supplement school-based practices with homework that transfers instruction at school to the home.
- Maximize success by engaging in homework in a manner that fits routines and schedules at home.
- Determine with the team the extent to which it is important to use the same materials, language, and incentive systems that are used at school.

There is a myriad of relevant factors when resolving the lack of observed independence in a learner with ASD's behavior. The cases presented here provide a sample of issues where the primary basis for the problem is unrelated to the learner's skill level. Educators and family members are in the best position for resolving problems in independence by identifying those factors relevant to the presenting problem. In doing so, they are conducting a functional assessment. Functional assessments are most commonly applied in the context of addressing problematic, socially inappropriate, or aberrant forms of behavior, but can also be helpful in assessing difficulties seen in learning and performance. For example, Ferraioli, Hughes, and Smith (2005) described a systematic means for identifying problems that might arise during teaching procedures with learners with ASD. Daly III, Witt, Martens, and Dool (1997) applied functional assessment methods to identify the likely cause for academic performance issues. They applied a rigorous analysis to improve oral reading fluency. Studies such as these represent a growing level of support for evidence-based and objective methods for assessing problems in skill acquisition and academic performance. Familiarity with these techniques will provide educators and parents of learners with ASD with an understanding of the variety of factors that influence independence and assist in the development of efficient and effective educational and therapeutic programs for people with ASD.

## References

American Psychiatric Association. (2013). *Diagnostic and statistical manual of mental disorders* (5th ed.). Arlington, VA: American Psychiatric Publishing. doi:10.1176/appi.books.9780890425596.893619

Baron-Cohen, S., Leslie, A. M., & Frith, U. (1985). Does the autistic child have a "theory of mind"? *Cognition, 21*(1), 37–46. doi:10.1016/0010-0277(85)90022-8

Becraft, J. L. & Rolider, N. U. (2015). Reinforcer variation in a token economy. *Behavioral Interventions, 30*(2), 157–165. doi:10.1002/bin.1401

Betz, A. M., Higbee, T. S., Kelley, K. N., Sellers, T. P., & Pollard, J. S. (2011). Increasing response variability of mand frames with script training and extinction. *Journal of Applied Behavior Analysis, 44*(2), 357–362. doi:10.1901/jaba.2011.44-357

Charlop-Christy, M. H., Carpenter, M., Le, L., LeBlanc, L. A., & Kellet, K. (2002). Using the picture exchange communication system (PECS) with children with autism: Assessment of PECS acquisition, speech, social-communicative behavior, and problem behavior. *Journal of Applied Behavior Analysis, 35*(3), 213–231. doi:10.1901/jaba.2002.35-213

Christophersen, E. R., Arnold, C. M., Hill, D. W., & Quilitch, H. R. (1972). The home point system: Token reinforcement procedures for application by parents of children with behavior problems. *Journal of Applied Behavior Analysis, 5*, 485–497. doi:10.1901/jaba.1972.5-485

Cooper, J. O., Heron, T. E., & Heward, W. L. (2007). *Applied behavior analysis* (2nd ed.). Upper Saddle River, NJ: Pearson Education Inc.

Daly III, E. J., Witt, J. C., Martens, B., & Dool, E. J. (1997). A model for conducting a functional analysis of academic performance problems. *School Psychology Review, 26*(4), 554–574.

Dorow, L. G. (1975). Conditioning music and approval as new reinforcers for imitative behavior with the severely retarded. *Journal of Music Therapy, 12*(1), 30–39. doi:10.1093/jmt/12.1.30

Dozier, C. L., Iwata, B. A., Thomason-Sassi, J., Worsdell, A. S., & Wilson, D. M. (2012). A comparison of two pairing procedures to establish praise as a reinforcer. *Journal of Applied Behavior Analysis, 45*, 721–735. doi:10.1901/jaba.2012.45-721

Ferraioli, S., Hughes, C., & Smith, T. (2005). A model for problem solving in discrete trial training for children with autism. *Journal of Early and Intensive Behavior Intervention, 2*(4), 224. doi:10.1037/h0100316

Fiske, K. E. (2008). Treatment integrity of school-based behavior analytic interventions: A review of the research. *Behavior Analysis in Practice, 1*(2), 19–25. doi:10.1007/bf03391724

Fleming, C. V., Wheeler, G. M., Cannella-Malone, H. I., Basbagill, A. R., Chung, Y. C., & Day, K. G. (2010). An evaluation of the use of eye gaze to measure preference of individuals with severe physical and developmental disabilities. *Developmental Neurorehabilitation, 13*(4), 266–275. doi:10.3109/17518421003705706

Frith, U. & Hill, E. (Eds.). (2003). *Autism: Mind and brain.* New York, NY: Oxford University Press.

Geiger, K. B., Carr, J. E., & LeBlanc, L. A. (2010). Function-based treatments for escape-maintained problem behavior: A treatment-selection model for practicing behavior analysts. *Behavior Analysis in Practice, 3*(1), 22–32. doi:10.1007/bf03391755

Hagopian, L. P., Wilson, D. M., & Wilder, D. A. (2001). Assessment and treatment of problem behavior maintained by escape from attention and access to tangible items. *Journal of Applied Behavior Analysis, 34*(2), 229–232. doi:10.1901/jaba.2001.34-229

Hanley, G. P., Iwata, B. A., Lindberg, J. S., & Conners, J. (2003). Response-restriction analysis I: Assessment of activity preferences. *Journal of Applied Behavior Analysis, 36*(1), 47–58. doi:10.1901/jaba.2003.36-47

Hawkins, R. P. (1979). The functions of assessment: Implications for selection and development of devices for assessing repertoires in clinical, educational, and other settings. *Journal of Applied Behavior Analysis, 12*, 501–516. doi:10.1901/jaba.1979.12-501

Levy, F. (2007). Theories of autism. *Australian & New Zealand Journal of Psychiatry, 41*(11), 859–868. doi:10.1080/00048670701634937

Lovaas, O. I., Koegel, R. L., & Schreibman, L. (1979). Stimulus overselectivity in autism: A review of the research. *Psychological Bulletin, 86*, 1236–1254. doi:10.1037//0033-2909.86.6.1236

Lovaas, O. I., Schreibman, L. Koegel, R., & Rehm, R. (1971). Selective responding by autistic children to multiple sensory input. *Journal of Abnormal Psychology, 77*, 211–222. doi:10.1037/h0031015

Matson, J. L. & Boisjoli, J. A. (2009). The token economy for children with intellectual disability and/or autism. A review. *Research in Developmental Disabilities, 30*, 240–248. doi:10.1016/j.ridd.2008.04.001

McLaughlin, T. F. & Williams, R. L. (1988). The token economy in the classroom. In J. C. Witt, S. N. Elliott, & F. M. Gresham (Eds.), *Handbook of behavior therapy in education* (pp. 469–487). New York, NY: Plenum. doi:10.1007/978-1-4613-0905-5

Reed, S. R., Stahmer, A. C., Suhrheinrich, J., & Schreibman, L. (2013). Stimulus overselectivity in typical development: Implications for teaching children with autism. *Journal of Autism and Developmental Disorders, 43*(6), 1249–1257. doi:10.1007/s10803-012-1658-x

Rimland, B. (1964). *Infantile autism. The syndrome and its implications for a neural theory of behavior*. New York, NY: Appleton-Century-Crofts.

Rodriguez, N. M., Levesque, M. A., Cohrs, V. L., & Niemeier, J. J. (2017). Teaching children with autism to request help with difficult tasks. *Journal of Applied Behavior Analysis, 50*(4), 717–732. doi:10.1002/jaba.420

Smaby, K., MacDonald, R. P., Ahearn, W. H., & Dube, W. V. (2007). Assessment protocol for identifying preferred social consequences. *Behavioral Interventions, 22*(4), 311–318. doi:10.1002/bin.242

Taylor, B. A. & Harris, S. L. (1995). Teaching children with autism to seek information: Acquisition of novel information and generalization of responding. *Journal of Applied Behavior Analysis, 28*, 3–14. doi:10.1901/jaba.1995.28-3

Tullis, C. A., Cannella-Malone, H. I., Basbigill, A. R., Yeager, A., Fleming, C. V., Payne, D., & Wu, P. F. (2011). Review of the choice and preference assessment literature for individuals with severe to profound disabilities. *Education and Training in Autism and Developmental Disabilities*, 46(4), 576–595. Retrieved from www.jstor.org/stable/24232368

Wacker, D. P., Harding, J. W., & Berg, W. K. (2008). Evaluation of mand-reinforcer relations following long-term functional communication training. *The Journal of Speech and Language Pathology—Applied Behavior Analysis, 3*(1), 25–35. doi:10.1037/h0100229

Wilder, D. A., Schadler, J., Higbee, T. S., Haymes, L. K., Bajagic, V., & Register, M. (2008). Identification of olfactory stimuli as reinforcers in individuals with autism: A preliminary investigation. *Behavioral Interventions, 23*(2), 97–103. doi:10.1002/bin.257

Yoon, S. & Bennett, G. M. (2000). Effects of a stimulus-stimulus pairing procedure on conditioning vocal sounds as reinforcers. *The Analysis of Verbal Behavior, 17*, 75–88. doi:10.1007/bf03392957

# 10 Understanding Learning Disabilities

## Implications for Teachers and Parents

*Jason P. Kaplan and Gayle Macklem*

Children with learning disabilities (LD) account for almost 39% of the approximately 5.9 million school-aged children who received special education services in the United States (Cortiella & Horowitz, 2014). It is further estimated another 15% or more students struggle because of unidentified and unaddressed problems (National Center for Learning Disabilities, n.d.). Despite the prevalence of LD, several misconceptions and misunderstandings persist about the definition, evaluation, and diagnosis of LD (National Joint Committee on Learning Disabilities, 2011). Unfortunately, these fallacies create a lot of confusion for parents and teachers working with students and often result in delays of appropriate services and/or timely intervention. By correcting some of these fallacies, parents and teachers will be better poised to provide support and intervene sooner with struggling learners.

This chapter will cover common misconceptions and misunderstandings related to the definition, characteristics, cognitive ability, and perceived laziness of children with LD. Additionally, we will discuss the labeling of reading disabilities; the effects of a learning disability on a student, such as the social and emotional complications of LD; and how to increase the success of students with LD in post-secondary education.

### Why It Matters

Learning disabilities are one of the least understood and hotly debated disabilities (Bradley, Danielson, & Hallahan, 2002). Since the introduction of the term LD in 1963, many groups and organizations have offered definitions leading to even more confusion and resulting in many unidentified children (Shifrer, Muller, & Callahan, 2011). The consequences of not identifying students who may have LDs can be devastating to children, their families, and society. Those children who are not identified are at a higher risk for repeating a grade, being suspended or dropping out of school, being involved with the juvenile justice system, not finishing college, and/or not being employed (Horowitz, Rawe, & Whittaker, 2017).

### *What Is a Learning Disability?*

Since the introduction of the term learning disability, many groups and organizations have offered definitions. Perhaps the most common definition of LD used in education is the one that appears in the Individuals with Disabilities Education Act (IDEA). This is the definition used to determine whether a child is eligible for special education services in school. IDEA defines a specific learning disability as:

> A disorder in one or more of the basic psychological processes involved in understanding or in using language, spoken or written, which disorder may manifest itself in the imperfect ability to listen, think, speak, read, write, spell, or do mathematical calculations. Such term includes such conditions as perceptual disabilities, brain injury, minimal brain dysfunction, dyslexia, and developmental aphasia. Such term does not include a learning problem that is primarily the result of visual, hearing, or motor disabilities, of mental retardation, of emotional disturbance, or of environmental, cultural, or economic disadvantage.
>
> (20 U.S.C. §1401 (30)

While the definition of LD provides one way to think about the disability, there is a basic consensus among most professionals that learning disabilities are neurologically-based and make the process of learning difficult. They interfere with a child's ability to efficiently and effectively learn specific academic skills (e.g., reading, writing, math). This difficulty learning is often inconsistent with a student's overall intellectual abilities. Because students with LD often, but not always, function at least within the average range of ability, the differences in a student's functioning are often referred to as the gap between the child's potential and actual achievement (Cortiella & Horowitz, 2014). It is important to be aware of the fact that LDs manifest regardless of factors such as culture, race, language, gender, or socioeconomic status (National Joint Committee on Learning Disabilities, 2011).

### *Characteristics of Common Types of LD*

Some of the more common labels for LD include dyslexia (reading), language-based learning disabilities, dyscalculia (math), and dysgraphia (writing), (Horowitz et al., 2017). Despite the designation *Specific Learning Disability* (SLD), children with LD often underachieve in several academic areas; their difficulties are not limited to a single area. There are common similarities in reading and math disabilites. Research indicates there are shared weaknesses in working memory, processing speed, and verbal comprehension (Willcutt et al., 2013). While researchers have found an overlap between different types of disabilities, there are some distinct differences. Reading disabilities are more associated with weaknesses in Phonemic awareness and naming speed, while deficits in math are more closely associated with weaknesses in task shifting (Willcutt et al., 2013).

Understanding the charactertics and symptoms of learning difficulties is important in order to provide early support to struggling learners. Many children with LDs are likely to also have poor planning and organizing (Locascio, Mahone, & Eason, 2010), while others may present with social or emotional difficulties as a result of a learning issue (Backenson et al., 2015). As Backenson et al. (2015) found, children with processing deficits (difficulty using information) had higher of levels of internalizing (sadness or anxiety) symptoms and poorer adaptive functioning than those with other subtypes of LD and those without LD. This highlights the need for parents and teachers to be aware of the many ways in which LD may present.

To clarify some of the terms used to identify various LDs, the Office of Special Education and Rehabilitation Services (OSERS) issued a letter to schools. This letter was the result of parent and advocacy group concerns that some schools and state agencies were avoiding or refusing to use the technical labels for different types of learning disabilities that have been identified in the literature. In the letter, the Assistant Secretary made it clear that nothing in the law prohibits the use of the terms dyslexia, dyscalculia, or dysgraphia by schools (Yudin, 2015). Schools must identify students who exhibit disabilities through a comprehensive evaluation. They must provide evidence-based interventions for those who are eligible, monitor their progress, and adjust the interventions as needed. Teachers providing remediation benefit from knowing the specific areas a student has difficulty with, such as decoding skills in the case of dyslexia.

### *ADHD Is Not a Learning Disability*

Even though LDs are distinct disabilities, several related conditions can also significantly affect learning. Some of the more commonly associated weaknesses include executive functioning deficits, which involve planning, organizing, strategizing, remembering details, and managing time effectively; memory deficits; and auditory and visual processing deficits (Cortiella & Horowitz, 2014). Despite the fact these deficits are not labeled LDs, they can interfere with the ability to process information efficiently and can help explain why a student may have problems with learning.

Another disability which can impact learning is attention deficit hyperactivity disorder (ADHD). Even though ADHD is a different condition, estimates indicate that there is a about a 45% overlap between these two conditions, with many children with ADHD experiencing problems in reading, math, and/or writing (DuPaul, Gormley, & Laracy, 2013). Mattison and Mayes (2012) found that children with ADHD and LD scored significantly lower than children without learning disabilities on measures associated with academic competence (i.e., processing speed and working memory). This underscores the need to screen for ADHD when evaluating a child for LDs, and screening for LDs when evaluating a child for ADHD. Although ADHD is not a learning disability, students with ADHD may need and be eligible for various supports in school.

### *Are Learning Disabilities Mild Disabilities?*

Because we cannot "see" learning disabilities, some parents or school personnel may think that this condition is not serious and may mistakenly relate a child's inability to make progress to laziness, poor motivation, or low ability (National Joint Committee on Learning Disabilities, 2011). This may not be the case. Many students with LD have uneven patterns of strengths and weaknesses (Miciak, Fletcher, Vaugh, & Tolar, 2014) that affect the severity and pervasiveness of their learning difficulties. Based on the demands of the learning task and the nature of the presenting problems, a child's learning difficulty may be more apparent when they attempt one learning task and be nonexistent in another (National Joint Committee on Learning Disabilities, 2011).

One common question that parents and teachers ask is whether there is a medical test that can be given to find out whether a child has a learning disability and how severe it may be. Even though LDs have a neurological basis, there are no specific medical tests that can be given to identify a learning disability.

However, parents or teachers suspecting that a child may have a learning disability can obtain a comprehensive evaluation from their school's special education eligibility team. This team will use a variety of different psychological and academic tests to help determine whether a child has a learning disability. Key components of a comprehensive evaluation include obtaining information from multiple data sources, including, but not limited to: standardized tests, informal measures, student observations, student self-reports, parent reports, progress monitoring data, and general education work samples (Learning Disabilities Association of America, 2010).

### *Social and Emotional Complication of LD*

In addition to struggling with difficulties when learning, children with LD may also present with associated mental health issues. For example, students with LDs who under-achieve are more likely to experience decreased self-esteem and report symptoms of anxiety and depression compared to their typical peers (Alesi, Rappo, & Pepi, 2015). Alesi et al. (2015) identified depressive symptoms in students with LDs as young as nine years of age. These students additionally experienced higher school-based anxiety and lower academic self-esteem than their non-disabled peers.

A meta-analysis (comprised of many studies) of parent- and teacher-reported symptoms of depression showed that depressive symptomatology in students with LDs were significantly higher than in typically developing students (Nelson & Harwood, 2011). Interestingly, parents reported more symptoms than students did themselves. This may be because parents observe behavioral symptoms of depression, and/or because parents of students with LD experience more stress than parents of students without learning disabilities. Students reported internally experienced symptoms. An evaluation for possible symptoms of depression may be warranted based on reports of depressive symptomatology on the part of parents, teachers, or students themselves. Additionally, it is important for educators and parents to focus on teaching strategies to cope with stress while also helping students master academic strategies.

Mammarella et al. (2016) looked at students with LDs in grades 3 to 6. They found that students in the 8–11 age range were experiencing anxiety about school. Specifically, children with reading disabilities experienced more severe symptoms of anxiety than other handicapped and non-handicapped children. These students also experienced social anxiety. The fact that students were experiencing social anxiety is not surprising given Elias (2004) described difficulties with social relationships as a "common feature of most students with learning disabilities" (p. 53); these students had both difficulty with social interaction and a tendency to be rejected by their peers. Elias felt that difficulties associated with learning disabilities could affect understanding one's social world, taking the perspective of others, and recognizing feelings in themselves and others.

### *Late Emerging Reading Disabilities*

Research suggests the signs of reading disabilities are often present as early as preschool (Papadimitriou & Vlachos, 2014). However, there is a subset of children who develop reading disabilities at an older age. Leach, Scarborough, and Rescorla (2003) identified students whose reading achievement dropped in grade 4. They described these students as having late emerging reading disabilities (LERD). In the Leach et al. study, 47% of students with LD were found to be late-identified (p. 221). These students were not missed by schools; instead, the LDs were simply emerging late.

Another group of researchers was interested in how many children developed poor reading skills for the first time when in fourth grade (Etmanskie, Partanen, & Siegel, 2016). This group determined that there were about equal proportions of students who had early- versus late-emerging reading difficulties. Most of the students who evidenced early, or inconsistent reading difficulties, continued to score within the below average range when they were in grade 7. However, of the children who experienced late developing reading difficulties in grade 4, most (67%) scored in the average range by grade 7. Researchers also explored whether or not the students whose reading problems surfaced in grade 4 could be identified as early as Kindergarten. In fact, the late emerging difficulties in reading comprehension were predicted by poor scores on a working memory task in Kindergarten.

### *Increasing Success in Post-Secondary Education*

Researchers have found that high school seniors with LD tend to experience more school disengagement and emotional stress when transitioning from secondary school to college compared to other students (DuPaul, Pinho, Pollack, Gormley, & Laracy, 2015). They are less likely to pursue post-secondary education in general (Joshi & Bouck, 2017). Because increasing numbers of students with LD want to obtain post-secondary education of some kind (Joshi & Bouck, 2017), we need to know how to help them.

First, high school teachers and specialists can help by determining *exactly* what students with LD actually need in order to succeed (Weis, Dean, & Osborne, 2016); and second, educators must carefully consider the academic placement of students with LDs who have the cognitive ability to succeed in college while they are still in high school (Joshi & Bouck, 2017). High school students who earned 80% or more of their high school credits in general education classrooms compared to special education tutorial settings were more likely to attend colleges and stay enrolled compared to those who continued to receive support in special education settings (Rojewski, Lee, & Gregg, 2013). Transition planning teams need to consider placing bright students with LDs in general education classrooms for core subjects when possible. Other predictors of success for students with LD include students' grade point average (Joshi & Bouck, 2017), self-awareness, proactivity, perseverance, appropriate goal setting, use of available supports, and emotional stability (Goldberg, Higgins, Raskind, & Herman, 2003; Raskind, Goldberg, Higgins, & Herman, 1999).

Another potential issue for students is that the laws which protect students with LDs in college are different in that these laws are designed to keep disabled students from being discriminated against, rather than being designed to remediate disabilities (Weis et al., 2016, p. 484). Colleges report that many accommodations written for high school students with LD were not supported by evidence from psychoeducational report test data, current functioning toward the end of high school, or the past history of students with LDs (Weis et al., 2016). Teachers and parents need to develop specific recommendations to share with colleges, including exactly which academic areas need accommodations, and for what length of time they should be provided. The risk of providing students with accommodations they do not need in high school is that colleges may not honor generalized accommodations.

## Notes from the Field

*Trey is an eight-year-old third grader who did relatively well in school academically and socially in the early grades. Trey often met grade level expectations, or was just barely below, and his parents were told not to worry. Recently, at Trey's mid-year parent–teacher conference, his teacher informed Trey's parents that he was below grade level in reading and was having trouble with writing. The teacher also mentioned she was concerned about Trey's attention and suggested talking with the family's pediatrician about an attention disorder. Trey's teacher concluded the conference by saying that Trey was lazy. She said: "When he wants to do well, he can." She went on to say that Trey was starting to act out during reading period and he often asked to go the bathroom during the writing block. At home Trey had always been reluctant to practice reading but he would sit and listen to stories read to him. Lately, Trey has been coming home saying that school is boring and that he does not want to go anymore. Trey's parents left the conference feeling concerned and unsure of what next steps to take.*

This story is typical of a child who may have a learning disability. It is not uncommon for children with LDs to be successful in the primary grades and then begin to have trouble. In Trey's case, it is likely that the demands of the first and second grade curriculum were somewhat manageable for him, but as the work became more complex, his ability to perform independently decreased. Additionally, in most cases, emotional, behavioral, and attention issues in school do not spontaneously appear as they have in Trey's case. This suggests that his recent behavior may well be related to the achievement difficulties he is currently experiencing in school. There is enough evidence to suggest that additional information is warranted in order to begin to understand the changes in Trey's academic and behavioral functioning. The good news is that Trey is only in fourth grade and there is a lot of time to intervene and teach him compensatory strategies.

For students who are identified as experiencing learning difficulties even earlier in their school careers, parents and teachers need to know that this does not necessarily predict failure. With appropriate instruction and support, children with learning disabilities can be successful (Cortiella & Horowitz, 2014). Instruction needs to be matched to the student's individual needs, and if the child does not make progress, it is important to make instructional changes and/or move to more intensive services early, rather than simply waiting and watching (Miller, Vaughan, & Freund, 2014).

## Practical Tools for School-Based Professionals

- Teachers can provide strong support and encouragement for students with LDs, and can help them identify their strengths (Idan & Margalit, 2014).
- It is important to be aware of the fact that even when students with LDs perform as well as their peers academically, they may still experience considerable emotional distress (Idan & Margalit, 2014).
- Teachers can model the following productive learning behaviors:
  - Viewing mistakes as a normal part of learning.
  - Asking for clarification and asking for help.
  - Talking about productive and unproductive strategies for mastery in the relevant content area.
- Discourage students from comparing themselves to others. Emphasize that everyone has personal strengths and weaknesses.
- Relating concepts taught in class to real-life situations makes ideas more meaningful for students with LD.
- Including extra practice and review improves the mastery levels of all students, including those with LDs (Steele, 2005).
- Teachers need to be aware that some students with LDs have deficits in working memory. These students benefit from routines, procedures, and structure. Additionally, visual clues, modeling, and rehearsal of desired behaviors along with short, simple, and sequential directions can make a big difference for these students (Virginia Department of Education, 2017, p. 3).
- Teachers and specialists should consider which accommodations students with LDs actually need. Students at the high school level may be able to make these judgments for themselves and will share their thoughts if asked (see Lovell and Landowski, 2015).
- It is important to determine each student's very specific needs to share with colleges. Teachers can help by working with students to determine what actually helps and what does not really make a difference.

## Take Home Ideas for Parents

- Parents of students with LDs are likely to have to play a more active role in regard to assisting their children with schoolwork than parents of typically developing children (Idan & Margalit, 2014).
- Be the expert on your child. Learn as much as you can about your child's needs. As a parent, you need to be the advocate for your child.
- If you suspect that your child has a LD and is struggling to learn, many proactive steps can be taken. First, collect as much information as you can about your student's academic, social, and emotional functioning.

Talk with teachers and keep notes of meetings and conversations (including those with specialist teachers, such as the music, physical education, and art teachers, coaches, and extracurricular instructors). While LDs may have the greatest impact on school performance, symptoms of LDs may also manifest themselves outside of school at a dance class or soccer practice. Other sources of information that can provide insight include old progress reports and report cards (even those from pre-K can sometimes be helpful), and work samples from your child's current and past grades.

- Talk with your pediatrician to make sure that your child does not have any medical issues that could be interfering with his or her learning. For example, children with undiagnosed sleep disorders can appear inattentive or disabled (Shochat, Cohen-Zion, & Tzischinsky, 2014).
- Meet with the learning specialist, special education teacher, or school psychologist at your child's school to discuss your concerns. Opening the lines of communication with school professionals and sharing your experiences at home is a very important component to your child's success. Also, ask what you can do at home to help.
- In many states, a response-to-intervention (RTI) process must be implemented prior to, or as part of, the evaluation for a LD. If your child is receiving intervention services as part of RTI or other multi-tiered systems of support, ask the school to describe their progress-monitoring plan, including the types of data collected and at what intervals. It will also be important to develop specific goals for your child, and understand how the school will determine whether an evaluation is needed. Finally, arrange for a follow-up meeting with your child's teacher(s) to review intervention data and evaluate progress toward goals.
- While many schools do an excellent job of supporting struggling learners, if your concerns persist, it is within your legal right as a parent or teacher to request a comprehensive evaluation for a learning disability; school professionals will initiate an evaluation if they agree or will explain their rationale if they disagree. When requesting an evaluation, you should address your letter to the school principal and/or special education administrator. In the letter, be sure to clearly state that you are concerned that your student may have a learning disability and provide examples to support your concern along with a list of questions you would like the school to address. For example; "My student has consistently not met grade level expectations and struggles to write cohesive paragraphs. I would like to know why he/she is having so much difficulty."

## References

Alesi, M., Rappo, G., & Pepi, A. (2015). Emotional profile and intellectual functioning: A comparison among children with borderline functioning, average intellectual functioning, and gifted intellectual functioning. *Sage Open, 5*(3). doi:10.1177/2158244015589995

Backenson, E. M., Holland, S. C., Kubas, H. A., Fitzer K. R., Wilcox, G., Carmichael, J. A., ... Hale, J. B. (2015). Psychosocial and adaptive deficits associated with learning disability. *Journal of Learning Disabilities, 48*(5), 511–522. doi:10.1177/0022219413511861

Bradley, R., Danielson, L., & Hallahan D. P. (2002). *Identification of learning disabilities: Research to practice.* Mahwah, NJ: Erlbaum.

Cortiella, C. & Horowitz, S. H. (2014). *State of learning disabilities: Facts, trends, and emerging issues.* New York, NY: National Center for Learning Disabilities. Retrieved from www.ncld.org/wp-content/uploads/2014/11/2014-State-of-LD.pdf

DuPaul, G. J., Gormley, M. J., & Laracy, S. D. (2013). Comorbidity of LD and ADHD: Implications of DEM-5 for assessment and treatment. *Journal of Learning Disabilities, 46*(1), 42–51. doi:10.1177/0022219412464351

DuPaul, G. J., Pinho, T. D., Pollack, B. L., Gormley, M. J., & Laracy, S. D. (2015). Differences in engagement, positive core self-evaluation, school preparation, and college expectations. *Journal of Learning Disabilities, 50*(3), 238–251. doi:10.1177/0022219415617164

Elias, M. J. (2004). The connection between social-emotional learning and learning disabilities: Implications for intervention. *Learning Disabilities Quarterly, 27*(1), 53–63. doi:10.2307/1593632

Etmanskie, J. M., Partanen, M., & Siegel, L. S. (2016). A longitudinal examination of the persistence of late emerging reading disabilities. *Journal of Learning Disabilities, 49*(1), 21–35. doi:10.3102/0013189X10378400

Goldberg, R. J., Higgins, E. L., Raskind, M. H., & Herman, K. L. (2003). Predictors of success in individuals with learning disabilities: A qualitative analysis of a 20-year longitudinal study. *Learning Disabilities Research & Practice, 18*(4), 222–236. doi:10.1111/1540-5826.00077

Horowitz, S. H., Rawe, J., & Whittaker, M. C. (2017). *The state of learning disabilities: Understanding the 1 in 5.* New York, NY: National Center for Learning Disabilities. Retrieved from www.ncld.org/the-state-of-learning-disabilities-understanding-the-1-in-5.

Idan, O. & Margalit, M. (2014). Socioemotional self-perceptions, family climate, and hopeful thinking among students with learning disabilities and typically achieving students from the same class. *Journal of Learning Disabilities, 47*(2), 136–152. doi:10.1177/0022219412439608

Individuals with Disability Educational Improvement Act, Pub. L. No. 108–446, 118 Stat. 2647 (2004).

Joshi, G. S. & Bouck, E. C. (2017). Examining postsecondary education predictors and participation for students with learning disabilities. *Journal of Learning Disabilities, 50*(1), 3–13. doi:10.1177/0022219415572894

Leach, J., Scarborough, H., & Rescorla, L. (2003). Late-emerging reading disabilities. *Journal of Educational Psychology, 95*, 211–224. doi:10.1037/0022-0663.95.2.211

Learning Disabilities Association of America (2010). *White paper on evaluation, identification, and eligibility criteria for students with specific learning disabilities*. Pittsburgh, PA: Author.

Locascio, G., Mahone, M., & Eason, S. H. (2010). Executive dysfunction among children with reading comprehension deficits. *Journal of Learning Disabilities, 43*(5), 441–454. doi:10.1177/0022219409355476.

Lovell, B. J. & Landowski, L. J. (2015). *Testing accommodation for students with disabilities: Research-based practice.* Washington, DC: American Psychological Association.

Mammarella I. C., Ghisi, M., Bomba, M., Bottesi, G., Caviola, S., Broggi, F., & Nacinovich, R. (2016). Anxiety and depression in children with nonverbal learning disabilities, reading disabilities, or typical development. *Journal of Learning Disabilities, 49*(2), 130–139. doi:10.1177/0022219414529336

Mattison, R. E. & Mayes, S. D. (2012). Relationships between learning disability, executive functioning, and psychopathology in children with ADHD. *Journal of Attention Disorders, 16*(2), 138–146. doi:10.177.1087054710380188

Miciak, J., Fletcher, J. M., Vaugh, S., & Tolar, T. D. (2014). Patterns of cognitive strengths and weaknesses: Identification rates, agreement, and validity for learning disabilities identification. *School Psychology Quarterly, 29*(1), 21–37. doi:10.1037/spq0000037

Miller, B., Vaughan, S., & Freund, L., (2014). Learning disabilities research studies: Findings from NICHD funded projects. *Journal of Research on Educational Effectiveness, 7*(3), 225–231. doi:10.1080/19345747.2014.927251

National Center for Learning Disabilities (n.d.). *The State of LD: Identifying struggling students.* Retrieved from www.ncld.org/understanding-learning-and-attention-issues

National Joint Committee on Learning Disabilities (2011). Learning disabilities: Implications for policy regarding research and practice: A report by the national joint committee on learning disabilities, March 2011. *Learning Disabilities Quarterly, 34*(4), 237–241. doi:10.1177/0731948711421756

Nelson, J. M. & Harwood, H. (2011). Learning disabilities and anxiety: A meta-analysis. *Journal of Learning Disabilities, 44*(1), 3–17. doi:10.1177/0022219409359939

Papadimitriou, A. M. & Vlachos, F. M. (2014). Which specific skills developing during preschool years predict the reading performance in the first and second grade of primary school? *Early Child Development and Care, 184*(11), 1706–1722. doi:10.1080/03004430.2013.875542

Raskind, M. H., Goldberg, R. J., Higgins, E. L., & Herman, K. L. (1999). Patterns of change and predictors of success in individuals with learning disabilities: Results from a twenty-year longitudinal study. *Learning Disabilities Research & Practice, 14*, 35–49. doi:10.1207/sldrp1401_4

Rojewski, J. W., Lee, I. H., & Gregg, N. (2013). Casual effects of inclusion on postsecondary education outcomes of individuals with high-incidence disabilities. *Journal of Disability Policy Studies, 25*(4), 201–219. doi:10.1177/1044207313505648

Shifrer, D., Muller C., & Callahan, R. (2011). Disproportionality and learning disabilities: Parsing apart race socioeconomic status, and language. *Journal of Learning Disabilities, 44*(3), 246–257. doi:10.1177/0022219410374236

Shochat, T., Cohen-Zion, M., & Tzischinsky, O. (2014). Functional consequences of inadequate sleep in adolescents: A systematic review. *Sleep Medicine Reviews, 18*(1), 75–87. doi:10.1016/j.smrv.2013.03.005

Steele, M. M. (2005). Teaching students with learning disabilities; Constructivism or behaviorism. *Current Issues in Education, 8*(10). Retrieved from http://cie.asu.edu/ojs/index.php/cieatasu/article/view/1607

Virginia Department of Education (revised 2017). *Virginia's guidelines for students with specific learning disabilities*. Richmond, VA. Retrieved from www.doe.virginia.gov/special_ed/disabilities/learning_disability/learning_disabilities_guidelines.pdf

Weis, R., Dean, E. L., & Osborne, K. J. (2016). Accommodation decision making for postsecondary students with learning disabilities: Individually tailored or one size fits all? *Journal of Learning Disabilities, 49*(5), 484–498. doi:10.1177/0022219414559648

Willcutt, E. G., Petrill, S. A., Wu, S., Boada, R., DeFries, J. C., Olson, J. K., & Pennington, B. F. (2013) Comorbidity between reading disability and math disability: Concurrent psychopathology, functional impairment, and neuropsychological functioning. *Journal of Learning Disabilities, 46*(6), 500–516. doi:10.1177/0022219413477476

Yudin, M. K. (2015, October 23). *Dear colleague letter*. Washington, DC: U.S. Department of Education, Office of Special Education and Rehabilitation Services. Retrieved from www2.ed.gov/policy/speced/guid/idea/memosdcltrs/guidance-on-dyslexia-10-2015.pdf

# 11 Efforts to Prevent Bullying and Cyberbullying by Understanding Student Motivations

*Gayle Macklem and Barbara Miller*

Bullying is an age-old phenomenon, yet only relatively recently have there been serious efforts to study and address it. In spite of the fact that researchers have not as yet fully agreed upon a formal definition of bullying, we have some knowledge of the effects of face-to-face bullying as well as cyberbullying on both students and schools. Since bullying often takes place within a social context, we are also beginning to understand the various motivations that determine the role a student may play in a bullying episode. Fortunately, many schools are answering the call to address bullying by implementing prevention programs. In fact, there is some evidence that bullying may be decreasing somewhat (Waasdorp, Pas, Zablotsky, & Bradshaw, 2017; Zhang, Musu-Gillette, & Oudekerk, 2016). However, in light of the disappointing outcome data for some anti-bullying programs, we need to determine which interventions may have the best chance of working in schools, and what both parents and teachers can do to help.

## Notes from the Field

### *Sarah*

*Sarah is a happy seventh grader whose family moves to a new community just as she enters the eighth grade. In the new school, Sarah feels desperate to make new friends and recreate the social life she has left. She begins to spend time with some girls who are part of a popular group and soon discovers a social pressure that makes her feel really uncomfortable. The girls insist that in order to be accepted as a real friend she has to share her clothes with them. Sarah complies and lends items of clothing in fear of their threats that she will otherwise be rejected and isolated. She also finds that getting the clothing back is not so easy. Sarah's mother notices that things are missing when she does the laundry. Sarah becomes hysterical when confronted by her mother and she says that she has no choice because the girls will make her life miserable if she doesn't go along with the group behaviors.*

### *Jen and Bill*

*Jen and Bill have been high school sweethearts who know everything about each other, even secret passwords. When Jen decides that it would be good for the two of them to begin to date other people, Bill becomes enraged. He leaves Jen with no choice but to break up with him. Bill goes on a rampage and decides that he will ruin her social life. He represents himself as Jen and posts hateful comments about some of their friends on social media. When Jen begins to realize what is happening, she is terrified of what else Bill might do given how much personal information he has about her.*

### *Michael*

*Michael Jones is an athletic fifth grader whose father is a basketball coach. He has a lot of social status because many of the other boys admire his athletic prowess and envy that he has a dad who is well known in the community. Michael is very aggressive toward certain students during recess. When these boys try to shoot baskets, he calls them losers, takes the ball, throws it at them, and trips them as they run. His friends laugh. After several mothers complain, the principal asks Mrs. Jones to come to school to discuss this behavior. Her response is that the school is totally overreacting. She believes that boys play hard and she has read that male social interaction tends to be physical. She insists that is how boys relate. Furthermore, if anyone's child should know about sportsmanship, it would certainly be hers.*

### *Laura*

*Laura is a fourth-grade student who is very studious and socially awkward. A clique of girls who consider themselves to be very cool make fun of her behind her back and call her a bookworm. They post pictures on the internet of worms reading books with her name and with negative comments about her.*

These examples of bullying and cyberbullying reflect behaviors that are all too common. The general public has become increasingly concerned about bullying in recent years. Parents and school professionals are both frustrated and mobilized to deal with these incidents.

## Why It Matters

Dan Olweus, a Swedish researcher, is considered the most influential authority on bullying. His expanded description of bullying behavior includes the behaviors most people associate with bullying such as hitting and shoving, and also includes behaviors such as ignoring and excluding a student, telling lies, spreading rumors, and both mean and hurtful behaviors.

There has been considerable discussion among researchers in regard to which behaviors should be considered bullying behaviors. The bottom line for Olweus is that bullying is aggressive behavior that is intentional, involves an imbalance of power in the eyes of the targeted child, and is usually repeated (Olweus, 2013). One of the points of contention in regard to bullying behaviors has been what to call a single incident of aggression which would be considered bulling if repeated. Olweus has responded to the debate by revising his criteria and pointing out that repetition is common, but he actually never considered repetition an absolutely necessary criterion. This reconsideration is certainly helpful when formulating a definition of cyberbullying behaviors or bullying through electronic media. In the case of cyberbullying, a single hurtful posting can be read repeatedly by the target of the bullying and shared with an enormous audience. The power differential in cyberbullying may rely on a difference in technical expertise.

### *Bullying Occurs in Groups*

It is important to think of bullying as a group phenomenon because it is influenced by the media and technology and also because bullying behaviors are witnessed in schools, neighborhoods, and even in some homes (Swearer & Hymel, 2015). Bullying typically occurs in small groups and in situations where children consider aggression to be normal. The participants in a bullying incident may include the bully, a child who is sometimes the bully and is also victimized, the victim who is typically passive, and the children who are present when bullying takes place, who are referred to as bystanders.

### *Victims of Bullying*

Anything that makes a child different from the peer group might trigger bullying. Victims of school bullying can be hurt both physically and psychologically (Jeong, Kwak, Moon, & San Miguel, 2013). Bullied victims tend to perform less well in school. They are at risk for mental health difficulties and for relational problems with peers. Children who are vulnerable to bullying need to be identified early (Arseneault, Bowes, & Skakoor, 2010). The risk for being victimized is not equal for all children (Menesini & Salmivalli, 2017). Vulnerable children include students who tend to be isolated, anxious, depressed, cry easily, have low self-esteem, and are not assertive. They may wander around the outskirts of the playground trying not to be seen and appear to be stressed (Arseneault et al., 2010). Students with disabilities, those who are obese, or students belonging to ethnic or sexual minorities are at greater risk (Menesini & Salmivalli, 2017). Some victims of bullying are aggressive in the early grades and are later rejected. Some children tend to be bullied chronically and may show signs of severe psychological problems.

Although many students tend to be able to adapt and cope when victimized, some children bullied even less than two to three times a month experience detrimental effects in regard to their feelings of well-being and happiness (Fullchange & Furlong, 2016). Bullying undermines personal and social supports, leading to difficulties in coping for these children as their belief in others decreases. Victims of frequent victimization and by several bullies suffer more than those bullied less frequently or by fewer peers (Menesini & Salmivalli, 2017). In the short term, these students can experience severe symptoms of mental health problems. The effects of bullying on children's adjustment can last a long time. The children who are bullied and then bully others have the most negative outcomes.

Cyberbullying refers to bullying using electronic means such as email, blogs, instant messages, Snapchat, or text messages (Kowalski, Giumetti, Schroeder, & Lattanner, 2014). The consequences of cyberbullying are many, including anxiety and depression, decreased school performance and truancy, physical symptoms, and in rare cases suicide (Kowalski et al., 2014). Risk factors for becoming a cybervictim include stress, anxiety, depression, loneliness, substance use, emotional problems, and also somatic problems (Kowalski et al., 2014). Cybervictims tend to be lonely, anxious and/or depressed, spend a good deal of time online, are rejected and isolated by peers, and have low self-esteem (Guo, 2016). Victims of cyberbullying are often, but not always, victims of physical and verbal bullying as well.

### *Bullies*

Children who bully have various motivations for their behaviors (Peeters, Cillessen, & Scholte, 2010; Rigby, 2012). Some bullies are quite aggressive and have little empathy or social understanding of their victims. They justify their aggressive actions and feel no guilt or remorse. When caught, these students may say that the victim annoyed them or that they were getting even over some perceived slight. Other bullies are aggressive because they misinterpret the actions of others. This group of children is reactive in confrontational social situations. Some bullies have a good deal of social power and are popular, even though at the same time their peers dislike them. Other bullies with less developed emotional understanding may not realize they are causing harm at the time they engage in bullying. They may explain that they were bored and were just having fun, or were just involved because others were doing it, with little awareness of the pain they cause (Macklem, 2015; Rigby, 2012).

Bullies with a strong understanding of social relationships, along with the ability to manipulate the group, tend to use nonphysical or relational bullying (Peeters et al., 2010). Relational bullying involves hurtful behavior designed to damage the targeted child's position in the social group or reputation. These bullies use relational bullying to become powerful among their peers and then to retain their power. They are able to convince others to ignore the victimized child and side against her/him. Some bullies may be unpopular. These bullies also use relational aggression to make themselves feel powerful. The difference between unpopular and popular bullies is that unpopular bullies openly ignore and exclude others, whereas popular bullies use indirect strategies like gossip to manipulate the group. Classmates do not tend to like popular and socially skilled girls who bully, for example, because these bullies reject or exclude girls who have less status.

Large studies of the research on cyberbullying (meta-analyses) list the risks for getting involved in cyberbullying to include: participating in traditional bullying, engaging in risky behaviors online, frequent use of the internet, and individual characteristics such as low empathy (Kowalski et al., 2014, pp. 1124, 1127). The correlations or relationships between traditional bullying and cyberbullying are high but not perfect, as some students involved in cyberbullying are not involved in traditional bullying. Some cyberbullies believe that bullying is an acceptable way to behave, and others do not make the connection between what they are doing and the consequences of their behavior. When students engaging in cyberbullying act intentionally but are just having fun without really intending to hurt the child they target, they are considered to be *inadvertent* cyberbullies (Sabella, Patchin, & Hinduja, 2013). These students may need education rather than punishment when the consequences for bullying involve zero tolerance.

### *Bystanders*

Bystanders are the students who are present when a bullying incident occurs. The bystander effect suggests that individuals are less likely to offer assistance when others are present (Hudson & Bruckman, 2004). Bystanders may encourage bullying just by the fact that they are present when bullying is taking place. They may support the bully by joining in. Some bystanders may speak up and defend the targeted child, although the likelihood of someone supporting the victim decreases as children go through the grade levels. Other bystanders may join in because they feel that it is the safest thing to do at the time (Rigby, 2012). Still others admit that they were just going along with the crowd or didn't want to miss out on the fun.

The bystander effect has to do with group behavior. If other bystanders are present, the individual student is less likely to support the victim (Howard, Landau, & Pryor, 2014). When an individual child in a group realizes that others are not going to act, any thought of stepping up and helping is crushed. A young child is less likely to speak up if there is a parent or teacher present. Some children who watch but don't help cope with the uncomfortable feelings they experience by using self-talk to distance themselves from what is going on. Their sense of safety is affected. Still other children may not intervene because they believe that bullying is normal and therefore okay. They may see aggressive behavior as culturally acceptable and may devalue or blame the victim.

Bystanders' decisions about how to respond to a bullying situation may depend on a variety of factors (Howard et al., 2014). An individual student may consider whether speaking up will affect what is happening. A student may consider whether or not the bully will retaliate if challenged because the person who speaks up may become the next victim. A bystander may worry about losing his or her position in the group. Another consideration may be the relationship of the bystander to the child being bullied. The targeted child may or may not be a friend. An individual child's relationship with the victim or bully will influence a bystander's response.

Girls are more likely to react with empathy and concern to a bullying incident than boys (Howard et al., 2014). They are also more likely to experience distress when viewing a bullying incident as compared to boys. Boys who believe aggressive behavior is okay are more likely to think bullying is okay. They may watch, laugh, cheer, or join in. Children want to be accepted by their peers and this desire influences their behavior. Boys who believe that aggressive behavior is not okay are more likely to include a victim in their games or to support the victim in some way. Boys' beliefs about aggression make a difference in whether or not they will react positively in a bullying situation.

### *Bullying in the Classroom*

At the classroom level, when popular students are involved in frequent bullying and classmates laugh or join in, the popular bullies are rewarded with attention. Bullying becomes acceptable behavior (Menesini, Palladino, & Nocentini, 2015). When the most-liked students in the class are the bullies, their behavior becomes attractive to their classmates. When children are in classes with bystanders who smile, enjoy watching bullying, and by their reactions support bulling, this behavior encourages other well-liked students to take on bullying roles. When bystanders reinforce bullying behavior, individual students who may not otherwise engage in bullying behavior on their own are influenced to join in.

Group dynamics in the classroom have an effect on cyberbullying as well. When victims are supported by classmates, there is significantly less cyberbullying in those classes. Interestingly, studies have found cyberbullying was higher in classes where students believed that teachers would intervene when they learned about bullying (Elledge et al., 2013). Bullies in these classes may have simply found another way to be aggressive toward peers.

### *Prevention of Bullying*

Because of the intense interest bullying has received by the general public, educators, and researchers, there are a number of bullying prevention efforts in schools not only in the U.S., but also in many other countries. There have been sufficient efforts to prevent bullying in schools for researchers to conduct major reviews and large analyses (meta-analyses) to try to determine whether or not preventive efforts are working (Bradshaw, 2015). Bradshaw reviewed a large group of studies and determined that the overall prevention effect is somewhat mixed (p. 323). She determined that the programs worked better for children in the 11- to 14-year age group and worked better in Europe than in the U.S. or Canada. Programs that worked best involved close adult supervision both inside and outside of the classroom, teaching and enforcing expected rules of behavior, and involving parents. In order for any bullying prevention program or curricula to work, it must be taught as closely as possible to the way the designers and researchers intended.

Implementation has to do with how well a program is delivered in the real world. It strongly determines the effectiveness of an intervention (Low, Van Ryzin, Brown, Smith, & Haggerty, 2014). Implementing whole-school bullying prevention programs is quite a challenge in regard to complexity of various stakeholders' interests and the needed coordination among a large contingent of staff, students, parents, and the local community. School staff must pay attention to the following:

- Lesson components;
- The quality of instruction;
- Efforts to generalize skills;
- Training teachers to coach students both within the classroom and in less structured areas of the school;
- Ensuring student engagement;
- Involving parents; and
- Working with both mental health staff and administrators around actual bullying incidents.

It is not unusual to find out much later after bullying has been taking place that students did not tell adults about the incidents. There is considerable peer pressure on students not to tattle in schools. Students may not report they are being bullied for a number of other reasons as well, including:

- Blaming themselves for provoking the bullying;
- Fear of being ridiculed;
- Concern the bullying will get worse (Cortes & Kochenderfer-Ladd, 2014); and

- Worry that teachers will simply tell them unsympathetically to deal with the bullying themselves. Girls in particular tend to want emotional support from their teachers around bullying (Cortes & Kochenderfer-Ladd, 2014).

Students who are victims and also pick on others may worry that telling would make the teacher pay attention to their own involvement in bullying. Boys may not want teachers involved because, when they tell the teacher, it puts them at risk for rejection when classmates find out that they told (Cortes & Kochenderfer-Ladd, 2014, pp. 21–22).

Students' expectations for how teachers may react if they are told about bullying is a determining factor in whether or not students tell the teacher about bullying (Cortes & Kochenderfer-Ladd, 2014). In classrooms where students were willing to tell teachers, teachers strongly discouraged bullying and took reports seriously. In these classrooms, teachers reacted to reports by separating the students who were involved in bullying, and/or by involving parents. Students considered these actions helpful. Bullying in these classrooms decreased. The helpful teachers considered punishment a last resort and protected the identity of the child who told.

Prevention efforts with the greatest likelihood of some success include implementation of well-researched bullying prevention interventions, interventions focused on improving the school climate, and evidence-based social-emotional programs (Bradshaw, 2015). Although action by schools is complex in regard to cyberbullying, the good news is that efforts to address traditional bullying may defer cyberbullying as well (Olweus, 2013).

School professionals must consider several factors when they work to prevent bullying and cyberbullying. These include the general disciplinary approach of the school, the school climate, and student beliefs about aggression and bullying in particular. When school professionals deal with specific incidents of bullying, it is important to separate poor judgment, roughhousing, general teasing with no intention of hurting someone, and harmless bantering between students from behavior that involves aggressive attacks.

Because there are differences among the children who bully others, a single response to bullying is inappropriate (Peeters et al., 2010). It may also be unfair. When discipline is fair in a school and rules are clear, there is less bullying (Rigby, 2012). If the perceived level of fairness increases in a school, researchers believe the risk of bullying would decrease in turn (Jeong et al., 2013). Additionally, teachers' frequent use of punishment facilitates both physical and relational bullying.

In some cases, the best approach might be to target the whole school, or an entire class (Peeters et al., 2010). In other situations, the response that might have the best outcome would be an individualized response to those children involved in the incident. It is important to make these distinctions given the less-than-hoped-for success of bulling prevention efforts in schools. Schools can make an effort to improve the school culture and to influence the peer group, so that bullying and cyberbullying are not acceptable without using zero-tolerance as a deterrent. It is critically important to support victims of bullying and cyberbullying, and for school professionals to identify and work with vulnerable students before bullying becomes part of the local culture. At the same time, a school's response to bullying cannot be the same for all bullies, and for all incidents of bullying (Howard et al., 2014).

## Practical Tools for School-Based Professionals

- Teachers need to appreciate that they have a role to play in prevention of bullying. This involves how they respond to bullying incidents reported to them. At the same time, teachers need to help students understand which peer conflicts should be reported and should involve adults, and which do not need adult intervention.
- When teachers ignore or react in ways that do not help children who complain about bullying, students do not have good relationships with their teachers; and when school climates are not positive, schools report higher levels of victimization (Swearer & Hymel, 2015).
- For schools considering the use of surveys or questionnaires to measure the extent of bullying in their school or district, Olweus (2013) strongly recommends that measures include a definition of bullying in order to obtain accurate information.
- Schools need intensive and sustained efforts to prevent bullying. Schools in urban areas in particular will need programs with a broad focus addressing aggressive behaviors with multiple components (Bradshaw, 2015). School staff members must be careful in regard to selecting programs which use peer mediation or peer mentoring, as researchers have found that these can increase victimization (Ttofi & Farrington, 2011). Appointing a single trusted person to whom students can report incidents may encourage reporting.
- School climate interventions to address respect and acceptance of individual differences are related to decreases in bullying in schools (Gage, Prykanowski, & Larson, 2014). Improving school climate is an important strategy for school leaders to tackle in order to reduce bullying.
- School psychologists and school counselors should assist in determining the motivation for bullying, which will influence choice of response and the appropriateness of education and/or punishment (Peeters et al., 2010). Bystanders' motivation may be of interest as well, particularly in relation to mobilizing bystanders to help with preventive efforts. Additionally, school psychologists can work with victimized

children who experience early bullying, as this can be associated with chronic victimization and intensely negative outcomes (Arseneault et al., 2010).

- One way to deal with bullying behavior is to focus on changing children's motivation for bullying others. This means school staff would have to individualize their response according to the differing motivations for bullying. For example, for bullies who are having "fun," an intervention to increase empathy might be effective.

## Take Home Ideas for Parents

- Parents can prevent bullying behaviors outside their homes by monitoring bullying between siblings at home and by labeling the hurtful behavior as bullying. Parent–child talk about bullying needs to be ongoing (Couvillon & Ilieva, 2011).
- Parental monitoring has a significant role in curbing physical and verbal bullying and can make a huge difference in controlling cybervictimization and cyberbullying as well (Guo, 2016). Parents can let their children know that they will monitor online communications if they become concerned. At the same time, children who are victimized online need to be taught to print out and date cyberbullying messages.
- Empathy offers a child protection from getting involved in bullying and cyberbullying (Kowalski et al., 2014). Parents can model empathetic behavior and talk a good deal about caring for, and responsibility for, those children who are less skilled.
- Help children understand that even shy children can do something when they see others bullied. At the very least, they can walk away and not reinforce the bully by their presence.
- If your child becomes involved in cyberbullying or is bullied online, do not take away electronic devices as a way to protect your child from cyberbullying (Couvillon & Ilieva, 2011). Electronic media can also be positive and allow a child to be part of the group.
  Additionally, children have access to electronic devices away from home and can be hurt even if hurtful messages are not sent directly to them as bullying messages can be posted on sites that everyone in their peer group will see.
- In case of either a bullying or a cyberbullying incident in which your child is involved, talk with your child calmly. Write down details and dates of bullying or cyberbullying. Ask questions, be supportive, and do not criticize your child or how your child handled the situation. Use this data to talk with the school later, or to inform your ISP provider if your child is being bullied online. If your child has been threatened online, contact law enforcement. Do not try to contact the parents of the child or children who bullied your child. This could make things worse.

- Obtain a copy of the school's anti-bullying policy to determine if it has been violated according to your child's story. Meet with your child's teacher(s) and document what will be done to keep your child safe. Follow the school's chain of command when working with the school. Start with the teacher, go on to the assistant principal or principal if things do not improve, and then to the superintendent, and, if needed, the school committee.
- If your child has been bullied and is very distressed, contact the school psychologist and ask for help for your child.

## References

Arseneault, L., Bowes, L., & Skakoor, S. (2010). Bullying victimization in youths and mental health problems: "Much ado about nothing"? *Psychological Medicine, 40*(5), 717–729. doi:10.1017/S0033291709991383

Bradshaw, C. P. (2015). Translating research to practice in bullying prevention. *American Psychologist, 70*(4), 322–332. doi:10.1037/a0039114

Cortes, K. I. & Kochenderfer-Ladd, B. (2014). To tell or not to tell: What influences children's decisions to report bullying to their teachers? *School Psychology Quarterly, 29*(3), 336-348). doi:10.1037/spq0000078

Couvillon, M. A. & Ilieva, V. (2011). Recommended practices: A review of schoolwide preventive programs and strategies on cyberbullying. *Preventing School Failure, 55*(2), 96–101. doi:10.1080/1045988X.2011.539461

Elledge, L. C., Willford, A., Boulton, A. J., DePaolis, K. J., Little. T. D., & Salmivalli, C. (2013). Individual and contextual predictors of cyberbullying: The influence of children's provictim attitudes and teachers' ability to intervene. *Journal of Youth Adolescence, 42*, 698–710. doi:10.1007/s10964-013-9920-x

Fullchange, A. & Furlong, M. J. (2016). An exploration of effects of bullying victimization from a complete mental health perspective. *Sage Open, 6*(1). doi:10.1177/215824401562359

Gage, N. A., Prykanowski, D. A., & Larson, A. (2014) School climate and bullying victimization: A latent class growth model analysis. *School Psychology Quarterly, 29*(3), 256–271. doi:10.1037/spq0000064

Guo, S. (2016). A meta-analysis of the predictors of cyberbullying perpetration and victimization. *Psychology in the Schools, 53*(4), 432–453. doi:10.1002/pits.21914

Howard, A. M., Landau, S., & Pryor, J. B. (2014). Peer bystanders to bullying: Who wants to play with the victim? *Journal of Abnormal Child Psychology, 42*, 265–276. doi:10.1007/s10802-013-9770-8

Hudson, J. M. & Bruckman, A. S. (2004). The bystander effect: A lens for understanding patterns of participation. *Journal of the Learning Sciences, 13*(2), 165–195. doi:10.1207/s15327809jls1302_2

Jeong, S., Kwak, D., Moon, B., & San Miguel, C. (2013). Predicting school bullying victimization: Focusing on individual and school environment security factors. *Journal of Criminology*. (Article ID 401301). doi:10.1155/2013/401301

Kowalski, R. M., Giumetti, G. W., Schroeder, A. N., & Lattanner, M. R. (2014). Bullying in the digital age: A critical review and meta-analysis of cyberbullying research among youth. *Psychological Bulletin, 140*(4), 1073–1137. doi:10.1037/a0035618

Low, S., Van Ryzin, M. J., Brown, E. C., Smith, B. H., & Haggerty, K. P. (2014). Engagement matters: Lessons from assessing classroom implementation of *Steps to Respect:* A bullying prevention program over a one-year period. *Prevention Science, 15*, 165–176. doi:10.1007/s11121-012-0359-1

Macklem, G. L. (2015). *Boredom in the classroom: Addressing student motivation, self-regulation, and engagement in learning.* New York, NY: Springer International Publishing.

Menesini, E., Palladino, B. E., & Nocentini, A. (2015). Emotions of moral disengagement, class norms, and bullying in adolescence: A multilevel approach. *Merrill-Palmer Quarterly, 61*(1), 124–143. doi:10.13110/merrpalmquar1982.61.1.0124

Menesini, E. & Salmivalli, C. (2017). Bullying in schools: The state of knowledge and effective interventions. *Psychology, Health & Medicine, 22*(sup1). doi:10.1080/13548506.2017.1279740

Olweus, D. (2013). School bullying: Development and some important challenges. *Annual Review of Clinical Psychology, 9*(14), 751–780. doi:10.1146/annurev-clinpsy-050212-185516

Peeters, M., Cillessen A. H. N., & Scholte, R. H. J. (2010). Clueless or powerful? Identifying subtypes of bullies in adolescence. *Journal of Youth and Adolescence, 39*, 10141–1052. doi:10.1007/s10964-009-9478-9

Rigby, K. (2012). Bullying in schools: Addressing desires not only behaviors. *Educational Psychology Review, 24*, 339–348. doi:10.1007/s10648-012-9196-9

Sabella, R. A., Patchin J. W., & Hinduja, S. (2013). Cyberbullying myths and realities. *Computers in Human Behavior, 29*, 2703–2711. doi:10.1016/j.chb.2013.06.040

Swearer, S. M. & Hymel, S. (2015). Understanding the psychology of bullying: Moving toward a social-ecological diathesis stress model. *American Psychologist, 70*(4), 344–353. doi:10.1037/a0038928

Ttofi, M. M. & Farrington, D. P. (2011). Effectiveness of school-based programs to reduce bullying: A systematic and meta-analytic review. *Journal of Experimental Criminology, 7*(1), 27–56. doi:10.1007/s11292-010-9109-1

Waasdorp, T. E., Pas, E. T., Zablotsky, B., & Bradshaw, C. P. (2017). Ten-year trends in bullying and related attitudes among 4th- to 12th graders. *Pediatrics, 139*(6), e20162615. doi:10.1542/peds.2016-2615

Zhang, A., Musu-Gillette, L., & Oudekerk, B. A. (2016). *Indicators of school crime and safety: 2015.* (NCES 2016–079/NCJ 249758). National Center for Education Statistics, U.S. Department of Education, and the Bureau of Justice Statistics, Office of Justice Programs, U.S. Department of Justice. Washington, DC.

# 12 Understanding, Exploring, and Responding to Challenging Behavior in Elementary School Students

*Craig Murphy*

Students with emotional and behavioral disabilities consistently compromise the learning environment for themselves and their classmates. In addition, these students often challenge authority and undermine efforts to establish a positive classroom climate, and decisions about how to manage their behavior and emotional presentation often take precedent over discussions about classroom instruction and academic achievement. Many of these students drop out or leave school unprepared for the future (Stormont, Thomas, & Van Garderen, 2012). No single group of educators understands the challenges of these students as well as classroom teachers, and yet they often report feeling unprepared to teach them or to intervene with their social, emotional, and behavioral problems (Reinke, Stormont, Herman, Puri, & Goel, 2011). Children with emotional and behavioral disabilities are equally challenging for parents in the home environment. The role of the school psychologist has never been so important, as these students continue to enter classrooms at record levels (Nelson, Benner, Lane, & Smith, 2004). Specifically, school psychologists must play a critical role in building the capacity of classroom teachers for educating students with emotional and behavior disabilities and collaborating with the families of these students to promote a consistent approach across the home and school settings.

## Notes from the Field

Challenging students are not a recent phenomenon. In fact, the 1997 Amendments to the Individuals with Disabilities Education Act (IDEA) included substantial revisions requiring positive behavior support (PBS) plans and strongly encouraged the use of functional behavioral assessments (FBA). These revisions were due to the dramatic increase in student behavior problems and the significant impact of those problems on both the individual child and their respective classrooms. In addition, Landrum and Tankersley (1999) contend that students who present with behavior problems do so at enormous expense to both the educational and human service systems. The dropout rates for challenging students are consistently among the highest of any particular subgroup of students (Carson, Sitlington, & Frank, 1995). Although the literature has a great deal to say about challenging students, the following anecdote from a classroom teacher working to support a challenging student might say it best.[1]

*One Friday morning in mid-September the class was called down to the school-wide assembly. Johnny was on the computer. Earlier we had told him that when the class was called down, he would need to get off the computer and join us. The class was called down and all of the students lined up. Johnny refused to get off the computer. After repeated warnings, he remained at the computer. When I tried to quickly quit the browser, Johnny blocked my hand. We were headed to a dead-end. The class was lined up waiting patiently watching what was taking place. After another warning, I pulled the power cord out from the wall. The computer was off. I knew at the time that there was a chance that this would make the situation much more volatile, but I needed to draw a line. Johnny did not get up or react.*

*Johnny's aide took my class to the assembly and I stayed with him. None of the strategies I was using helped resolve this impasse. I was backed into the same corner as Johnny. If he got up, I won. If he remained, he won. Johnny was not getting up. Finally, I stated, "I really did not want to start my Friday morning like this." Johnny looked at me and said, "Me neither." This different strategy captured how I was truly feeling, and Johnny saw that I was vulnerable. At the time, my comments were not expressed for Johnny's benefit. In retrospect, I think Johnny responded to the authenticity, and he recognized that imposing my power over him is something that I did not want to do. It also allowed him to share how he truly felt. Like me, he wanted a better Friday. "Let's go to the assembly and later today we can find some time for you to continue what you were doing on the computer. We joined the class at the assembly."*

*I found a way out of the corner but knew that my instructional and classroom management strategies were going to be tested each and every day moving forward until I developed a better understanding of Johnny's challenges.*

Working with challenging students and raising children who demonstrate challenging behaviors require taking the time to understand their behaviors and managing one's own frustration and emotional responses. This can be difficult for teachers trying to meet the needs of 25 students, and equally exhausting for a parent who is trying to juggle the myriad demands of raising a family. These students need our unconditional support and dedication more than ever, however, and are often dependent on their school experiences and connections to help them develop the skills they need to be successful, both academically and socially.

## Why It Matters

The following is a brief description of the "challenging student" referred to throughout the chapter, followed by a proposed model for teachers and school psychologists supporting these students, "The Four Pillars of Collaboration." Although each of the pillars is discussed in detail, actual quotes from classroom teachers who are currently supporting challenging students are integrated into the discussion to provide context and practical examples from the front lines of education—the classroom.

### *What Is a Challenging Student?*

Challenging students are not defined by their diagnoses, although they often come with several. Their level of difficulty cannot be measured by a rating scale or computed through a structured classroom observation. These tools do, however, provide valuable information and data that will guide our initial hypotheses and interventions. Although the continuum of challenging students is substantial, the following characteristics consistently set them apart from their peers and make them instantly recognizable for classroom teachers and other educators working in the schools:

- Challenging students change the classroom learning environment and overall classroom climate simply by being present.
- Challenging students compromise the authority of the adults working in the room and influence the behavior of all of the students in the classroom.
- Challenging students consistently disrupt instruction and make it extremely difficult for classroom teachers to complete lessons, follow daily routines, and navigate the social and academic expectations of the school day.
- Challenging students are volatile, making it nearly impossible for classroom teachers to prepare for each day and to feel good about their overall effectiveness.

## Practical Tools for School-Based Professionals

The tale of a challenging student resonates with classroom teachers and school psychologists without exception. The fact remains, students with challenging behaviors are an important part of our community and we need to decide how to truly practice collaboration in order to improve outcomes for these students and the staff who work with them. Classroom teachers need to be prepared to welcome them and school psychologists need to be prepared and available to help build capacity. The following beliefs serve as the Four Pillars of Effective Collaboration between classroom teachers and school psychologists working to support these challenging students.

### *Belief #1: Shared Vision*

The most important belief, and therefore the first of the Four Pillars of Collaboration, is that challenging students are important and their success in the classroom benefits everyone. The first belief was shaped by Dr. Ross Greene's Collaborative and Proactive Solutions (CPS) model (Greene, 2014). One of the guiding mantras to the CPS model is "kids do well if they can." Although this sounds intuitive to educators and parents at first, alternative explanations are far more common when school-based teams are discussing challenging students. In fact, the most prominent theory operating in schools today is the traditional behavioral approach to understanding challenging behavior. The behavioral approach argues that kids do well if they are motivated, if they are rewarded, if they can get out of completing work, or if their challenging behavior is reinforced by others. Educators subscribing to the behavioral approach often conduct A-B-C analyses and set up behavior intervention plans (BIPs) based on their functional hypotheses of why the student is demonstrating challenging behaviors. Although these approaches and strategies have merit, it is critical that classroom teachers and school psychologists recognize the limitations of the approach when working with their most challenging students.

In addition to Dr. Greene's influence, the second part of this shared vision is unconditional support. Extending his mantra, classroom teachers and school psychologists must share the belief that challenging students do well when they can, and when they know that the classroom teacher believes in them and supports them unconditionally. When educators collaborate on behalf of challenging students believing that the student will do well when they can and committing to supporting them unconditionally, it changes the approach dramatically. Consider the following quote from a classroom teacher:

*During the first week of school, I was told that Matt's previous teacher had a plan in which he could earn points so that he could use the computer. I recognized early on that the computer was actually something Matt needed to help him adjust to the classroom. It was a time that he could spend in the room doing something that he enjoyed. I was not eager to continue this behavior modification program from the previous year; in general, I have had a hard time with these programs. It is hard for me to maintain, and what if Matt made some poor choices at the start of the day and lost the chance to use the computer—then what? How is the day going to get better? Would we be bartering all day to try to get back the time for something that I believe he NEEDS?*

*Given that I thought the computer time was therapeutic for Matt, I promised him something the first week of school. I promised him that no matter what kind of day he was having, he would ALWAYS be able to use the computer two times each day for ten minutes. I would tell him when that would be, but it was a guarantee that I made to him that I would keep; it was unconditional. Currently, Matt comes to school a few minutes early and uses his first ten minutes, and he often uses the second ten minutes during snack/recess. He does not miss any academic work while he's using the computer, and we never barter or negotiate. I realized that Matt was missing a sense of unconditional support in his life. A sense that no matter what, someone cares about you and wants to have things in place that will help you. The message that this approach sends to Matt is simple: I will do what I can to make your day a good day, and in return, I expect you to do the same. Like all children, Matt is more than willing and eager to have good days. Simply put, I believe that he does well when he can, and therefore I support him unconditionally.*

### *Belief #2: The 2% Need Something Different*

An alternative to defining challenging students diagnostically is to do so mathematically. The normal curve, a critical component for all school psychology statistics courses, clearly depicts a majority (just over 84%) of students falling within or below the average range for problem behaviors; these are the students who demonstrate minimal to no problem behaviors in the school setting. Approximately 14% of students fall above one standard deviation, but below two standard deviations from the mean; these students demonstrate increasing levels of problem behaviors in the school setting and often require specific accommodations and/or support plans to manage their behaviors and/or emotions. Truly challenging students are the 2% of kids on the far-left end of the normal curve who need something different, and, often, something *very* different. Strict behavioral programs do not work. Token economies and response cost systems may make the behavioral difficulties far worse. Delegating teaching and behavior management responsibilities to paraprofessionals can lead to social isolation and sub-standard instruction.

For this 2% of students, classroom teachers are faced with tough decisions each and every day. They are expected to balance the changing academic demands of their curricula and the everyday pressures of high-stakes testing while simultaneously building and fostering a positive classroom climate for all students. The 2% make this balancing act nearly impossible. Stormont, Thomas and Van Garderen (2012) indicate that several factors make these demands on teachers extremely daunting, including a lack of confidence, knowledge, or skills. It is critical that classroom teachers do not feel alone in their commitment to the 2% of students who are testing them at every turn. School psychologists need to (a) have an active presence in these classrooms; (b) engage in frequent conversations with these teachers about what is working and what needs to be changed; and (c) respect the professionalism and experience of the classroom teacher and validate their efforts. The following anecdote from a classroom teacher captures the impact of the 2% perfectly.

*Typically, when I work with support staff around social-emotional issues, I am not discussing the vast majority of kids. As a veteran classroom teacher, I have learned numerous strategies that work successfully with 98% of the students: perhaps a missed recess here, a call to parents there, a stern lecture, or more importantly, taking proactive steps to create positive relationships with every student in the room. For 2% of the students I work with, however, my most effective strategies have not been consistently successful. Developing a positive relationship continues to be vital, but it is not as easy to do and I am not always as persistent as I must be. In my early teacher years when working with difficult students, I had no other strategies other than to continue to try things that did not work, and since the strategies worked with almost all other students, I could feel comfortable in knowing that the problem was the child.*

*Like most people, I am willing to admit a mistake, but rarely am I willing to admit it readily. During the second week of school, the students needed to do a writing assessment. Before school I had made a mental note to check in with Miles about the prompt and give him a heads-up about what we would be doing. The day started, and I forgot to talk with him. At writing, I started to tell the class about the assignment. Miles began to get agitated and started saying he could not do it; he had nothing to write about. When we started to write, Miles fled the room followed closely by his aide. At the end of writing time, I found Miles in a small office with his aide standing outside the room. Miles had been given a computer to do the writing. It was clear that he was not using the computer to write; rather he was playing a game. In the past, I might have reprimanded him for leaving the room and then not doing the work. I might have told him that he would not be allowed back in the room until the work was complete. I might have told him that he now lost computer privileges for a week. All of these things would work effectively with most students, but not for Miles. When Miles is agitated, he is unwilling and unable to take any responsibility for his actions; of course, as a teacher I want to teach him accountability.*

*I realized with Miles that my usual strategies were counterproductive. Instead of following my usual strategies for the 98%, I told Miles that I messed up, that I meant to talk with him in the morning, and that I had simply forgot. I apologized to him for that. As I was talking, his body language changed. He sat up and looked directly at me. We talked a bit more and then returned to the classroom. I did not ask him to reflect on his behavior. This was not a reciprocal apology. Do I really think I was totally at fault? No, but I wanted to model for Miles what it looks like when someone takes responsibility, and I wanted the writing done. Had I threatened him or given him an ultimatum, he might still be sitting in that room.*

***Belief #3: One Good Day***

Students who demonstrate challenging behavior on a consistent basis have far too many "bad days." These students perform significantly below normally achieving peers in numerous academic areas, including vocabulary, listening comprehension, literacy, science, and social studies (Nelson et al., 2004). Therefore, their learning experience is often frustrating, reinforces their negative attitude toward school, and sets the stage for challenging behavior on a daily basis. In addition, Mattison, Spitznagel and Felix (1998) found that challenging students often present with behavioral characteristics consistent with conduct disorder, oppositional defiant disorder, and attention disorders. These behavioral characteristics make it extremely difficult for these students to function in a traditional classroom environment, which in turn challenges the classroom teacher to establish a learning environment that is both truly welcoming and supportive.

This is a challenge that classroom teachers and parents must be prepared to meet. They must recognize the importance of emotional regulation and a child's sense of security. Specifically, Boekaerts (1993) contends that students exert time and energy on regulating their emotions, which directly compromises their learning. In addition, Koomen, van Leeuwen, and van der Leij (2004) found that emotional security plays a critical role in student learning, and "that in stressful situations a relatively unfamiliar adult can serve as a substitute attachment figure and provide children with a secure base" (p. 270). Developing teachers' understanding of emotional regulation and discussing the importance of a student's emotional security in the classroom increases the likelihood that the challenging student will enjoy "a good day." The following story illustrates the impact that classroom teachers can have on challenging students when they are confident in their ability to dictate whether or not it will be a "good day."

*All teachers have had tough students. When having a difficult student, every second of every day can be trying. Teachers have to consider these students when creating lessons, handing out materials, and making groups. Teachers begin each day hoping that the student will come to school in a good frame of mind and get through the day without a problem. I always told the student that he could decide whether it would be a good day or not based on his actions. I have come to learn that this is not entirely true. My actions are ultimately what control whether or not a student has a good day. And, in turn, if a student has a "bad day," the first person I should look at is myself. Furthermore, I have never met a teacher whose difficult student had a bad day while they had a good day. In the end, it is either win-win or lose-lose. Good and bad days are not random.*

### *Belief #4: The Bottom of the Pyramid*

Response to Intervention (RTI) is a three-tiered model of educational problem solving for providing academic and behavioral interventions for students with increasing levels of need (Riley-Tillman & Burns, 2009). The 2% typically burn through Tier 1 supports prior to the end of the first month of school. Tier 2 supports are often equally ineffective. Therefore, school-based teams are often gathering to discuss the Tier 3 options very quickly for these students, options that often include hiring an assistant, exploring alternative classroom placements, and possibly outside placements altogether.

The fundamental flaw in this approach is that, like the pyramid itself, Tier 1 supports lay the foundation for all subsequent levels of supports, interventions, and strategies. Classroom climate takes center stage for these students, and if the climate is not welcoming and supportive, these students will fail. Intensive clinical work or academic remediation taking place outside of the classroom will rarely allow a challenging student to transition back into their classroom environment if it is not welcoming and supportive.

Despite the clear connection between the three tiers of supports, teachers justifiably worry about the impact the challenging student's behavior will have on his/her classmates. Similarly, parents worry about the impact one child's behaviors and dysregulated emotions can have on their other children and their family as a collective unit. Therefore, teachers and parents need support to build strong and supportive classroom and home environments, respectively.

## Take Home Ideas for Parents

Parents who are struggling to understand and support their children due to challenging behaviors can learn from the work being done in schools. Specifically, newer parents should start by learning the basics of mental health for children. An excellent website to help parents get started is provided by Dr. Ross Greene (www.livesinthebalance.org). For more experienced parents, collaborating with a mental health specialist, such as a school psychologist, should help them eliminate the "noise" so they can reflect on their own beliefs and how they are affecting their child's challenging behaviors in the home environment. Veteran parents will most likely benefit from a genuine partnership with a mental health professional, a relationship that is mutually beneficial for understanding the 2% of challenging children.

For all parents, a mental health professional can support their goals of becoming more effective by taking on a coaching role. Just as literacy and math coaches are expected to build teacher capacity for teaching reading and math, respectively, mental health professionals working with parents build their capacity for supporting challenging children. The following is a teacher reflection of how this collaboration affects life in the classroom for a challenging student, which illustrates the potential of a coaching relationship with parents.

*The most complicated students come with many different levels and methods of support. When I first met Andrew, there were many behavior plans in place. And given that he had been removed from the classroom in fourth grade, some of those plans were created and implemented by central administration staff. During the second week of school, as I was getting to know Andrew and the rest of my class, I got an email from a support person about the behavior modification program Andrew was going to begin the following Monday. Why? Things were going smoothly in class, I was getting a feel for what might work and now we were going to be doing something that I felt, at the time, was unnecessary. For a variety of reasons, it was necessary the previous year, but I not only felt it was not needed this year, I was concerned that it would interfere with the relationship that I was working hard to develop this year.*

*I did not have the history with Andrew, so I was in a tough spot because the trained professionals who knew him felt that this was what was best. Over the years, I had developed a good relationship with the school psychologist and used him for the support I needed. I explained to him what I was doing, where I was headed, and why I did not want to start any behavior plans yet. Fortunately, he had faith in my work, and was able to write to the other support staff and suggest we delay starting any plan. As a less experienced classroom teacher, I might not have been able to insist that we do not immediately start what was on the IEP; however, with the support of the school psychologist we were able to do something that supported what I was doing in the classroom. Fortunately, the school psychologist, along with other support staff, had developed a positive relationship with the parent over the years. The school psychologist and I were able to talk with the parent and explain what we were doing. We had the parent's support.*

*In working with difficult students, I have found that the relationship I have with the school psychologist is essential. Rarely do I use him to "take the kid and talk to him." But rather, we talk several times each week about difficult students and what I am doing to support them. The school psychologist is not coaching the students, he is coaching me. As a classroom teacher, I need the school psychologist to listen to what I am doing, what I am struggling with, and then ask me questions that will help me improve my work related to mental health issues. There are times when I want the school psychologist to talk with a child to reinforce some of the things we are talking about in the classroom. That cannot be done, however, unless the school psychologist and I are consistent in our understanding of the situation. Our core beliefs need to be the same and must be unwavering.*

### *When We Fail To Act, Kids Suffer*

Succeeding with the 2% benefits everyone. Most importantly, the child, who may have had some very difficult days in school, realizes that there are other possibilities. Schools and homes should not be battle grounds, but rather places where one is unconditionally supported. For classroom teachers and parents, when a difficult child makes progress, the rewards are immeasurable. We no longer go home hoping that the child is absent the next day, or that one of our children will go away for four weeks of camp in the summer. We are not tense every second of every day. We do not behave in ways that we are not proud of when in the midst of dealing with the difficult student or child. We have time to focus on other students or children. We have good days. In closing, consider the final teacher reflection:

*In the past when I have had difficult students in the room, I would always worry about all of the other students in my classroom. I still do, but now I look at the issue differently. Previously, I would give the difficult student a chance to do what everyone else was doing. If the student did not do it, I would usually engage in some type of confrontation. The student would then be told to sit somewhere else in the room if they were not going to do the assignment. The student would sit there and not do the work or sit out in the hall and not do the work, or I would have a support person take him somewhere and not do the work. If things went well, the student would comply or leave the room. If not, the confrontation escalated, and the classroom became an unsafe place for everyone. Fortunately, no student ever got hurt, but all students witnessed the aggression and confrontation.*

*Needless to say, when these occasions occurred, and with complicated students it can be daily, no students learned. So, in the past, when I talked about worrying about the other students, what was I worried about? I worried that if they saw this fellow student behave like this and "get away with it," maybe they could too, and then there would be no control. I had to show students that I was in control, so they wouldn't behave like that too. The 98% of the students we work with will never demonstrate defiant or challenging behavior simply because they have observed another student doing so in the classroom; this is a common, but extremely unrealistic belief held by many of my colleagues.*

*This year, my students observe something different. Students see that complicated students can work productively in the classroom, they are able to follow directions, they do have something positive to add to the classroom climate, and they can demonstrate growth and improvement. Students also see what happens when everyone works hard to make every day a great day for everyone in the room. It is nice to end the day knowing that 100% of my students were part of that valuable lesson.*

## Note

1. All names and identifying information used in teacher reflections have been revised to protect anonymity.

## References

Boekaerts, M. (1993). Self-regulated learning: A new concept embraced by researchers, policy makers, educators, teachers, and students. *Learning and Instruction, 7*(2), 161–186. doi:10.1016/S0959-4752(96)00015-1

Carson, R. R., Sitlington, P. L., & Frank, A. R. (1995). Young adulthood for individuals with behavioral disorders: What does it hold? *Behavioral Disorders, 20*(2), 127–135. doi:10.1177/019874299502000201

Greene, R. W. (2014). *Lost at school.* New York, NY: Guilford Press.

Koomen, H. M. Y., van Leeuwen, M. G. P., & van der Leij, A. (2004). Does well-being contribute to performance? Emotional security, teacher support, and learning behavior in kindergarten. *Infant and Child Development, 13*(3), 253–275. doi:10.1002/icd.352

Landrum, T. J. & Tankersley, M. (1999). Emotional and behavioral disorders in the new millennium: The future is now. *Behavioral Disorders, 24*, 319–330. doi:10.1177/019874299902400404

Mattison, R. E., Spitznagel, E. L., & Felix, B. C. (1998). Enrollment predictors of the special education outcome for students with SED. *Council for Exceptional Children, 23*(4), 243–256. doi:10.1177/019874299802300404

Nelson, J. R., Benner, G. J., Lane, K., & Smith, B. W. (2004). Academic achievement of K-12 students with emotional and behavioral disorders. *Exceptional Children, 71*(1), 59–73. doi:10.1177/001440290407100104

Reinke, W. M., Stormont, M., Herman, K. C., Puri, R., & Goel, N. (2011). Supporting children's mental health in the schools: Teacher perceptions of needs, roles, and barriers. *School Psychology Quarterly, 26*(1), 1–13. doi:10.1037/a0022714

Riley-Tillman, T. C. & Burns, M. K. (2009). *Evaluating educational interventions: Single case design for measuring response to intervention.* New York, NY: Guilford Press.

Stormont, M., Thomas, C. N., & Van Garderen, D. (2012). Introduction to the special issue: Building capacity to improve student outcomes through collaboration—current issues and innovative approaches. *Psychology in the Schools,* 45, 3999–401. doi:10.1002/pits.21605

# 13 Tackling Challenging Behavior with Adolescents in School Settings

*Daniel B. Jacobs*

Adolescence can be a difficult time for all youth, as they go through physical, emotional, and social changes. Interpersonal relationships can change from day to day and the "sense of self" that we hope to have as adults is quite fluid at that age. Adolescents dealing with mental health and emotional concerns can have an even tougher time managing the balancing act required of them. Those who cannot quite stay on top of all of their concerns in a socially appropriate or acceptable manner can be seen as "*acting out*," both at home and in the school setting.

Adolescents who exhibit externalizing and destructive patterns of behavior in home and at school often also have difficulties meeting the academic demands placed upon them; they can be known to lash out and act in angry, aggressive, and distancing ways. At best these patterns of behavior are simply disruptive, problematic, and distracting. These challenging behaviors need to be tackled effectively through direct and timely interventions in order to avoid the development of much more concerning and destructive patterns of behavior, such as self-destructive acts (e.g., self-inflicted violence, substance abuse, suicide attempts; e.g., Reed, Nugent, & Cooper, 2015) or violence toward property or others (e.g., bullying, criminality, assaulting others; e.g., Johnson et al., 2014). The interventions utilized to address these concerns need to be directly linked to actual behavior changing consequences and not just serve as more punishments to the challenging behaviors.

Pushing others away is perceived as a way to "protect" oneself, but the youth exhibiting these challenging behaviors are also actually driving away those who are able to be of help to them. In working with these students, school psychologists and other school-based clinicians need to be able to maintain their own perspective, not get pulled into needless struggles, and keep their focus on interventions and strategies which address problematic behavior and actually help the troubled adolescent. These clinicians also have to manage the competing needs of academic colleagues and systemic pushback that demands quick answers to complex problems that actually require greater nuance if genuine change is desired.

To truly and effectively tackle these challenging behaviors in a manner that leads to positive and lasting change, we have to understand the root causes and motivations behind the problematic behaviors, and then work to use this knowledge to develop plans that make sense as we try to help these students find their way. While none of this is easy, it is possible and is certainly one of the most important tasks we can accomplish in our work with adolescents in need.

## Why It Matters

One of the primary missions of schools is to educate students in a range of academic subjects to prepare them for later success in life. An adolescent displaying behavioral problems is much less likely to meet the academic demands placed upon him/her. Meeting the needs of adolescents exhibiting these challenging behaviors may not be easy; however, not meeting their needs and letting the behavior continue is a much worse alternative. The costs are higher in terms of time, school resource allocation, and ongoing negative impact on the academic learning process for the adolescent and his/her classmates.

We need to care about finding ways to tackle the challenging behavior of adolescents in a way that actually works because of the spillover effect, and the direct and indirect costs of these patterns of behavior when interventions fail. Adolescents exhibiting challenging behavior are often labeled as problematic or out of control, and this frequently leads to a loss of perspective regarding the actual person as someone in need, often impacted by neglect or abuse. The most useful interventions with youth exhibiting the challenging behavioral patterns described above focus on identifying the problematic behavior, understanding the motivating forces behind the behavior, determining which intervention to employ, and evaluating progress toward positive outcomes. Effective behavior change programs for adolescents, including those linked to mental health and substance abuse concerns, share commonalities such as clear presentation of information, fostering motivation to change, offering skills training and practice, and promotion of self-esteem and a sense of self-efficacy (Flannery, Fenning, Kato, & McIntosh, 2014; Kuhn, Ebert, Gracey, & Epstein, 2015).

Unfortunately, many school responses to challenging behavior are linked to punitive and reactive response patterns rather than proactive, consequence-driven interventions that actually result in lasting change. School psychologists are uniquely trained and positioned to engage in effective behavior change interventions, and also have potential to lead the development of school-based programs that actually work to address extremely challenging student behaviors fueled by trauma, anger, and emotional pain (Dou et al., 2015; Li et al., 2011; Reed et al., 2015).

One of the most important points to understand is that the adults involved need to be able to "put their emotions on the shelf" while engaging in interventions. The adult cannot respond in an emotional or reactive manner and hope to expect positive change. An adolescent in emotional pain may say or do things that are offensive or frustrating and when he or she sees that the adult involved in the scenario (e.g., teacher, counselor, parent) is "losing their cool" (i.e., not managing their own affect or emotion in an objective and calm fashion), there can be a range of reactions leading to more conflict. One likely reaction would be the adolescent feeling empowered by the adult showing his or her frustration, leading to the student engaging in more, not less, of the problematic behavior. Another common reaction when the student sees the adult become unnerved is a sense of lack of containment (e.g., "Oh, she cannot help me, she cannot even handle what is happening"), which can also lead to an increase in the problematic behavioral pattern.

A more effective intervention style for the adult involved is to remember, at all times, that the adolescent's behavior is in no way personal (even if one thinks it is frustrating), and to maintain an even and steady sense of empathy and calm as he/she engages in limit setting or intervention planning (Flannery et al., 2014; Fullchange, 2016; Kuhn et al., 2015; Walker & Sprick, 2016). It is very unlikely that an angry or scared adolescent who is feeling out of control will respond in a positive manner and then say: "I am so glad Ms. Shepherd screamed at me just then—it really did the trick to relax me and get me to pull it together." However, the same adolescent, might say: "I really lost it earlier, but Ms. Shepherd hung in there with me and helped me get my act together," assuming appropriate limit setting was indeed put in place.

Appropriate limit setting is an integral part of the intervention process and is directly linked to establishing effective consequences. Unfortunately, many school officials instead choose to respond to challenging behavior with various forms of punishment (e.g., detention) which are intended to be part of the intervention process but are destined to fail as lasting behavioral change initiatives. Punishment is emotion-driven, reactive, and often not fully thought out in terms of the desired behavior change effect. Consequences are logically planned out, preferably proactive, and should be directly linked to the problematic behavior in question. Effective intervention planning also always involves a feedback loop, or evaluation process, put in place to determine what is and is not working in the intervention process (Johnson et al., 2014; Kuhn et al., 2015; Li et al., 2011).

Many schools have "catch all" interventions (e.g., sending students to the front office) that are fine for short-term disruption of problematic behaviors but are actually rather ineffective at generating longer-term change. Put another way, if punishment was actually effective, adolescents engaged in challenging behavior such as verbal disruption or physical aggression would receive one detention or one suspension and then not repeat that behavior again. Obviously, this is not what happens, and no one at any level in the process is happy about the situation. While more effective "consequence plans" can take longer to develop than reactive punishment plans, the amount of time and school resources saved on the intervention side can be substantially significant.

## Notes from the Field

### *Zoe*

*Zoe is a 12-year-old girl who acted up in every class session with the same teacher until being sent to the office to "think about" what she had done. Her behaviors involved talking back to the teacher, telling inappropriate jokes, talking over others, and disrupting the teacher's lesson. Over the course of the semester, she eventually received 32 detentions for her behavior (all from the same teacher, and none from other teachers). When the external behavioral consultant for the school was brought in, the school psychologist explained that the school was committed to keeping Zoe "no matter what," but they were just not sure what to do next. The consultant then met with Zoe, and he asked her why this problem with the teacher was happening. After initially saying "History is a really hard class" and "Ms. Washburne just hates me," Zoe eventually admitted that she did not like the class or the teacher but she really just wanted to be expelled so she could go to another school in the system where her friends from the neighborhood were attending. "What do I need to get thrown out of this place?" she asked the consultant.*

### *Derriel*

*Derriel is a 14-year-old boy with a pattern of refusing to listen to the teacher, making inappropriate jokes, and talking over the teacher, particularly before quizzes and exams. When this occurs, he is typically sent to the office and receives a zero on the quiz/exam. He later explains to his school psychologist that he is unable to study or do homework at home due to conflict and (drug-related) chaos in the home, and he is exhausted most mornings when he gets to school. His explanation for his in-class behavior:*

> *If I get thrown out for acting up and being funny and I get a zero, I can just say the teacher hates me and is out to get me. If I take the test and I fail, everyone will think I'm stupid.*

### *Amara*

*Amara is a 16-year-old girl who was caught punching a female peer in class, which led to a fight that the school resource officer had to break up. The consequence was suspension for both girls with threat of expulsion if they fought again. The other girl was mad that Amara had started dating her former boyfriend and had been taunting Amara about it and threatened to "come after" her after school ended that day, with her friends. Amara later said she was not scared of fighting one person but was worried about the threat of being jumped by a large group of girls. "This way I just had to fight her, and now if she tries anything again she can get expelled too and I don't think she's that stupid."*

### *Jayne*

*Jayne is a 17-year-old senior who was seen punching a sophomore by the locker room in the gym after school. When asked what was going on, Jayne's response was simply: "I don't know—it just sort of happened." The sophomore appeared too scared to "go on the record" and later insisted: "We weren't fighting, we were just messing around." The teacher who witnessed the event spoke with the assistant principal and it became clear that this was at least the fourth episode in the past two months that involved violence and Jayne at the school. No significant interventions had been put in place to address Jayne's behavior due to missed communications from different faculty and student witnesses. Jayne's parents refused to come in when asked to attend a conference to explore possible solutions to this challenging pattern of behavior. It was later discovered that Jayne had recently been placed on probation after being caught for mugging a younger adolescent and then faced an assault and battery charge in the community.*

### *Kaley*

*Kaley is a 15-year-old girl who was observed acting confused, loud, and disruptive in a morning class session. She appeared unfocused and odd, and rather than engaging in class activities later in the session, she appeared to be sleeping at her desk. When the teacher asked Kaley to engage in class discussion more appropriately, she cursed at the teacher and was sent to the office. In discussions with Kaley later, she explained to her school psychologist that she was "acting all weird and stuff" due to still being drunk from the night before when she had consumed 13 beer and vodka-based drinks. Kaley also explained that she was trying to "sleep it off" in the back of the classroom, but her teacher "just kept calling on me to answer stuff and I had such a headache and I told her to stick it, which did not go over well, but she did stop calling on me."*

### *Malcolm*

*Malcolm is a 15-year-old boy who seemed to be having a hard time in class one day and then even more so afterwards in the hallway in between fourth and fifth periods at school. The hallway was crowded and, when someone bumped into him, or even just walked close to him as they passed, he appeared to flinch and grimace. Malcolm leaned up against one of the lockers and just started crying and sobbing very loudly, and he seemed very confused. When another student came over to ask if he needed help, Malcolm pushed him away and yelled: "Just leave me the hell alone!" and ran out the side door of the school. He was later found by the bleachers next to the soccer field just staring straight ahead and shaking. Malcolm agreed to come inside with his school psychologist but refused to talk at all. His parents were called and he went home with them later that day. Later Malcolm's mother explained that he has a trauma history, had recently started talking about his concerns with his outpatient therapist, and he had begun having "flashbacks" related to the abuse he suffered when he was a child.*

### River and Simon

*River and Simon are sister and brother, 14 and 16 years old respectively, who were caught by a teacher after school in the math classroom that had been covered by graffiti and had holes punched in the walls. They were in possession of a bag of spray paint cans and Simon had plaster on his hands and sleeves that matched the drywall that had been damaged. Initially neither student would admit to causing the damage, and they were both charged with destruction of property. River was suspended and the principal began proceedings to expel Simon, but then River took full responsibility for everything and claimed that Simon had just "been trying to look out for me and get me out of there" after she had already caused the damage. School officials suspected that other students were involved but were unable to prove this theory and neither Simon nor River would identify anyone else involved in the episode.*

Each of the scenarios described above involved adolescents engaging in behavior that could be labeled as acting out, or challenging, by teachers or other adults who were observing these students. However, the root of each behavioral episode or pattern (the motivation, or intent) was not the same. Using the same type of response or intervention (e.g., punitive detention or suspension) with each student clearly does not make sense. If all of the school officials tasked with addressing student concerns do not clearly communicate with each other, and if they do not understand the root cause of the behavior, the interventions put in place are likely to have minimal or ineffective impact and the challenging behavior is likely to continue beyond the intervention (Dou et al., 2015; Flannery et al., 2014; Fullchange, 2016; Walker & Sprick, 2016).

### *Discussion*

If we look at each of the seven scenarios described above, we can see that seemingly similar behavioral patterns were actually caused by very different motivating forces, as summarized in Table 13.1.

If the school officials involved in each of these scenarios were to take a punitive, reactive, or punishment-based stance, the most common response or choice of intervention would be to remove the student from the class, send him or her to the office, and perhaps also levy a detention or suspension on the student if it were deemed appropriate. In the short term, removal of a disruptive influence in class makes perfect sense. The student is removed and the teacher can continue to teach the remaining students—problem solved (for the short term). However, when the student eventually returns to class there is no guarantee that being punished had any actual impact on the behavioral concern in question. The simplest form of the feedback loop described above has only one question: "Has the behavior stopped?" If the answer is in the affirmative then there is a belief that the

*Table 13.1* Motivating Factors Behind Challenging Behaviors in Case Examples

| *Note* | *Student:* | *Observed behavior/condition* | *Motivating factors behind behaviors* |
|---|---|---|---|
| 1 | Zoe | Verbal "acting up" in class | Desire to be expelled to be able to go to another school |
| 2 | Derriel | Verbal "acting up" in class | Desire to avoid shame or embarrassment of failing exams |
| 3 | Amara | Fighting with peer in school | Acting out of fear and desire to avoid greater potential violence with a "pre-emptive strike" |
| 4 | Jayne | Fighting with peer in school | Desire to dominate and cause harm to others |
| 5 | Kaley | Loud, disruptive, odd, and confused | Decreased emotional and behavioral control due to alcohol abuse |
| 6 | Malcolm | Odd, tearful, loud, and agitated | Decreased emotional and behavioral control due to symptoms linked to trauma |
| 7 | River and Simon | Destroying property; graffiti and punching holes in walls of math classroom | Unclear due to lack of information Possible explanations could include:<br>• desire for retaliation;<br>• sense of nihilism;<br>• adrenaline rush from destruction;<br>• desire for recognition from peers;<br>• frustrated artistic expression;<br>• under the influence of alcohol and/or other drugs. |

interventions employed have worked, and if the answer is no, then the assumption is that this has not occurred. Obviously, there are many potentially confounding factors in proving what does or does not work, but repeating the same ineffective intervention never leads to the desired outcome, and possibly increases the likelihood of recurrence of the problematic behavior.

In the scenarios described above (all based on real cases in the field, with identifying information disguised), Zoe and Derriel were both seen as challenging due to their verbal acting up in class that served as a disruption to the planned or expected activities of the teacher and the learning of the other students. In addition, while both of their behavioral patterns could clearly be described as challenging, they often might also be described as out of control, which is actually not accurate at all. Zoe's inappropriate behavior is volitional and she engages in her class disruption hoping to be removed from the school so she can go to another school (which, to her 12-year-old brain, is actually quite logical). Derriel's behavior as described is also not out of control, as he is clearly choosing and timing his behavior to get sent to the office and to not have to take a quiz or test that he perceives as shaming or extremely negative to his self-esteem. Zoe needs help sorting out her reasons for wanting to leave the school (and learning that even if she does leave, she will not go to the desired school) and Derriel needs significant help with study skills and with a chaotic home environment. Without addressing their actual needs by tackling the root causes of their problematic behavior, school officials are likely to fail repeatedly.

The other obvious sign of failed behavioral change interventions was Zoe's 32 detentions. Detentions seldom achieve lasting behavioral change (unless linked by reparative work and/or specific social skills training), but no intervention that actually works would need to be employed 32 times. The teacher in that scenario got trapped in a reactive, emotional cycle with Zoe and eventually had no other tool in her behavioral toolbox but to remove her from the room and assign detention. The clinicians and administrators in that school knew something was wrong but kept backing the teacher's actions to avoid undermining her (until bringing in a consultant), and because they had no other explanation or plan. Work was done with Zoe to improve and shape her behavior, but it was later determined that she needed to move to a different teacher's classroom to achieve lasting change, as the two could not give up their learned roles as "combatants." In the new classroom, with the support of her family and regular meetings with the school clinicians, Zoe did much better at the school; and while she certainly got frustrated at times in class, the number of perceived challenging episodes dropped considerably.

In the scenarios described above, Amara and Jayne were examples of two adolescents engaged in fights on school grounds with very different motivating factors. Amara reportedly felt threatened for her safety and made a strategic decision to start a fight with the one person, in view of others and with a reasonable expectation of it being stopped by school officials, rather than face the uncertainty and perceived danger of being jumped by a large group of attackers. She was willing to face the suspension and actually appreciated the risk of expulsion for future fighting, as she saw it as a security policy to help with de-escalating the situation. In work with her school counselor, Amara was able to identify more positive ways to help herself—for example, by focusing on her long-term interest in joining the military (which she learned she could jeopardize by fighting). Her counselor helped her to get involved in sports and avoid the drama surrounding the relationship with the boyfriend.

Jayne apparently had a pattern of picking on younger students at school and in the community and later reported finding gratification in hurting others. Jayne relied on victims to be too scared to press charges, and, based on past events at the school not resulting in significant consequences, Jayne had learned that it is very possible to get away with this type of behavior. Once the school started to focus on Jayne's situation more proactively and with improved communication, every future event was recorded and it was later determined that this particular school was not a fit for someone with these concerns (e.g., criminal pursuits, desire to harm others). Jayne was transferred to a more structured therapeutic program within the system. Two other adolescents similar to Amara and Jayne might both be seen as fighters, but their situations are clearly very different and the interventions necessary to address their needs would certainly need to be different as well if the school hoped to tackle their challenging behavior effectively (e.g., Griffiths & Hart, 2016).

The scenarios described above with Kaley and Malcolm describe adolescents exhibiting disruptive classroom and inappropriate on-campus behavior. Both have trouble focusing, are not following appropriate behavioral guidelines, and end up lashing out at teachers or peers. However, as discussed above, Kaley's problems are linked to substance abuse concerns and Malcolm's challenges are linked to a pattern commonly seen in youth with concerns linked to Post-Traumatic Stress Disorder (or PTSD). Both of these adolescents clearly need therapeutic intervention beyond the training of the teachers, and perhaps even the school personnel, and to best help them there needs to be coordination and sharing of information between the family, any outpatient providers, and the school team. Adolescents displaying challenging behaviors fueled by significant mental health or substance abuse concerns will not respond to pure punitive behavioral responses. They need therapy or counseling, ongoing progress monitoring, and regular communication between the adults in their lives to help them understand and respond to their concerns, and to explore positive coping strategies.

With regard to alcohol and substance abuse, most school policies are designed to address a student's drinking or drugging on campus and result in punitive consequences, and/or perhaps referral to treatment.

Kaley drank off campus, the night before, but consumed so much that her body still had enough alcohol in it to be intoxicated the following day. This is a very different, and very concerning, outlier type of behavior; that is, even for adolescents who engage in substance usage. Her specific usage is very alarming. A 15-year-old who consumes 13 alcoholic drinks on a school night warrants a substance abuse evaluation by a trained professional.

Simon and River's scenario is ambiguous as written because it is unclear specifically who engaged in which challenging behavior. What is clear is that there is a sense of loyalty and connection between them (e.g., River being willing to take the full responsibility to help Simon not be expelled). In addition, graffiti and punching holes in walls are not the same behavior, and questions persist about why that classroom was targeted on that particular day. Suspension or expulsion might serve as a deterrent to other students when consistently enforced, but would still not address the actual problematic behaviors involved. Both students would have potentially learned more if they had, with written parental permission, been assigned supervised "clean up duty" in the damaged classroom. The more appropriate choice to punishment for someone who causes damage or destruction is to give them the consequence of repairing the damage they have caused (e.g., plaster the holes and repaint the walls). With enough time, they could also be trained how to do this repair work correctly (and perhaps in other parts of the school), and this would engineer a scenario in which adults could give positive reinforcement for the repair work they have done, instead of just negative feedback for the damage caused. Meeting with school-based mental health providers to explore reasons behind the behavior would also be crucial. In addition, some students who engage in graffiti often have artistic skill but no training or opportunity, and they can do exceptionally well in structured art programs if they choose to participate. This avenue could be explored after reparations have been made.

In all of the scenarios described above, punishment would be the quickest and easiest response pattern by school officials. However, an effective intervention also needs to be designed such that the student is not simply equated with the behavior and then lost to the system (Flannery et al., 2014; Griffiths & Hart, 2016; Ttofi, Farrington, Losel, Crago, & Theodorakis, 2016). The true measure of the effectiveness of each consequence and intervention plan would be to monitor and observe the adolescents' subsequent behaviors and performance in school and see whether the challenging or destructive behavioral patterns ceased or began to re-occur. Quick and easy responses might seem a good plan in the short term, but for true behavioral change, more planning and thought needs to go into the development of interventions. Each of the interventions described above also clearly benefited from the coordination of information between family, school, and community supports, and the importance of this open collaboration cannot be stressed enough. The adolescents who engage in challenging behaviors will have the greatest chance of success if the adults in their lives collaborate.

## Practical Tools for School-Based Professionals

- Punishment fails, and proactive consequences can succeed as long-term behavior change interventions.
- Identify root causes of challenging behavior before designing interventions.
- Have a range of proactive intervention options available.
- Avoid punitive interventions when possible and use a "feedback loop" to evaluate the effectiveness of interventions to actually result in a change in behavior.
- Generate scenarios for the adolescent to have an opportunity to succeed and earn positive reinforcement.

## Take Home Ideas for Parents

- Punishment fails, and proactive consequences can succeed as long-term behavior change interventions.
- Engage in clear communication with school officials to avoid confusion or cross-purpose actions.
- Maintain consistency in proactive interventions with school officials' interventions to avoid undermining one another.
- As appropriate, share key data about mental health treatment with school clinicians.
- Generate scenarios for the adolescent to have an opportunity to succeed and earn positive reinforcement.

Adolescents engaged in challenging or disruptive behaviors as described above are clearly at risk of not being able to function up to their full academic potential. School officials must respond to challenging episodes, and the results will be longer-lasting and more effective when the interventions are linked to consequences designed to change the behavior, as well as tailored to the specific adolescent. Punitive interventions that are reactive and implemented without an evaluation process, or feedback loop, are much less likely to result in lasting change.

Tackling challenging behavior exhibited by adolescents in schools is difficult work, but very important for us to address in a manner that leads to lasting results for the good of the specific adolescents, and for the good of the larger community. It is hard but very possible to address these challenges in an effective manner, and one of the most important factors is the ability to maintain positive and open communication between families and school officials so we can all work together to help our students succeed.

## References

Dou, C., Wei, Z., Jin, K., Wang, H., Wang, X., & Peng, Z. (2015). Family and social environmental factors associated with aggression among Chinese adolescents. *School Psychology Quarterly, 30*(3), 421–430. doi:10.1037/spq0000103.

Flannery, K. B., Fenning, P., Kato, M. M., & McIntosh, M. (2014). Effects of school-wide positive behavioral interventions and supports and fidelity of implementation on problem behavior in high schools. *School Psychology Quarterly, 29*(2), 111–124. doi:10.1037/spq000039.

Fullchange, A. (2016). Empathy and potential for positive outcomes for at-risk youth. *Communique, 45*(1), 8 & 10. Retrieved from www.nasponline.org

Griffiths, A. J. & Hart, S. (2016). DSM-5 and school psychology: Conduct disorder. *Communique, 45*(2), 1, 26–27. Retrieved from www.nasponline.org

Johnson, M., George, P., Armstrong, M., Lyman, D., Dougherty, R., Daniels, A., ... Delphin-Rittmon, M. (2014). Behavioral management for children and adolescents: Assessing the evidence. *Psychiatric Services, 65*(5), 580–590. doi:10.1176/appi.ps.201300253.

Kuhn, T., Ebert, J., Gracey, K., & Epstein, R. (2015). Evidence-based interventions for adolescents with disruptive behaviors in school-based settings. *Child and Adolescent Psychiatric Clinics of North America, 24*(2), 305–317. doi:10.1016/j.chc.2014.11.005.

Li, Y., Zhang, W., Liu, J., Arbeit, M., Schwartz, S., Bowers, E., & Lerner, R. (2011). The role of school engagement in preventing adolescent delinquency and substance use: A survival analysis, *Journal of Adolescence, 34*(6), 1181–1192. doi:10.1016/j.adolescence.2011.07.003.

Reed, K., Nugent, W., & Cooper, R. (2015). Testing a path model of relationships between gender, age, and bullying victimization and violent behavior, substance abuse, depression, suicidal ideation, and suicide attempts in adolescents. *Children and Youth Services Review, 55*(C), 128–137. doi:10.1016/j.childyouth.2015.05.016.

Ttofi, M., Farrington, D., Losel, F. Crago, R., & Theodorakis, N. (2016). School bullying and drug use later in life: A meta-analytic investigation. *School Psychology Quarterly, 31*(1), 8–27. doi:10.1037/spq0000120.

Walker, H. & Sprick, R. (2016). Coordinated intervention when children first start school prevents destructive outcomes. *Communique, 44*(7), 1, 26, 28–30. Retrieved from www.nasponline.org

# Part III

# Proactive, Systemic Strategies in Schools

# 14 How Schools Organize Their Mental Health Services

*John Desrochers*

In years past, there was relatively little awareness among the public about the role of mental health professionals employed in the public-school system, and most of that awareness focused on the role of school counselors at the high school level helping students with adjustment problems and post-secondary planning. Indeed, many once questioned the appropriateness of expanding mental health services within the schools, believing that mental health was not the school's province, and that the family, along with services available within the community, should attend to these needs. This situation has changed dramatically in recent times, with most people understanding that school mental health professionals play a role in all kinds of mental health matters, from mental wellness to crisis intervention. What may not be appreciated as fully is the extent of the need for mental health services in schools and how those services are staffed and organized. This chapter will outline the extent of student needs addressed by school mental health professionals, describe a framework (known as *multi-tiered systems of support*) for delivering mental and behavioral health services, and offer practical suggestions to professionals and parents for improving school-based mental health systems.

## Notes from the Field

*When Ms. Barnaby looks out over her English class, she keeps an eye on Alex, who has had severe behavior difficulties this year and whose scowl today means that trouble may be brewing. In the back is Alondra, who is clearly depressed and totally disengaged from school. James, who doesn't have a friend in the world, is so anxious that he can hardly talk to you. Two students are on medication for attention deficit disorder. How many others, she wonders, have problems she doesn't even know about? Cutting, abusive families, drugs, suicidal behavior?*

*She started at this school six years ago and immediately sought out help for her students, but quickly discovered the school only had access to two school counselors and a school psychologist who came once a week to attend to students who were in intensive special education programs.*

*It quickly became clear that, while well-meaning, these professionals were overworked and focused mostly on the students with the most severe mental and behavioral problems. Alex sees the school counselor once a week and gets some support from special education, but Ms. Barnaby is pretty much left on her own to deal with the others.*

*In a nearby district, Ms. Alonzo looks out over a similar set of students with a set of problems that are not too different from those experienced by Ms. Barnaby's students. But her school has a much better developed set of programs to address the mental and behavioral health needs of its students. Staffing is much better, more attention is devoted to sustaining a positive school climate, and a comprehensive range of services is available to students. In Ms. Alonzo's school, Alex would have additional services such as a behavioral intervention plan featuring systematic positive reinforcement strategies and evaluation of progress monitoring data. Alondra would be seen for counseling by a school psychologist who would reach out to her family to provide support. A social worker would refer James to a community-based clinic which would provide counseling and medication. Some of the other children she was worried about would be screened and given support as needed and their progress monitored. As a result, her students' behavior is better and their mental health issues are being addressed, so Ms. Alonzo is able to devote more time to instruction and her students are better able to benefit from that instruction.*

## Why It Matters

Ms. Barnaby and Ms. Alonzo may not know it, but they are not alone. Every school in the country contains students with the same range of mental and behavioral health issues. But the quality of the mental health services available to those students varies widely from well-staffed mental health programs that feature prevention and multiple tiers of increasingly intensive interventions to schools that do not have even one full-time school-based mental health professional. For example, only 22% of public schools nationwide have a full-time school psychologist, and the difference between states is huge, with a high of at least 81% of schools in Connecticut and New York to a low of less than 1% of schools in Alabama having a full-time school psychologist. Moreover, poor children and children of color suffer disproportionately (Baffour, 2016). This state of affairs contrasts dramatically with recommended staffing ratios for school-based mental health professionals provided by each of the relevant professional associations. For example, the National Association of School Psychologists (2010) recommends a ratio of one school psychologist per 500–700 students, depending on the intensity of services they are called upon to provide. Both the American School Counselor Association (2012) and the School Social Work Association of America (2013) recommend a ratio of 1 to 250.

Why should we be concerned about this? Because when it comes to access to mental health services for most of our nation's children and adolescents, schools may be the only game in town. Approximately 13% to 20% of students have or will have a diagnosable mental illness or significant behavioral disorder in any given year, and that percentage seems to be increasing (Perou et al., 2013). Only a third of young people who need mental health services receive them at all (Merikangas et al., 2011) and, of those who do, it is commonly estimated that the number who access those services in school is approximately 70–80% (mostly from school psychologists and school counselors; Committee on Pediatric Emergency Medicine, 2011). There is some variability in these estimates (e.g., a national study found that 36% of students who receive services access those services at school, and about 47% access them through community mental health clinics and hospitals; Merikangas et al., 2011), but there is no doubt that schools are a major provider of mental health services in the United States.

The sense of urgency felt by Ms. Barnaby and Ms. Alonzo is justified: Every teacher routinely has four or five students in her class with significant mental or behavioral health issues and many more will have mental and behavioral health issues that are significant but do not reach the level of a diagnosable condition. These difficulties reduce the ability of students to perform well in school and cause them and their families significant and sometimes long-term suffering. Finally, the economic cost to families of dealing with children's behavioral and mental health problems is huge—estimated as approximately 250 billion dollars (National Research Council and Institute of Medicine [NRC & IOM], 2009).

Every common mental or behavioral disorder that children or adolescents can be prone to may be found in public schools today. In other words, children and adolescents overwhelmingly depend upon their schools for mental health services, but most schools are not adequately staffed to meet the need. In some schools, access to mental health professionals may be nearly impossible. In these cases, mental health services for children and adolescents are essentially nonexistent because if they are not available in schools, the children must go without. Ms. Barnaby would be lucky if even one of her needy students had access to a mental health service provider.

Providing services to meet the increasing frequency and severity of problems exhibited by students is no small challenge, but many school districts are working hard to change this situation and to build comprehensive school mental health programs within their schools. Examples abound all across the country in districts large and small. For example, for over a decade, the Westport Public Schools, a prosperous suburban school district in Connecticut, have intentionally built a comprehensive program of mental and behavioral health supports in all its schools. At this point, each building is well-staffed with school mental health personnel and has several tiers of increasingly more intensive mental and behavioral health services for all students. Of greatest interest is the emphasis on mental and behavioral wellness within the schools, including an emphasis on high behavioral and academic expectations, positive school climate, and full participation in social and emotional learning programs (see Desrochers, 2015, for a description of this program).

In a very different sort of community, the Boston Public Schools began using the Comprehensive Behavioral Health Model (CBHM) in 2012 (Pearrow, Amador, & Dennery, 2016; Pearrow et al., 2016), introducing it in 10 schools with an additional 10 added each year. The CBHM features several tiers of mental and behavioral health services, including a social and emotional learning curriculum provided to all students; universal screening for mental and behavioral health problems; extensive staff development; and collaboration with community providers (for more information, see cbhmboston.com). Analysis of outcomes from the program indicates improved social skills and attendance, reduced disciplinary referrals, and increased academic achievement, including improved state test scores (Pearrow, Snyder, & Kay, 2017). Many other school districts are also implementing comprehensive, integrated, multi-tiered systems of support in their schools (e.g., see Barrett, Eber, & Weist, n.d.).

As teachers like Ms. Barnaby and Ms. Alonza can tell you, mental and behavioral health problems have a significant impact not only on the students who have these kinds of difficulties, but also on the entire climate of the school, and on the ability of other students to take advantage of the instruction being offered in their classes. It is hard to imagine how a student coping with depression, anxiety, or conduct problems could possibly be completely available for instruction or for healthy engagement with everything a school has to offer. Likewise, it is obvious that classroom disruption or bullying by even one student essentially halts instruction for the entire class and creates a climate that encourages further disruption and lack of engagement. Teachers know that students who exhibit problems with mental and behavioral health represent some of the most significant challenges in their day-to-day work. On the other hand, it is easy to understand how students who are well adjusted, happy, and engaged with their schooling not only achieve more than students who do not possess these qualities, but also contribute positively to the instructional quality of classroom life as well as the overall climate of the school. In other words, school-based mental health programs cannot be focused exclusively on mental illness; mental and behavioral wellness must also be actively promoted (Miles, Espiritu, Horen, Sebian, & Waetzig, 2010).

### *Mental and Behavioral Health Problems Can Be Prevented*

The positive news that has developed over the last two decades is that there are treatments for most mental and behavioral health problems and that many can be prevented through the use of wellness promotion activities such as social and emotional learning programs, screening for potential problems, and early intervention for those at risk for the development of such problems (e.g., NRC & IOM, 2009). In fact, research has shown that, in addition to improving the mental and behavioral health of individual students, such programs improve overall school climate as well as reduce suspensions, grade retention, special education referrals, and drop-out rates (e.g., Bruns, Walrath, Glass-Siegel, & Weist, 2004; Keeton, Soleimanpour, & Brindis, 2012; Shonkoff & Phillips, 2000). Moreover, in a meta-analysis of more than 270,000 students from urban, rural, and suburban districts, it was found that those who have access to social and emotional learning programs in their schools have significantly higher academic achievement (on average by 11 to 17 percentile points) than students whose schools do not provide such programs (Durlak, Weissberg, Dymnicki, Taylor, & Schellinger, 2011). Many interventions for students' mental and behavioral health are specifically designed for use in schools and implementation by school personnel (Desrochers & Houck, 2013).

### *Advantages of Providing Mental and Behavioral Health Services in Schools*

Schools are ideal places to provide mental health services to children and adolescents. Students are in school for a good part of every day for a long period of time during the developmental period when most mental disorders are beginning to develop. About half of all lifetime cases of mental illness are identified by age 14 and three-fourths by age 24, with many starting their development earlier, often before the appearance of symptoms (Kessler, Berglund, Demler, Merikangas, & Walters, 2005). Schools are uniquely positioned to offer services delivered on a continuum that is always appropriate to students' changing needs, starting with prevention activities before problems begin to appear. Because of this, school-based screening and early intervention could reduce the severity of the disorders or prevent them altogether (Kessler et al., 2007). The early age of onset of most mental illness, their prevalence, the impact these problems have on children and their families and schools, and the availability of programs and treatments that can help prevent mental illness strongly suggest the need to shift from a focus on treatment to prevention and early intervention (Merikangas et al., 2010).

Availability of parents and teachers for collaboration, opportunities for generalization and practice of social and emotional skills in the classroom, and opportunities for carefully monitoring student progress are other important advantages of school-based mental and behavioral health services. Moreover, because these services can be woven into the routine of school programming, students are more likely to take advantage of them when they are provided in school (Rivet-Duval, Heriot, & Hunt, 2011; Slade, 2002).

### *Multi-Tiered Systems of Support*

School mental health programs take many forms, but the consensus among experts in school-based mental health service delivery is that these services are best organized within a framework called multi-tiered systems of support (MTSS). Such a system features several key components that are similar to most other curriculum areas within the school:

- A comprehensive and coordinated continuum of programs and services focused on the mental and behavioral health of all the students in the school. Services and programs range from wellness promotion and screening to increasingly intensive levels of intervention. Collaboration among the family, school personnel, and community professionals ensures that all services are aligned and coordinated.
- The programs and services are integrated into the total functioning of the school and all staff (including administrators) are committed to implementing the mental health program to the same extent as all the other programs in the school.
- Interventions are matched to the needs of the students and are evidence-based as well as culturally and linguistically relevant to all students.
- Assessment is used systematically for screening, intervention planning, monitoring student progress, and program evaluation.
- Staffing and professional development activity is sufficient to operate and sustain the program.

MTSS frameworks are frequently represented in the form of a pyramid, such as in Figure 14.1. Resting on a foundation of the key components listed above, the pyramid illustrates the continuum of mental and behavioral health interventions from least to most intensive, with least intensive services being provided universally to *all* students in the school, whether they are exhibiting problems or not (Tier 1); targeted (Tier 2) interventions provided to fewer students (typically 10–15%); and intensive services (Tier 3) provided to the least number of students (typically 5–10%). Movement of students up and down the intensity level in the pyramid is fluid and based upon data indicating the outcomes of each intervention. Only students for whom a less intensive intervention has been unsuccessful move up the pyramid to more intensive interventions. Students who no longer need the intensity of their current intervention move down the pyramid to less intensive levels of intervention. Permeating the entire MTSS framework is an orientation toward *prevention*: The idea is to intervene early at less intensive tiers of service to prevent students from developing further problems and needing the more intensive levels of intervention.

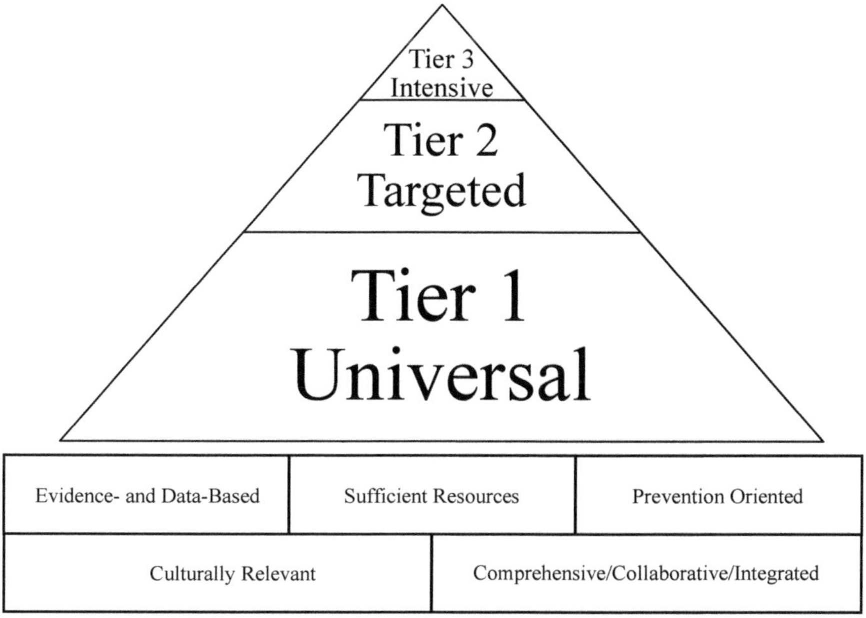


*Figure 14.1* Multi-Tiered Systems of Support for a School Mental and Behavioral Health Program.

### *School-Based Interventions for Mental and Behavioral Health*

School-based mental and behavioral health services extend well beyond counseling and behavioral intervention. For example, Tier 1 interventions, which are provided school-wide to all students regardless of whether they currently exhibit problems, might include: programs to support positive behavior and school climate; staff and parent education about mental health issues; character education and social–emotional learning programs; anti-bullying and suicide prevention activities; and school-wide screening for social, emotional, and behavioral concerns.

Tier 2 interventions, designed for students who are at risk of developing social, emotional, or behavior problems, might include: student support groups that address specific concerns (e.g., adjustment to a new school, LGBTQ issues, and substance use); group counseling to address specific risk factors for and concerns about such issues as anxiety, depression, divorce, and anger management; behavioral assessment and intervention; social skills instruction; psychoeducation and consultation with parents and school staff regarding at-risk students; and progress monitoring and evaluation of ongoing mental health or behavioral interventions.

Tier 3 interventions, which are designed for students who are at elevated risk or who already experience a significant mental or behavioral health problem, might include: comprehensive psychoeducational and functional behavioral assessments; development of treatment plans, special education programs, and case management; individual counseling; crisis prevention and intervention; family and teacher consultation and support; and intensive progress monitoring and program evaluation. The continuum of services extends to community-based providers, with school personnel providing referral services and collaboration. Schools and community agencies account for about 82% of all mental health services delivered to children and adolescents (Merikangas et al., 2011).

School mental health professionals are capable of providing most of these services. For example, all school psychologists are qualified to provide Tier 1 services, most are qualified to deliver Tier 2 services, and most are qualified to provide the majority of Tier 3 services. In many cases, these most intensive services are provided by a combination of school-based and community-based practitioners (e.g., psychiatrists, hospitals, family therapists). In some schools, community-based services are housed within the schools themselves (as in full service community schools and programs using a coordinated school health model); in other cases, school personnel maintain close collaboration with their community-based counterparts. The professional associations of each school-based mental health profession provide descriptions of the skill sets of their respective professionals (e.g., for school psychologists, see the National Association of School Psychologists (2010) *Model for Comprehensive and Integrated School Psychological Services*).

Not all districts have a fully realized MTSS in place. Some have most, but not all aspects; others are less well developed. Ms. Alonzo would recognize an MTSS continuum of services in her school. Ms. Barnaby would find several important features of MTSS missing in hers. Most importantly, outcomes for students in each school would be different. Schools that come closest to conceptualizing and organizing their mental and behavioral health delivery system according to this framework tend to produce the best outcomes in terms of mental, behavioral, and academic functioning of their students, with especially high gains for those students who previously had the lowest performance in these areas (Kutash, Duchnowki, & Green, 2011).

### *Who Are School-Based Mental Health Professionals?*

School-based mental health professionals include school psychologists, school counselors, adjustment counselors, and school social workers. School nurses are also often important members of many school mental health teams.

School psychologists have, as a minimum, master's and specialist degrees (60 or more graduate semester hours) in school psychology, including a year-long supervised internship, and are certified or licensed by state departments of education for school practice. School counselors have a minimum of a master's degree in school counseling and are certified or licensed by state departments of education. Most school social workers also have a master's degree and state department of education certification or licensure. School nurses have a minimum of a bachelor's degree and licensure as a registered nurse. Many of these professionals have additional training and credentials (e.g., state department of health psychologist licensure, licensed educational psychologist, licensed professional counselor, licensed social worker, advanced practice nurse). Other specialists (e.g., board certified behavior analysts) may also be part of these school teams. While there is a degree of overlap in the roles and functions of these professionals, each specialty has unique training, and each is needed in a comprehensive school mental health program.

## Practical Tools for School-Based Professionals

- School professionals interested in developing or building upon existing multi-tiered programs that promote student mental and behavioral health in their districts might consider forming a professional learning community related to multi-tiered systems of emotional and behavioral support. Start with discussion of a general document such as *Advancing education effectiveness: Interconnecting school mental health and school-wide positive behavior support* (link available in our eResource at www.routledge.com/9781138293571). The websites of the Collaborative for Academic, Social, and Emotional Learning (www.casel.org) and UCLA Center for Mental Health in Schools (smhp.psych.ucla.edu) are also sources of much information, especially for school-wide or district-wide programs at the universal (Tier 1) level. Work hard to enlist school mental health professionals and school administrators to join your group. Focus not only on the improvements in school climate and student mental and behavioral health that result from these programs, but also on the impact on overall levels of school academic achievement associated with such programs. Note the Every Student Succeeds Act allows states and school districts to provide high-quality instruction, professional development, and *learning supports*, and permits the use of funds (including Title I, Title II, and Title IV) to support multi-tiered systems of support.
- Review the extent to which your program incorporates features of high-quality multi-tiered school mental health programs. Key indicators include: a comprehensive, coordinated continuum of services integrated into the overall functioning of the school; collaboration and buy-in from families, school personnel (including administrators), and community providers; assessment data used for screening, progress monitoring, and program evaluation; interventions matched to the needs of students; and adequate staffing and professional

development opportunities. Identify gaps and areas of weakness in your continuum of services and develop plans to improve services in those areas.

- Advocate for improvements to your school's mental and behavioral health program. To get started, see Vaillancourt, Cowan, and Skalski (2013a, b).

## Take Home Ideas for Parents

- If you have concerns about the emotional or behavioral health of your child, discuss them with your child's teacher or with a school-based mental health professional. Explore what services are available within the school and in the community. Ask for referral to community social agencies if needed. Consider other sources of help in your community (counseling agencies, churches, town social services, local university clinics). Refer your child to special education personnel if you believe your child has a disability (to get started, see *Special Education: A Basic Guide for Parents*, link available in our eResource at www.routledge.com/9781138293571).
- When deciding on a mental health provider, ask questions such as: (a) How do you define the problem? (b) What are the goals of treatment and how will they be accomplished? (c) How will you measure progress? (d) What training and experience have you had providing service for this problem? (e) Have you worked before with students who had similar problems? And, (f) How can I help? The professional associations for each type of school-based mental health professional have websites that describe their profession. For example, the National Association of School Psychologists publishes *Who Are School Psychologists?* (link available in our eResource at www.routledge.com/9781138293571) and other publications describing their work.
- Find out to what extent your school or district implements a multi-tiered system of supports for mental and behavioral health. Advocate for the district-wide use of such a system, perhaps starting with a strong Tier 1 program featuring a social and emotional learning program (see the Collaborative for Academic, Social, and Emotional Learning website: www.casel.org).

## References

American School Counselor Association. (2012). *Student-to-school-counselor ratios*. Retrieved from www.schoolcounselor.org/asca/media/asca/PositionStatements/PS_ComprehensivePrograms.pdf

Baffour, P. (2016). *Counsel or criminalize? Why students of color need supports, not suspensions*. Center for American Progress. Retrieved from https://cdn.americanprogress.org/wp-content/uploads/2016/09/21142816/SupportNotSuspensions-brief.pdf

Barrett, S., Eber, L., & Weist, M. (Eds.). (n.d.). *Advancing education effectiveness: Interconnecting school mental health and school-wide positive behavior support*. Retrieved from www.pbis.org/common/cms/files/Current%20Topics/Final-Monograph.pdf

Bruns, E. J., Walrath, C., Glass-Siegel, M., & Weist, M. D. (2004). School-based mental health services in Baltimore: Association with school climate and special education referrals. *Behavior Modification, 28*, 491–512. doi:10.1177/0145445503259524

Committee on Pediatric Emergency Medicine. (2011). Pediatric and adolescent mental health emergencies in the emergency medical services system. *Pediatrics, 127*(5). Retrieved from http://pediatrics.aappublications.org/content/127/5/e1356

Desrochers, J. E. (2015). Rx for mental health. *Educational Leadership, 73*(2), 46–50. Retrieved from www.educationalleadership-digital.com/educationalleadership/201510?pg=NaN#pgNaN

Desrochers, J. E. & Houck, G. M. (2013). *Depression in children and adolescents: Guidelines for school practice*. Silver Spring, MD: National Association of School Nurses.

Durlak, J. A., Weissberg, R. P., Dymnicki, A. B., Taylor, R. D., & Schellinger, K. B. (2011). The impact of enhancing students' social and emotional learning: A meta-analysis of school-based universal interventions. *Child Development, 82*(1), 405–432. doi:10.1111/j.1467-8624.2010.01564.x

Keeton, V., Soleimanpour, S., & Brindis, C. D. (2012). School-based health centers in an era of health care reform: Building on history. *Current Problem in Pediatric and Adolescent Health Care, 42*, 132–156. doi:10.1016/j.cppeds.2012.03.002

Kessler, R. C., Angermeyer, M., Anthony, J. C., De Graaf, R., Demyttenaere, K., Gasquet, I., ... Üstün, T. B. (2007). Lifetime prevalence and age-of-onset distributions of mental disorders in the World Health Organization's World Mental Health Survey Initiative. *World Psychiatry, 6*(3), 168–176. Retrieved from www.ncbi.nlm.nih.gov/pmc/articles/PMC2174588

Kessler, R. C., Berglund, P., Demler, O., Merikangas, K. R., & Walters, E. E. (2005). Lifetime prevalence and age-of-onset distributions of DSM-IV disorders in the National Comorbidity Survey Replication. *Archives of General Psychiatry, 62*(6), 593–602. doi:10.1001/archpsyc.62.6.593

Kutash, K., Duchnowki, A. J., & Green, A. L. (2011). School-based mental health programs for students who have emotional disturbances: Academic and social–emotional outcomes. *School Mental Health, 3*, 191–208. doi:10.1007/s12310-011-9062-9

Merikangas, K. R., He, J. P., Burstein, M., Swanson, S. A., Avenevoli, S., Cui, L., ... Swendsen, J. (2010). Lifetime prevalence of mental disorders in U.S. adolescents: Results from the National Comorbidity Study–Adolescent Supplement. *Journal of the American Academy of Child and Adolescent Psychiatry, 49*(10), 980–989. doi:10.1016/j.jaac.2010.05.017

Merikangas K. R., He, J., Burstein, M. E., Swendsen, J., Avenevoli, S., Case, B., ... Olfson, M. (2011). Service utilization for lifetime mental disorders in U.S. adolescents: Results from the National Comorbidity Survey Adolescent Supplement. *Journal of the American Academy of Child and Adolescent Psychiatry, 50*(1), 32–45. doi:10.1016/j.jaac.2010.10.006

Miles, J., Espiritu, R., Horen, N., Sebian, J., & Waetzig, E. (2010). *A public health approach to children's mental health: A conceptual approach*. Washington, DC: Georgetown University Center for Child and Human Development. Retrieved from http://gucchdtacenter.georgetown.edu/publications/PublicHealthApproach.pdf

National Association of School Psychologists. (2010). *Model for comprehensive and integrated school psychological services*. Bethesda, MD: Author. Retrieved from www.nasponline.org/standards/2010standards/2_PracticeModel.pdf

National Research Council and Institute of Medicine. (2009). *Preventing mental, emotional, and behavioral disorders among young people: Progress and possibilities*. Washington, DC: National Academies Press. Retrieved from www.nap.edu/catalog.php?record_id=12480

Pearrow, M., Amador, A., & Dennery, S. (2016). Boston Public Schools' Comprehensive Behavioral Health Model. *NASP Communiqué, 45*(3), 1, 20, 22. Retrieved from www.nasponline.org/publications/periodicals/communique/issues/volume-45-issue-3/boston-public-schools-comprehensive-behavioral-health-model

Pearrow, M., Amador, A., Dennery, S., Cohen, M. Z., Snyder, J., & Shachmut, L. (2016). Boston's Comprehensive Behavioral Health Model: Organizational structures. *NASP Communiqué, 45(4)*, 16–17. Retrieved from www.nasponline.org/publications/periodicals/communique/issues/volume-45-issue-4/bostons-comprehensive-behavioral-health-model-organizational-structures

Pearrow, M. M., Snyder, J., & Kay, A. (2017). Boston's Comprehensive Behavioral Health Model: Research and evaluation. *NASP Communiqué, 45*(6). Retrieved from www.nasponline.org/resources-and-publications/periodicals/communiqué-volume-45-number-6-(march/april-2017)/bostons-comprehensive-behavioral-health-model-research-and-evaluation

Perou, R., Bitsko, R. H., Blumberg, S. J., Pastor, R., Ghandour, R. M., Gfroerer, J. C., ... Huang, L. N. (2013). Mental health surveillance among children—United States, 2005–2011. *MMWR, 62*(2), 1–35. Retrieved from www.cdc.gov/mmwr/preview/mmwrhtml/su6202a1.htm?x_cid=su6202a1_w

Rivet-Duval, E., Heriot, S., & Hunt, C. (2011). Preventing adolescent depression in Mauritius: A universal school-based program. *Child and Adolescent Mental Health, 16*(2), 86–91. doi:10.1111/j.1475-3588.2010.00584.x

School Social Work Association of America. (2013). *School social workers helping students succeed: Recommended school social worker to student ratios* (Resolution). Retrieved from https://docs.wixstatic.com/ugd/426a18_4050422b3c41478f9ee0db83d1bc1f75.pdf

Shonkoff, J. P. & Phillips, D. A. (Eds.). (2000). *From neurons to neighborhoods: The science of early childhood development*. Committee on Integrating the Science of Early Childhood Development, Board on Children, Youth, and Families, National Research Council and the Institute of Medicine. Washington, DC: National Academy Press.

Slade, E. P. (2002). Effects of school-based mental health programs on mental health service use by adolescents at school and in the community. *Mental Health Service Research, 3*, 151–166. Retrieved from http://link.springer.com/article/10.1023/A%3A1019711113312

Vaillancourt, K., Cowan, K. C., & Skalski, A. K. (2013a). Providing mental health services within a multitiered system of supports. In J. E. Desrochers & G. M. Houck (Eds.), *Depression in children and adolescents: Guidelines for school practice* (Appendix, Handout K). Silver Spring, MD: National Association of School Nurses.

Vaillancourt, K., Cowan, K. C., & Skalski, A. K. (2013b). *Professional advocacy planning worksheet*. In J. E. Desrochers & G. M. Houck (Eds.), *Depression in children and adolescents: Guidelines for school practice* (Appendix, Handout L). Silver Spring, MD: National Association of School Nurses.

# 15 School-Wide Suicide Prevention

*Tracey Borriello Murphy, June Bowman, and Colleen Meigher*

In 2015, suicide was the second leading cause of death for adolescents ages 15–19 (Centers for Disease Control and Prevention [CDC], 2017). According to the 2015 Youth Risk Behavior Survey (YRBS), almost 18% of high school students seriously considered suicide in the previous 12 months (Kann et al., 2016). Although suicide is a public health problem worldwide, it is also the most preventable form of adolescent mortality. Correcting misconceptions, raising awareness of risk factors, and widely disseminating information regarding available resources provide the foundation for much-needed prevention efforts.

Often myths about suicide prevent family members, friends, caregivers, or adolescents themselves from seeking much-needed support. Deepening public understanding of risk factors that can lead to suicide and suicidal behavior allows for the provision of increasingly targeted and intensive prevention efforts. School-based suicide prevention programming is now part of the curriculum in approximately 74% of public high schools (CDC, 2014). School-wide efforts allow all students access to critical information and resources, and structured programming offers a means via which students at increased risk for suicide may be identified and targeted for treatment they might not otherwise receive.

## Notes from the Field

### *A Distressed Student*

When a student is struggling emotionally and feeling a pain they grapple to identify or put into words, they will often approach a trusted adult or friend in confidence. "I want to die" or "I feel like killing myself" are statements no parent, teacher, or friend ever wants to hear, but they are not all that uncommon. Examples taken from the experiences of school-based personnel reveal how suicidal ideation and behaviors come to the attention of friends and school staff.

*Imagine a student walking into a school office and when asked what is on her mind, she agrees to share five words provided the adult does not comment on those words. The student shares the words, "I want to kill myself." On another occasion, a student requests that a friend see a member of the school support staff.*

### *Friends Worried About a Friend*

*When two unfamiliar boys enter the office, the reason for the visit is abundantly clear: the friend has a pronounced raw rope burn around his neck. The boy looks at the support person and comments "the rope broke."*

When depression and anxiety lead to hopelessness, we must respond with urgency to develop both short- and long-term support plans. Parents and school staff can be integral in identifying students at risk for suicide and supporting access to effective treatment before a tragedy occurs (Substance Abuse and Mental Health Services Administration [SAMHSA], 2012).

## Why It Matters

### *The Rising Incidence of Suicidal Ideation, Attempts, and Completions*

The National Center for Health Statistics released data depicting a striking jump in suicide rates across the country between 1999 and 2014, indicating an increase of 24% (CDC, 2017). While the increase varied across groups sorted by demographics, the increase impacted every age group to some degree. No truly complete count of suicide-attempt data exists; however, according to the CDC (2015), for every reported death by suicide across the entire population, approximately 12 additional individuals have engaged in acts of self-harm; this number is thought to be higher for adolescents. Over the last several years, students are reporting increased suicidal ideation (17.7%) and, more importantly, the tendency to develop a concrete plan (14.6%). Similarly, suicide attempts have risen to 8.6% and attempts resulting in harm to 2.8% over the same seven-year period (Kann et al., 2016).

### *Risk Factors Associated with Suicidal Behaviors*

Undeniably, suicide is an attempt to solve the problem of intense psychological pain. Supports for those impacted by suicidal ideation and behaviors vary tremendously across the country and even amongst communities within proximity of one another. Today, treatment to manage risk factors associated with increased suicidal ideation and attempts are more effective than ever. Identifying those at increased risk as well as making treatment more accessible is critical.

Youth suicide represents a significant health problem worldwide, so it is particularly important to understand underlying factors (Cash & Bridge, 2009). While boys tend to have higher suicide rates, girls engage in more suicidal ideation and attempts (CDC, 2015). Psychiatric disorders are another significant risk factor for adolescents who die by suicide (Lieberman, Poland, & Kornfeld, 2014). Specifically, substantial struggles with mood, anxiety, overall conduct, and substance use may impact those who experience suicidal ideation and make attempts, as well as those who die by suicide. While depression is the single most concerning correlate, substance abuse also contributes substantially to the risk of suicide, particularly in the context of a comorbid mood disorder.

Familial challenges also play an important role in a child's risk profile. Parental struggles with mental health, family conflict, dramatic changes in family constellation (including death of a parent and divorce), and child abuse/neglect contribute to the potential development of suicidal thoughts and behaviors. A significant increase in the likelihood of suicide attempts amongst those with same-sex orientation is also consistently identified in the literature, particularly if the individual has experienced family rejection or a general negative response by those close to them (Cash & Bridge, 2009). Additionally, bullying involvement is also strongly associated with suicidal ideation and behavior but has not been shown to be a causal factor (Holt et al., 2015).

### *Resilience*

Risk factors can be counteracted by protective factors and resiliency. Protective factors are environmental or personal characteristics that can offset the risk of suicide. Resilience is the positive capacity to cope with risk factors (SAMHSA, 2012). According to the National Association of School Psychologists (NASP, 2015), children and adolescents who may be at risk should be actively supported in building protective factors, such as positive relationships with family and friends, well-developed problem-solving and coping skills, and a feeling of connectedness to their schools and communities.

### *Schools as a Resource*

By making resources widely available to adolescents, families, community members, and educators, it is possible to provide a tiered system of supports within both the context of the school as well as the community. Schools are primed to function as places where students can be readily identified as at risk for mental health concerns or suicidal behaviors. Schools are also access points where adolescents can gain support for a wide variety of mental health and behavioral needs.

Adolescents spend a minimum of seven hours per day, five days per week within their school communities. As such, educational settings have access to this highly vulnerable population and are in an excellent position to provide education around mental health and targeted suicide prevention programming. In the high school setting, multiple adults are in contact with each student regularly. Staff are trained to support student academic learning as well as help them gain access to systems that support emotional well-being. With so many contact hours, educators can notice changes in behavior, trends around changing friendships, and general student affect.

Additionally, adolescents are often able to find an adult with whom they connect in the school setting, providing an opportunity for introducing additional supports if warranted. There are specific mechanisms via which teachers can access elevated supports for students whom they are particularly concerned about. School systems often employ school counselors, mental health clinicians, and school psychologists, and have ongoing access to community referrals for students at risk or amidst an acute crisis. With early identification of youth at risk for suicide, treatment for the major risk factors associated with suicide, and increased availability of resources, adolescents can experience a reduction in the thoughts and behaviors associated with suicide.

### *School-Based Tiered Intervention, Tier 1*

A tiered system of supports provides for ongoing learning, screening, and targeted supports, as well as highly individualized interventions based upon student needs (Lieberman et al., 2014). Within the context of schools and suicide prevention, this tiered system can provide a structure to ensure the needs of students are met to the greatest extent possible. Many schools employ a variety of school-wide suicide prevention programming designed to support education around mental health and suicide, as well as identify students who may be experiencing suicidal ideation. These programs are designed to meet the needs of large groups of students with a variety of needs. They are both educational and supportive, and implemented by trained staff.

When working with large groups of students where students at risk for suicide are likely to be present, it is critically important to use evidence-based programming. One such prevention program is Signs of Suicide (SOS), developed by Screening for Mental Health, Inc. (link available in our eResource at www.routledge.com/9781138293571). SOS is a program that includes a training video with vignettes and personal stories embedded into a carefully crafted psychoeducational curriculum. The goals of the SOS program are two-fold: (a) to train students to identify the signs and symptoms of suicide and how to seek help; and (b) to identify students who are at high risk for suicidality.

SOS programs have been widely and effectively used in schools and communities (Lieberman et al., 2014). As part of a typical program, students view the SOS training video during a specified class and engage in a class-wide discussion about depression and suicide. The program includes information regarding the positive outcomes of interventions designed to treat depression and mental illness as well as what to do if you or a friend experiences suicidal ideation. Following the training video and discussion, students complete a corresponding short questionnaire in which they rate themselves on a seven-item depression inventory; two of the questions include information regarding past suicide attempts and suicidal ideation. The questionnaire also asks students to identify a trusted adult both in and out of school. Finally, students are asked whether they would like to speak with an adult once the program concludes.

Questionnaire results are reviewed by trained clinical staff the same day they are completed by students, and students who meet symptom criteria for high risk of depression and/or suicide are seen by a clinician in school before the end of the school day. The clinician gathers more information to further assess the current risk and generates a plan regarding the best way to move forward. After this follow-up assessment, some students are referred for check-ins with their school counselor or referred for regular outside counseling, a Tier 2 intervention. Some students who are deemed at high risk for clinically significant depression or suicidality are admitted for partial or inpatient hospitalization, a Tier 3 intervention. Parent/caregiver involvement is critical throughout the process.

Another example of a school-wide suicide prevention is Question-Persuade-Refer, or QPR (available at www.qprinstitute.com). The premise of the program lies in the belief that by broadly educating large populations of staff, parents, and community members, about the symptoms of depression and characteristics of suicidal individuals, they will be able to identify individuals in need of support and get them the help they require. Specifically, QPR is a training that is delivered to large groups via a combination of lecture, PowerPoint, and discussion. At the training, attendees learn the verbal, behavioral, and situational clues and warning signs of suicide; learn to directly ask whether a person is thinking of killing him/herself; persuade him/her to stay alive and get help; and refer him/her to qualified mental health supports.

Although some students are private, keeping their struggles with mood and suicidality hidden from those around them, others tend to be more forthcoming. Anecdotally, the bulk of experiences reported by school staff suggest that the majority of students will report their suicidal thoughts and behaviors when asked. Consider the data from SOS research: for the 2015/2016 school year, Screening for Mental Health (2018) distributed 1,327 SOS programs, reaching an estimated 500,000+ new students. Of those estimated 500,000+ new students that received the program, an estimate of 12% or 60,000+ students were identified for follow-up. Half of those students were identified through the student screening tool, while the other half actively sought help for either themselves or a friend. This tendency underscores the importance and effectiveness of school-based suicide prevention programming.

### *School-Based Tiered Intervention, Tier 2*

Students may experience or exhibit a variety of risk factors or warning signs that reflect a higher risk for suicidal ideation and/or behaviors; Tier 2 interventions are often appropriate for these students. Given the presence of various risk factors, a school may recommend individual or group counseling for specific students with the goal of reducing the risk of self-harm by enhancing coping mechanisms and changing maladaptive behavior patterns.

In some schools, specialized yearlong weekly Dialectical Behavioral Therapy (DBT) skill groups (Linehan, 2015) are offered for students who have been identified as needing additional support around managing their emotions and/or life circumstances in a healthy and productive manner. Students may have expressed suicidal ideation or exhibited prior suicide behaviors, particularly those who may have been previously hospitalized for depression or suicidality. Groups are run by two co-leaders who are clinicians in the school and primarily use the DBT curriculum created by Marsha Linehan (2015). Students are introduced to concrete emotion regulation skills, such as learning to ask themselves whether their emotions "fit the facts" of the situation and whether the intensity of their current emotions are "effective" for them. Students learn strategies for managing the identified intense emotions and are given the opportunity to practice the lessons under the guidance of the clinician.

Another recommended Tier 2 program for students who require additional mental health support is the Bridge for Resilient Youth in Transition (BRYT; link available in our eResource at www.routledge.com/9781138293571). BRYT combines: (a) clinical support (counseling, crisis intervention, psychoeducation, referrals); (b) academic support (partnership with teachers to develop an academic plan, help students manage schoolwork, and provide basic tutoring); (c) family support (frequent communication with families, crisis support, and education); and (d) care coordination and case management (transition planning, coordination and communications with school staff and community providers). Bridge programs do this by having a dedicated classroom available throughout the school day staffed by a leader/clinician (e.g., social worker, counselor, or psychologist) and an academic coordinator (e.g., a teacher or a classroom aide or tutor). Students are assigned to the BRYT classroom to counteract prolonged absences for mental and physical health reasons and to support the transition back to a full academic course load. BRYT programs equip schools to provide short-term intervention with academic and counseling support in a dedicated space, available all day, to effectively meet the needs of the school's most vulnerable students.

### *School-Based Tiered Intervention, Tier 3*

Suicide prevention and intervention also occurs at the individual level. At times, high-risk students are identified through a friend, through schoolwork (e.g., essay, art) and referred by a teacher or staff, through a Tier 1 or 2 intervention program, or through self-identification. This information should be immediately shared with school-based mental health professionals, and an individualized risk assessment should be conducted to explore suicidal intent, plans, actions, and history. Specific questions are typically developed and included in a school's safety protocol, often based on evidence-based methodologies, such as the Colombia Suicide Severity Rating Scale (available at cssrs.columbia.edu/) or Riverside Trauma Center Suicide Prevention Protocol (available at www.riversidecc.org). In-depth information regarding changes in behavior, sleeping, eating, and mood is assessed.

When a school has identified safety concerns for a student, the response typically involves immediately meeting with the student to gather more information. For example, a high school senior reported to his guidance counselor that he was having trouble finding the motivation to get his schoolwork done, whereas in the past the student had been quite motivated and hard-working. The counselor began asking other questions related to social life, sleeping and eating habits, and mood. Over the course of the conversation, it became clear that the boy had become increasingly isolated over the past several months, was having difficulty sleeping, had lost his appetite, and was feeling irritable much of the time. At this point, the counselor called in the school psychologist to meet with the student jointly and continued with the interview.

In this case, school professionals followed a carefully designed safety protocol, asking the student a variety of additional questions. When asked about whether he had ever felt so down that he wished that he would not wake up in the morning, the boy acknowledged having those feelings many days. He was also asked if he had ever thought about killing himself or if he had a plan to take his life. The boy reported that he had considered killing himself, but he had never thought about how he would accomplish that. He also denied having any intention of or urge to kill himself or having made any past suicide attempts.

After completing the in-depth interview, parents were contacted and this information was shared with them. Given his responses, he was not imminently at risk for self-harm or suicide, so hospitalization was not recommended. The school recommended that the student, with the aid of his parents, begin working with an outside therapist to help him understand his feelings and develop coping skills to manage his mood and behavior. In similar situations, it may also be appropriate to recommend group therapy or psychiatric consultation. Finally, the guidance counselor was assigned to meet with the student on a regular basis to reassess suicidality as well as to check in and determine whether additional supports or changes to the student's school program were required.

All students and situations differ. Important variables, such as presenting issues, current mental health status, and availability of supports, are all utilized in developing an individualized Tier 3 plan to support a student presenting with suicidal ideation or intent. School staff should be continually encouraged to evaluate their ability to assess an individual student, collaborate with colleagues, and coordinate increased supports, both within the school and in the community, for students at increased risk.

## Practical Tools for School-Based Professionals

There is no need for any teacher or other school personnel to feel alone in making decisions about a student's well-being. Schools are in a unique position to support the health and safety of all. Reducing the risk of youth suicide is essential in maintaining a safe and secure school environment by promoting the behavioral and emotional health of students. School staff should seek education and training in suicide prevention, identifying and responding to students who may be at risk of suicide, and following the school's protocols for referral and follow-up.

School staff may not feel comfortable or know what to do when they observe signs potentially indicative of suicidality. Concerns around student safety should be immediately shared with a supervisor or mental health person in the building in order to generate a swift plan. If a student does share their suicidal thoughts, NASP (2015) suggests:

- Remaining calm. If a student is opening up to you, it is an indication that they must trust you and feel comfortable with you. Try not to panic.
- Indicate concern for the student's well-being; try not to blame or cast judgment.
- Listen attentively.
- Provide reassurance that support is available, and this is a temporary feeling.
- Do not agree to keep secrets about the presence of suicidal thoughts.
- Take threats seriously.
- Supervise the youth, ensuring they are not left alone.
- Ensure they do not have ready access to items that could be used to cause self-harm.
- Seek help: School staff should escort the student to the school psychologist or another school-based mental health professional, the school nurse, or an administrator. There needs to be an immediate assessment of the student's state and school protocols should be followed.

Making a call to a parent regarding concerns is especially difficult if you feel a student is at risk for suicide. The parent on the other end of the phone will likely feel a mix of emotions, including panic, hysteria, guilt, and even anger, at their teen or the school; they may wonder how they "missed it." These are not uncommon reactions. Sharing reactions and concerns with a mental health professional like the school psychologist or school counselor will be helpful as they can make suggestions for next steps. The goal should be to triangulate supports with the school, a treatment provider, and the parent/caregiver to increase the level of supervision and monitoring of an at-risk teen to ensure their continued safety (King, Foster, & Rogalski, 2013).

Teachers need to know the school personnel such as the school psychologist, social worker, counselor, and/or school nurse who can immediately work with a student in distress. While it is not the responsibility of school staff to treat a student, any time a student is suspected of having suicidal thoughts or behaviors, procedures should be clearly followed, and the student's legal guardians should be notified. Links should be established with existing community mental health supports, local pediatricians, and hospital emergency rooms to facilitate assessment and referrals. Protocols should be developed as part of a comprehensive program of education for students, staff, and parents as outlined in prevention programs such as SOS (2018) and the SAMHSA (2012) publication *Preventing Suicide: A Toolkit for High Schools.*

### *Parent and Teacher Awareness*

To be aware, vigilant, and preventive of suicide, school personnel and parents need to be cognizant of the many myths surrounding suicide, particularly those most relevant in dealing with teens (Miller, 2011). Common myths about suicide include:

- It is better not to talk about suicide with an at-risk student. Extensive studies of school-based suicide prevention programs, suicide screening programs, and direct questioning through interviewing provide an abundance of support for the fact that adolescents who can openly and honestly engage with a trusted adult about the topic of suicide typically have better outcomes than their peers who may be at risk and do not engage in similar conversations (Miller, 2011).
- Parents or caregivers should have been aware of their child's suicidal thoughts or behaviors. Adolescents often do not readily communicate thoughts and feelings to parents, especially without probing. A study by Kashani, Goddard, & Reid (1989) found parents often did not know of their children's suicidal thoughts. This reinforces the need for coordinated school prevention programming and staff training around mental health and suicidal ideation.
- Suicide is impulsive. Most often individuals who attempt or die by suicide have given the act considerable thought, making specific plans

in regard to methods and locations (Joiner, 2010). This means there is time for prevention and intervention. Education, assessment, and tiered supports are critical in supporting reduction in suicide ideation, attempts, and completions.

- Students who talk about suicide are merely seeking attention. "For many suicidal people, suicide is more a 'cry of pain' than a 'cry for help.'" (Miller, 2011, p. 76). When a student touches upon the concept of suicide, regardless of how—through conversation, social media, or writing about suicide—it should be taken seriously and assessed immediately by a professional.
- A *primary* causal factor for suicide is family and/or social stress, rather than mental health problems/disorders. The largest single risk factor for suicide is the presence of a depressive disorder (SAMHSA, 2012). While this does not rule out the presence of other risk factors, it underscores the importance of school staff being aware of the signs and symptoms of depression, general emotional distress, and other mental health issues. The National Alliance on Mental Illness provides a good resource for identifying possible signs of a mental health condition (link available on our eResource at www.routledge.com/9781138293571).

School staff and parents/caregivers also need to be aware of concrete warning signs of suicide, as these are typically observable in those who are contemplating suicide (NASP, 2015). The American Foundation for Suicide Prevention provides a comprehensive list of suicide warning signs (link available on our eResource at www.routledge.com/9781138293571).

Issues of confidentiality, privacy, the teen's perception of what is happening, and parent concerns for their larger family need to be balanced with safety issues. It is also important to be aware of potential means of suicide and to remove access to items such as fire arms, medications (including prescription and over-the-counter), alcohol and other substances, and car keys.

## Take Home Ideas for Parents

- Informed parents and caregivers are those who are knowledgeable about the risk factors, protective factors, and warning signs of suicide. Fostering communication with your teen and knowing what to do if your teen feels suicidal is of critical importance along the journey of parenthood.
- Depression in teens is a contributing factor to youth suicide. As a parent, it is important to recognize the signs and symptoms of depression in an adolescent. With appropriate intervention, teenage depression is highly treatable.

- Ask for help by contacting your school psychologist, a mental health professional through your insurance provider, a local community mental health center, your primary care doctor, or by calling 1-800-273-TALK (National Suicide Prevention Lifeline) for a referral if you notice concerning behaviors in your teen.

## References

Cash, S. & Bridge, J. (2009). Epidemiology of youth suicide and suicidal behavior. *Current Opinion in Pediatrics, 21*(5), 613–619. doi:10.1097/MOP.0b013e32833063e.1

Centers for Disease Control and Prevention. (2014). *School health policies and practices study. Suicide prevention.* Retrieved from www.cdc.gov/healthyyouth/data/shpps/pdf/2014factsheets/suicide_shpps2014.pdf

Centers for Disease Control and Prevention. (2015). *Suicide facts at a glance.* Retrieved from www.cdc.gov/violenceprevention/pdf/suicide-datasheet-a.pdf

Centers for Disease Control and Prevention, National Center for Health Statistics. (2017). *Health, United States spotlight: Health status and determinants.* Retrieved from www.cdc.gov/nchs/hus/spotlight/2017-december.htm

Holt, M. K., Vivolo-Kantor, A. M., Polanin, J. R., Holland, K. M., DeGue, S., Matjasko, J. L., … Reid, G. (2015). *Bullying and suicidal ideation and behaviors: A meta-analysis. Pediatrics, 135*(2), e496–509. doi:10.1542/peds.2014-1864.

Joiner, T. (2010). *Myths about suicide.* Cambridge, MA: Harvard University Press.

Kann, L., McManus, T., Harris, W., Shanklin, S. L., Flint, K. H., Hawkinds, J., … Zaza, S. (2016). Youth risk behavior surveillance—United States, 2015. *Centers for Disease Control and Prevention, Morbidity and Mortality Weekly Report (MMWR), 65*(6), 1–174. doi:10/15585/mmwr.ss6506a1

Kashani, A. H., Goddard, P., & Reid, J. C. (1989). Correlates of suicidal ideation in a community sample of children and adolescents. *Journal of the American Academy of Child and Adolescent Psychiatry,* 28, 912–917. doi:10.1097/00004583-198911000-00016

King, C. A., Foster, C. E., & Rogalski, K. M. (2013). *Teen suicide risk: A practitioner guide to screening, assessment, and management.* New York, NY: Guilford Press.

Lieberman, R., Poland, S., & Kornfeld, C. (2014). Best practices in suicide prevention and intervention. In P. L. Harrison & A. Thomas (Eds.), *Best practices in school psychology: Systems-level Services* (pp. 273–288). Bethesda, MD: National Association of School Psychologists.

Linehan, M. (2015). *DBT skills training manual* (2nd ed.). New York, NY: Guilford Press.

Miller, D. N. (2011). *Child and adolescent suicidal behavior school-based prevention, assessment, and intervention.* New York, NY: Guilford Press.

National Association of School Psychologists. (2015). *Preventing youth suicide: Tips for parents & educators.* Retrieved from www.nasponline.org/resources-and-publications/resources/school-safety-and-crisis/preventing-youth-suicide/preventing-youth-suicide-tips-for-parents-and-educators

Screening for Mental Health, Inc. (2018). *Signs of Suicide (SOS).* Retrieved from https://mentalhealthscreening.org/programs/youth

Substance Abuse and Mental Health Services Administration. (2012). *Preventing suicide: A toolkit for high schools*. (HHS Publication No smA-12–4669.) Rockville, MD: Center for Mental Health Services, Substance Abuse and Mental Health Services Administration. Retrieved from https://store.samhsa.gov/shin/content/SMA12-4669/SMA12-4669.pdf

# 16 Schools, Substance Abuse, and Psychology

## Addressing Adolescent Substance Abuse in the School Setting

*Daniel B. Jacobs*

Substance abuse concerns are at the top of the list of challenges that overwhelm students and families, as well as those trying to help them. Substance abuse can impede academic progress, worsen mental health problems, and lead to significant behavioral impairment (e.g., class failure, school suspensions, expulsion, higher depression and rates of self-destructive acts, increased aggression, higher rates of criminality, death; Kliewer et al., 2016; Reed, Nugent, & Cooper, 2015). While students impacted by substance abuse problems and substance use disorders may vary in terms of drug of choice, all experience difficulty in school, home, and the community.

In addition, school psychologists and other clinicians working with children and adolescents directly and indirectly affected by substance abuse concerns are often undertrained and underprepared to respond in a timely and effective manner. There is an enormous need for better training and resources for these clinicians in the area of substance abuse intervention in schools (Benningfield, Riggs, & Stephan, 2015; Onrust, Otten, Lammers, & Smit, 2016; Plotts & Lasser, 2013). Despite the challenges involved, it is possible to help prevent substance abuse engagement, and schools are one of the best places for prevention—and intervention, when necessary—efforts in this area. (Boendermaker, Prins, & Wiers, 2015; Serafini, Shipley, & Stewart, 2016).

### Why It Matters

While there has been an increase in attention to addiction or substance use disorders (also known as SUDs) in recent years in the media and in governmental circles, much of this focus has been linked to abuse of opioids and death by overdose. Terms such as "epidemic" and "crisis" are applied to this abuse with a media emphasis on the increasing risk and dangers of the abuse, and less of an emphasis on the causes behind the usage. As stories appear in media circles regarding middle- or upper-class Caucasian young adults overdosing and dying from pain pill or heroin abuse, the implication is that drug abuse is a new problem that is barely understood. In fact, those working in the field of substance abuse treatment have witnessed similar substance abuse challenges impacting communities of color and those impacted by poverty and economic challenges for many years, without the same media attention. Drugs and addiction are not solely linked to one ethnic group or one geographic location and the "cure" is not going to come from aggressive or punitive legislation.

Drugs are not just a "community problem" or a "family problem"—they are clearly also a "school problem" and need to be addressed as such. Those who become addicted to drugs face many academic, behavioral, social, and emotional challenges that greatly decrease quality of life and hope for future advancement (Kann et al., 2016; LeNoue & Riggs, 2016; SAMHSA, 2014). The majority of adults with significant opioid problems started abusing other drugs as adolescents and "worked up" to opioids as they got older (e.g., SAMHSA, 2014). With more prevention efforts and earlier intervention efforts, we can reduce the number of young people who become those adults later harmed or killed by drug abuse.

### *Youth Drug Abuse Risk*

The number one drug abused by young people (and adults) in this country is *not* opioids, it is alcohol. According to the National Youth Risk Behavior Survey (Kann et al., 2016), the National Survey on Drug Use and Health (SAMHSA, 2014), and the Surgeon General's Report on Alcohol, Drugs, and Health (Murthy et al., 2016), we know that students in high school are more likely to become engaged in substance abuse behaviors as they get older, with 23% of ninth graders reporting current alcohol use in the past 30 days; and the rate increases to 29% for tenth graders, 38% for eleventh graders, and over 42% for students in twelfth grade. Students drinking in the ninth grade reporting first drinking alcohol before age 13 are at the highest rates of all those drinking in high school, indicating that earlier first usage is a high-risk factor for early and regular abuse at older ages in adolescence. High school students reporting "binge-drinking" episodes of five drinks or more in a couple of hours in the past 30 days before being surveyed, as well as binge-drinking episodes of ten or more drinks in a row, also followed a similar progression, increasing from ninth, tenth, eleventh to twelfth grade (10%, 15%, 22%, and 24% for the former, and 2.4%, 4%, 5%, and almost 6% for the latter; Kann et al., 2016). The heavier the drinking, the higher the correlation with other risk factors (e.g., deadly drinking and driving episodes, cigarette smoking, engagement in acts of violence and/or criminality, unprotected sexual activity, and/or psychological difficulties). Clearly, the earlier a youth begins drinking alcohol, the higher the risk of increased usage and subsequent behavioral problems.

The second most abused drug by young people in this country is marijuana. According to Kann et al. (2016) and SAMHSA (2014), the same pattern of increased abuse occurs as students age. Approximately 15% of ninth graders reported using marijuana in the past 30 days and this number increased to 20% for tenth graders, over 24% for eleventh graders, and over 27% for students in the twelfth grade. In a similar pattern as the statistics reported above for alcohol, the younger students using marijuana had also started using marijuana before age 13 at a higher rate than the older students using this drug (rates of 8.5%, 8.3%, 6.7%, and 6.1% for ninth, tenth, eleventh, and twelfth graders). As with alcohol, greater abuse of marijuana at an earlier age is associated with worse academic and behavioral difficulties for many youths. In addition, marijuana and alcohol, both classified as depressants with known negative effects on executive functioning (long-range planning, decision making), academic performance, positive adaption of social skills, and behavioral self-control, are much more greatly abused by youth in schools than are opioids or other illicit substances.

Prescription drugs, including OxyContin, Percocet, Vicodin, codeine, Adderall, Ritalin, or Xanax, are the next most abused group of drugs by high school students. Patterns of abuse suggest youth abusing these substances are trying to alter their brain chemistry and change their mood states in a destructive or self-medicating manner. Similar to alcohol and marijuana, abuse of these substances also increases as students get older, with rates of 13%, 15%, almost 19%, and 20%, linked to ninth, tenth, eleventh, and twelfth graders (Kann et al., 2016).

The comments above are not intended to suggest that, as school-based clinicians and educators, we should ignore abuse of other illegal substances (e.g., cocaine, hallucinogens, steroids, heroin) by young people. Nor is the omission above of statistics on cigarette and tobacco products abuse by youth meant to imply that it is also not an area with significant public health issue implications (while on the decline, these rates are lower than alcohol abuse but higher than marijuana abuse with the age groups discussed above). This chapter's focus is on other substances that have received less attention in the past in terms of school-based efforts. Clearly, reaching young people before they initiate any substance usage or begin engaging in increasingly risky and lethal drug abuse would be best, and understanding the range of motivators that can lead youth to engage in substance-abusing behaviors will help us make this happen.

### *Motivating Factors for Youth Substance Abuse*

Students commonly report the following reasons for abusing substances (Benningfield et al., 2015; Connors, DiClemente, Velasquez, & Donovan, 2013; Lenoue & Riggs, 2016; Winters, Lee, Botzet, Fahnhorst, & Nicholson, 2014):

- A desire to have fun by "getting high";
- A desire to "self-medicate" emotional pain such as seen in depression or anxiety;
- A need to "numb" psychological distress or "flashbacks" subsequent to sexual abuse;
- Familial role modeling that shows substance abuse as "normal" or acceptable behavior;
- Giving in to peer and social pressure; and
- Choosing to use due to a desire to fit in socially.

In addition, students with low self-esteem, lower sense of self-efficacy, and/or lack of knowledge about options to make their lives and circumstances better are more likely to engage in substance-abusing behaviors. If they believe there are no positive options ahead for them, why would they not want to self-medicate or alter their brains, if even just temporarily? Clearly, school-based interventions designed to address youth substance abuse need to be flexible enough to take into account the different range of motivators fueling seemingly similar substance-abusing behavioral patterns.

We can prevent and address student substance abuse in schools, but we need to consider the complexities discussed above as part of our road map to developing complex and multi-faceted interventions. Put quite simply, there is no "one size fits all" type of intervention that should or could be employed to fight substance abuse in schools, and thoughtful consideration of the different factors impacting actual student substance-abusing behavior can be crucial in effective program planning.

## Notes from the Field

### *Alexander*

*Alexander was a 17-year-old boy enrolled in the eleventh grade at Sunnydale High School. He had been marked as tardy or absent multiple times over the past two years after starting high school and this pattern had continued, and even increased, as he went into his junior year as well. The most commonly given excuses were "car trouble" and "he's not feeling well" from his father, and the school's policy of detentions had apparently had no impact on changing the pattern. Alexander's grades suffered, and there were questions about whether he would be able to pass the eleventh grade or need to be retained. Efforts to reach out to his father (his mother had passed away three years earlier) around this issue were not successful as, when he was reached, he said he was "really busy with work" and could lose his job if he took time off to come in to school for meetings. Alexander acknowledged the absences as a concern but offered no suggestions about how to change the situation and clearly did not want to talk about his family situation at all.*

***Willow***

*Willow was a 13-year-old girl in the ninth grade who, in December of the school year, began hanging out in the cafeteria or the school library with older juniors and seniors. She began skipping classes and going off campus with her friends at lunchtime (allowed for seniors but not for freshmen) and when she returned from these off-campus trips the whites of her eyes appeared quite red and she said she had "bad allergies." Willow also smelled like clothing freshener or perfume in her afternoon classes, to the point that other students did not want to sit next to her. She was a very bright girl and at first her academic performance remained the same as at the start of the school year, but after a few months she had much more trouble maintaining her grades. She denied having any concerns when asked.*

***Anya***

*Anya was a 15-year-old sophomore who began dating a 17-year-old junior named Oz. Oz was on the school's hockey team and on Friday nights after games the team members and their friends would congregate at one of the players' houses "to hang out and party." Anya had tried to drink beer on a few of the Friday nights but did not really like it; she drank to fit in. She saw how Oz changed when he was drinking and was more aggressive and loud than when the two of them were alone together, and it bothered her. One Friday night she told Oz that she wanted to leave early, but he got mad and refused, instead yelling at her and leaving with his friends. She cried and sat on a couch by herself for a while. Richard, one of the other players, came by, asked if she was OK and offered her a glass of what he said was orange juice and vodka. Anya appreciated the attention, took the drink and talked to him for a few minutes while they drank together. She began to feel hot, tired, and nauseous, and he suggested she lie down in one of the bedrooms. Anya passed out and woke up three hours later with no clothes on and found out later that weekend that Richard had taken nude pictures of her and posted them online. Anya was so distraught she told her parents that she was sick on Monday and refused to go to school.*

***Angel***

*Angel was a 15-year-old boy with a history of classroom misbehavior, including refusing to listen to the teacher, making inappropriate jokes, and talking over the teacher. He received a series of failing grades on three exams in his language arts class, and further investigation revealed he never actually took the tests, as he was sent to the office prior to each exam due to his disruptive behaviors. In counseling sessions, Angel later explained to his school psychologist that he was unable to study or do homework at home due to conflict and drug-related chaos in the home; he was exhausted most mornings when he got to school. His father had been out of the picture for many years and his mother got drunk or high each night with her boyfriend and other friends. Angel reported staying up late each night, vigilant, watching over his little sisters, Darla and Drusilla, to make sure none of the adults "come in and cause trouble." Angel had begun leaving all of his books and homework in his locker at school because the last time he brought work home from school one of "those adults" stole his backpack and spilled beer all over his papers, and then laughed when Angel complained. When Angel's mother tried to intervene, the man hit her and laughed some more.*

### *Buffy*

*Buffy was a 17-year-old student-athlete who was also very involved in the arts program at the high school. She loved to paint almost as much as she loved to play basketball and lacrosse. She had many friends and did fairly well academically but did need tutoring to complete her math course. Buffy had recently begun attending "raves" with some of her friends, parties that went all night, because she "just wanted to dance and dance, and dance some more." While at these dances she began trying different drugs offered to her, first marijuana, then Ecstasy, then acid or LSD. Initially she had fun at these dances and felt that the drugs were enhancing the experience. After the last dance that she went to, Buffy had a "bad trip" after taking acid, felt nervous and paranoid, had trouble controlling her emotions, and began acting erratically. Her thought processes were impaired, and she felt "disconnected from reality." She missed a few team practices and her art teacher reached out to the school psychologist regarding some "disturbing pictures" Buffy had painted. Her friends noticed a major change in her mood state and could not communicate with her when they tried. Buffy was not in school the next week, and all her friends heard was that she was getting some help to feel better.*

### *William*

*William was a 14-year-old freshman at the school who spent a great deal of his time alone, writing poetry, and reading books. He was not closely connected to anyone at the school but seemed to get along with most people. He did exceptionally well in language arts and history classes but struggled with science and math. He was being treated on an outpatient basis for anxiety and depression and had been taking antidepressants since the seventh grade, with some improvement. William had begun spending a little bit of time with some older students who wrote for the school's literary magazine, and he tried Vicodin for the first time when someone gave it to him during a study block. William found that it relaxed him, and he began trying different types of pills to "see how they would make me feel." He later found a bottle of OxyContin in his grandmother's medicine cabinet, left over from her hip replacement surgery, and he began taking those with alcohol taken from his parents' liquor cabinet. William repeated this pattern a few times and then decided to see what would happen if he took a number of pills all at once with some whiskey. He died later that afternoon, lying on his bed with music playing, and was found by his parents when they got home that evening.*

### *Rupert*

*Rupert was a 16-year-old student who had recently gotten his driver's license. His parents let him use one of the family's cars as long as he maintained his grades. He had a few male friends he had known since grade school but was uncomfortable around girls and did not know how to talk to them. Rupert talked with his school counselor about feeling shy and awkward at school and was not sure how "to fit in like everybody else does." He was an average athlete and was able to get on the junior varsity football team, which he enjoyed. Rupert went to a few of the football parties and started drinking beer "because everyone else was" and did not seem that affected by a "few beers." At one of the parties, he was challenged to a "drink off" by the team's captain. Rupert was nervous but joined in with the other students who were participating in the drink off. He was able to drink 14 beers in a row and handily won the competition as the next closest player drank eight beers and then vomited all over two other people. The players hoisted him on their shoulders and began chanting that he was "the man" and he reported feeling "pretty good" about receiving the positive attention. He drove home that night without incident.*

### *Discussion*

Each of the scenarios above involved adolescents engaging in problematic academic or social behavioral patterns influenced directly, or indirectly, by substance-abusing behaviors. The substances taken were not the same, the behavioral challenges or risks were not the same, and family histories were certainly varied, but there were some common themes connecting the cases. As we look closer at each of these seven students described in the scenarios above, we see common threads of insecurity, a desire to fit in, peer pressure, short-term choices having long-term risks on mental health, lack of knowledge about drug and family risk factors, and more severe consequences developing over time linked to longer-term engagement with substance abuse.

As we know from the data discussed above, all of the youth in the case scenarios have been negatively impacted by substance usage, and all but one could benefit from support and help, but the interventions they need are not the same. Willow is at great risk of developing future problems with a range of substances given the fact that at the age of 13 she had started smoking marijuana with older youth. We know that most of the youth in these scenarios are engaging in either underage drinking, illegal usage of illicit substances, or incorrect usage of legally prescribed medications. We know that Anya has been violated after having been drugged and this event perhaps could have been avoided had she felt she had more options regarding leaving the high-risk situation; it is extremely likely that she will need therapeutic support to avoid development of significant mental health concerns linked to this event. Buffy is potentially facing a complicated mental health challenge (i.e., possible development of a thought disorder subsequent to a drug-induced psychotic break), on top of substance abuse-related concerns.

While Rupert has not yet had his own difficulties linked to substance usage, and in fact has received primary and secondary reinforcement around his ability to drink more alcohol than his peers, he is at great risk of developing a significant problem with alcohol if he continues down the road he has started. Angel and Alexander are not necessarily using substances themselves at this point in time, but family members are using substances in a severely problematic manner (Alexander's father had an active drinking problem, and this was the real reason this student was late to school so often) and this pattern is causing a negative impact on the students' emotional, academic, and behavioral situations. To help these young men, we would have to be able to address familial concerns as the transgenerational risk of substance abuse concerns spilling over onto them at some point is very likely without proper supports.

The only student we cannot help is William—once someone has died, we cannot help them. We could be of support to his family and, with their permission, his story could prove helpful to other students at risk, but the time to have helped him was before he overdosed. As mentioned above, prevention and early intervention is key in substance abuse care and can help prevent accidental overdoses that take the life of a student such as William. One of the saddest parts of a narrative such as William's is that this senseless loss could have been avoided.

## Take Home Ideas for Parents

While the majority of this chapter has been focused on the role of school-based professionals in addressing adolescent substance abuse, obviously the student's parents and family are key in the plan to prevent and intervene in this area. There needs to be clear and open communication between school supports and the family, parents need to be informed of warning signs seen at school, and they also need to be aware of how to watch for early signals at home. One of the first steps in being prepared to do this is to be aware of the most common warning signs and symptoms of youth substance use, which include, but are not limited to (Connors et al., 2013; Kliewer et al., 2016; LeNoue & Riggs, 2016):

- Erratic or changing mood (e.g., anger, depression, tearfulness);
- Increased defensiveness or defiance;
- Disorganization, confusion, irresponsible or unreliable behavior;
- Loss of initiative, a drop in grades, decreased involvement in activities;
- Increase in isolative or secretive behaviors;
- Manipulating, lying, and self-centered bargaining;
- Physical concerns (e.g., blackouts, sleep impairment, concentration problems, increased tolerance, withdrawal symptoms); and
- Risky patterns (e.g., drug-using peer group, legal difficulties, missing possessions, impulsive decision making, participating in dangerous or frightening activities).

In addition, when applicable, awareness of family history of substance abuse and/or mental health concerns is crucial information for an adolescent to have; this does not mean he/she has to know all of the specific details of a family member's usage but rather more about their general concerns, risks, and recovery process.

## Practical Tools for School-Based Professionals

Just as students' families cannot know everything that is going on in the school setting, school-based clinicians cannot change family or genetic history, and we cannot change temperament or cultural expectations of what is acceptable or not regarding substance-abusing behaviors. As mentioned above, we can, however, work collaboratively with parents and families in the best interests of the student to bolster strengths and address motivating factors that contribute to substance use engagement. We can also work to develop school-based substance abuse prevention and intervention programs that are organically designed to meet the varied motivations behind the substance-using behaviors and that have realistic and practical steps to lead to effective behavioral change.

While including all of the details linked to the actual development of a school-based comprehensive substance use prevention and intervention program is beyond the scope of this chapter, the structure and general areas to address are clear. Those interested in developing effective interventions should consider the following findings and beliefs (Benningfield et al., 2015; Boendermaker et al., 2015; Flannery, Fenning, McGrath-Kato, & McIntosh, 2014; Fletcher, Bonell, & Hargreaves, 2008; Kliewer et al., 2016; Onrust et al., 2016; Serafini et al., 2016):

- The earlier that adolescent substance abuse engagement is identified the better; awareness of younger students spending great amounts of time with older, risk-taking students should be identified and addressed.
- "One-shot" drug abuse prevention programs are limited in effectiveness; multiple-session and ongoing programs are more useful and can have much greater impact.
- "Fear appeals" and "scare tactics" fail in the long term and waste precious resources.
- School clinicians and other staff need to receive in-depth training about alcohol and other drug risks, warning signs, and non-judgmental intervention options.
- There is a key difference between a student who has a problem with using substances and a student who is dealing drugs to others. They should not be treated the same way.
- Effective interventions in this area will address motivating factors such as depression, anxiety, a desire to foster social connection, desire for risk-taking, and misbeliefs about peer usage, and will involve awareness-raising about alternative ways to be challenged and excited in non-traditional manners (e.g., use of ropes courses and adventure programming, or involvement in poetry slams).
- Students who are more connected with their community and with school, and have higher self-esteem and self-efficacy, also have greater ability to utilize refusal skills when faced with risk situations.
- Peer leadership (small group) presentations and discussions on the topic of substance abuse (e.g., risks, positive choices) can carry much more weight with students than outside presenters. These peer groups are most effective when cross-led by a mix of student leaders (e.g., school athletes, student government representatives, artists, musicians, etc.).
- Develop role-play/case scenarios to foster discussion, based on real responses and concerns of students in school (generated in advance of intervention).
- Generate scenarios for adolescents to have an opportunity to succeed and earn positive reinforcement rather than just receive punitive responses.
- Open and clear communication between school officials and the student's family is key.
- School clinicians, school administration, and school athletic staff need to communicate about risks of minimizing substance usage and be open to discussing "group think" and risks associated with ignoring early warning signs of substance usage by athletes.
- Issues such as violence, child abuse, and risk of self-harm or risk of suicide must be addressed directly and separately.
- Issues such as risk of sexual assault, risk of STD-transmission associated with unsafe sex, and inability to consent when under the influence

should be discussed (possibly in same-sex groups), led by professionals trained to respond if complicated issues (e.g., trauma) arise.

- Referral to substance abuse specialists, appropriately trained to work with youth, when necessary. Communities should advocate to ensure such resources are available.
- Interventions designed to address substance abuse by students also need to take into account the risk of access to drugs on school grounds, as well as focus on the drugs being most abused by youth, in a manner that reflects the actual risk factors at play.
- Efforts should be prevention-focused and developmentally appropriate, and offer different programming for elementary-age and middle-school-age students in the community. In order for such programming to be effective, system leadership must fully support it.

### *Summary*

Clearly, adolescents engaged in substance-abusing behaviors represent a varied group and helping them requires a wide-range of intervention options. Positive communication and respectful relationships between students' families and school staff can absolutely foster smoother and more effective relational modeling and support. School staff can benefit from understanding key statistics about risks of adolescent substance usage and become informed enough to answer direct and frank questions about these concerns from students in appropriate venues. Students also have to feel that their school officials genuinely care about them. This is a complex issue, but there is much that can be done with a school commitment to be direct, open, and honest about the risks and challenges associated with substance abuse.

## References

Benningfield, M., Riggs, P., & Stephan, S. (2015). The role of schools in substance abuse prevention and intervention. *Child and Adolescent Psychiatric Clinics of North America, 24*(2), 291–303. doi:10.1016/j.chc.2014.12.004

Boendermaker, W., Prins, P., & Wiers, R. (2015). Cognitive bias modification for adolescents with substance use problems—Can serious games help? *Journal of Behavior Therapy and Experimental Psychiatry, 49*, 13–20. doi:10.1016/j.jbtep.2015.03.008

Connors, G., DiClemente, C., Velasquez, M., & Donovan, D. (2013). *Substance abuse treatment and the stages of change: Selecting and planning interventions* (2nd ed.). New York, NY: Guilford Press.

Flannery, K., Fenning, P., McGrath-Kato, M., & McIntosh, K. (2014). Effects of school-wide positive behavioral interventions and supports and fidelity of implementation on problem behavior in high schools. *School Psychology Quarterly, 2*, 111–124. doi:10.1037/spq0000039

Fletcher, A., Bonell, C., & Hargreaves, J. (2008). School effects on young people's drug use: A systematic review of intervention and observational studies. *Journal of Adolescent Health, 42*, 209–220. doi:10.1016/j.jadohealth.2007.09.020

Kann, L., McManus, T., Harris, W., Shanklin, S., Flint, K, Hawkins, J., … Zaza, S. (2016). Youth risk behavior surveillance—United States, 2015. *The Centers for Disease Control and Prevention Morbidity and Mortality Weekly Report Surveillance Summaries, 65*(6), 1–180. doi:10.15585.mmwr.ss6506a1

Kliewer, W., Riley, T., Zaharakis, N., Borre, A., Drazdowski, T., & Jaggi, L. (2016). Emotion dysregulation, anticipatory cortisol, and substance use in urban adolescents. *Personality and Individual Differences, 99*, 200–205. doi:10.1016/j.paid.2016.05.011

LeNoue, S. & Riggs, P. (2016). Substance abuse prevention. *Child and Adolescent Psychiatric Clinics, 25*(2), 297–305. doi:10.1016/j.chc.2015.11.0007

Murthy, V., Enomoto, K., Arends, M., Boyle, M., Castro, F., Chalk, M., … Zarkin, G. (2016). *Facing addiction in America: The Surgeon General's Report on alcohol, drugs, and health*. Washington, D.C.: U.S. Department of Health and Human Services (HHS), Office of the Surgeon General.

Onrust, S., Otten, R., Lammers, J., & Smit, F. (2016). School-based programmes to reduce and prevent substance use in different age groups: Systematic review and meta-regression analysis. *Clinical Psychology Review, 44*, 45–59. doi:10.1016/j.cpr.2015.11.002

Plotts, C. & Lasser, J. (2013). *School psychologist as counselor: A practitioner's handbook*. Bethesda, MD: National Association of School Psychologists.

Reed, K., Nugent, W., & Cooper, R. (2015). Testing a path model of relationships between gender, age, and bullying victimization and violent behavior, substance abuse, depression, suicidal ideation, and suicide attempts in adolescents. *Children and Youth Services Review, 55*, 128–137. doi:10.1016/j.childyouth.2015.05.016

Serafini, K., Shipley, L., & Stewart, D., (2016), Motivation and substance use outcomes among adolescents in a school-based intervention. *Addictive Behaviors, 53*, 74–79. doi:10.1016/j.addbeh.2015.10.004.

Substance Abuse and Mental Health Services Administration (2014). *Results from the 2013 National Survey on Drug Use and Health: Summary of national findings*, (NSDUH Series H-48, HHS Publication No. (SMA) 14–4863). Rockville, MD: Substance Abuse and Mental Health Services Administration.

Winters, K., Lee, S., Botzet, A., Fahnhorst, T., & Nicholson, A. (2014). One-year outcomes and mediators of a brief intervention for drug abusing adolescents. *Psychology of Addictive Behaviors, 28*(2), 464–474. doi:1037/a0035041

# 17 Level-Headed Responses to Students Who Make Threats

*Robert Kinscherff*

School professionals, parents, and others are frequently exposed to media accounts reporting instances of school violence, which range from the tragic to the ludicrous. On the one hand, memories of the Columbine High School mass shooting challenged assumptions that schools are reliably safe places for students and staff. On the other hand, common-sense is challenged by reports of an account (American Broadcast Corporation News, 2013) of a kindergartner initially ordered suspended for 10 days for a "terrorist threat" by suggesting to a friend that they shoot at each other with their plastic Hello Kitty bubble guns.

## Why It Matters

Landmark research that guided subsequent research and development of level-headed responses to threats of violence by students was published by the United States Secret Service and United States Department of Education in 2002. More recently, legal advocates and researchers (JustChildren & Cornell, 2013) demonstrated that threat assessment approaches can provide safety while limiting unwarranted school suspensions and the racially disparate impact of school disciplinary policies. Taken together, this and other research has yielded principles to guide development and implementation of evidence-based policies and practices to address threats of violence by a student:

- The core goal is determining whether a student who has *made* a threat does *pose* a threat. But preventing violence does not require successfully predicting who will behave violently, when, and under what specific circumstances—a virtually impossible task in most instances.
- Violence targeting a person, or a place, reflects a discernible trajectory arising from interactions among the student, the target, other persons, the setting, and situational factors.
- The student making a threat, peers, parents, school personnel, and others may be sources of information that allow positioning of the student on a trajectory that begins with contemplating a violent act,

passes through cognitive and behavioral preparations to engage in the act, and ends in commission of the threatened violent act. This trajectory may last only a few seconds, or it may emerge over a much longer period of time.
- This trajectory may be dissipated or disrupted before the violent act if it is identified, understood, and addressed, in a manner that holds the student accountable but also avoids punitive responses and provides supports to address the factors that were "driving" the trajectory toward violence.
- There are well-researched models of policy and practice available to schools which involve professionals, parents, and students that diminish instances of threatened or actual violence in the school setting.

Crafting approaches to level-headed responses to student threats is possible—and has already been done—if these principles are relied upon.

### *The Nature and Scope of the Problem*

"School violence" as used in this chapter is defined as violence committed on school property, on the way to or from school, or at school-sponsored events. It can involve students or adults as victims, perpetrators, or witnesses, although this chapter focuses upon students who threaten or perpetrate school violence. School violence also reflects a continuum of behaviors, from isolated fighting between two individuals, to bullying, to serious delinquent criminality and gang activity, to attempted or completed homicides by students, or at school-related activities.

The Centers for Disease Control and Prevention (2016) characterizes deaths from school violence as rare, and cites research by Zhang, Musu-Gillette, and Oudekerk (2016) finding that less than 2.6% of youth homicides occur at school (relatively unchanged over the past decade). However, Zhang and colleagues also report approximately 486,400 non-fatal violent victimizations in 2014 (students aged 12–18). Non-fatal victimization results in a range of physical injury, but even victimization that does not inflict significant physical injury contributes to elevated rates of school avoidance, depression and anxiety, substance abuse, and risk of suicide, while undermining academic achievement (CDC, 2016).

Viewing school violence from a prevention perspective draws attention to the greater prevalence of lower levels of threat and violence, such as bullying and student interpersonal conflicts. Consistent and effective attention to bullying, conflicts between individual students or groups of students, and criminal activity conducted by student gang members diminishes the likelihood of extreme events such as attempted or completed homicides.

Key to effective responses to lower levels of violence are: (a) fostering a climate of school engagement by students and school personnel that includes support for mutual respect and safety; (b) measures to identify and promptly respond to interpersonal conflicts, bullying, criminal misconduct, and/or emotional crisis; (c) clarity that any degree of threatened or actual violence is unacceptable and will prompt a proportionate but effective response to prevent harm and support safety; and (d) creation and implementation of policies and practices to identify and assess potential threats.

An important dimension of this work is establishing routine and respectful interactions with students and working to replace peer cultures which avoid "snitching" with peer cultures that value mutual safety. Similarly, it is important to directly address implicit or explicit cultures among school staff which protect some favored students or groups of students from consequences of misconduct and/or disproportionately impose disciplinary consequences on other students for similar misconduct. For example, schools must not tolerate abusive initiation rituals by sports teams or other groups, commonplace mocking and teasing, group rivalries that involve taunting and threatening, or other conditions likely to give rise to escalating conflicts among groups or significant emotional distress and escalating sense of desperation among individuals.

However, not tolerating these conditions does not mean embracing a "zero tolerance" approach that too often becomes punitive, risks escalation of conflicts, yields unnecessary suspensions or expulsions, risks being applied disproportionally to youth with special needs or who are racial minorities, and fuels desperation among youth at risk of engaging in a violent act. Research conducted by the Council of State Governments and the Public Policy Research Institute (2011) demonstrates that over-reliance upon suspensions increases the rates of grade retention, dropping out, and juvenile justice involvement. Similar research by the Virginia Department of Education (Cox, 2011) found that "traditional approaches to student discipline have not been effective in reducing disruptive behavior, vandalism, or the dropout rate" (p. 1).

Initiatives in Connecticut and elsewhere show promise in addressing the "school to prison pipeline" process, which disproportionately brings youth with behavioral health disorders, special needs, lower socioeconomic status, and minority status into contact with the juvenile justice system as a result of well-intentioned but failed zero tolerance policies.

### *Key Findings from the 2002 United States Secret Service Study*

This seminal study of 37 incidents of targeted school shootings and attacks was prompted by the Columbine High School attack by two students in April 1999 that killed 13 and wounded 20 others. The findings and their implications are given in *The Report of the Safe School Initiative* (2002) and are instructive for what they mean for addressing bullying, peer and school culture, and the use of threat assessment in school settings. The 10 key findings were:

1. Incidents of targeted violence at school rarely were sudden, impulsive acts.
2. Prior to most incidents, other people know about the attacker's idea and/or plan to attack.
3. Most attackers did not threaten their targets directly prior to advancing the attack.
4. There is no accurate or useful "profile" of student who engaged in targeted school violence.
5. Most attackers engaged in some behavior prior to the incident that caused others concern or indicated a need for help.
6. Most attackers had difficulty coping with significant losses or personal failures. Moreover, many had considered or attempted suicide.
7. Many attackers felt bullied, persecuted, or injured by others prior to the attack.
8. Most attackers had access to and had used weapons prior to the attack.
9. In many cases, other students were involved in some capacity.
10. Despite prompt law enforcement responses, most shooting instances were stopped by means other than law enforcement intervention.

Taken together, these findings indicate that most attackers had signaled their thinking or even their plan to attack (although not commonly by direct threat to their targets), had behaved in concerning ways, and were significantly emotionally distressed or desperate due to perceived rejection or harm by others, significant losses or personal failures, or other stressors. If their escalating movement toward intended lethal violence could have been identified and protective but non-punitive interventions put in place, the attacker may not have reached the lethal endpoint of their trajectory.

### *Developments Since the 2002 Secret Service Reports*

There have been significant developments in responding to school violence since the reports issued by the Secret Service and the U.S. Department of Education (2002). Although outside the scope of this chapter, one example is the development of universal programs for grades K-12 with demonstrated effectiveness in preventing violence and aggressive behavior (Centers for Disease Control and Prevention, 2007). From a prevention perspective, success of these strategies limits the number of youth likely to begin down a trajectory during which they make or pose a threat and subsequently engage in school violence.

A second major development has been research describing the kinds of risk factors that are associated with acts of violence by youth in school and other community settings. While inadequate to serve as a "profile" for purposes of predicting whether a specific youth will act violently under specific circumstances, these factors are important to consider. Hoge and Andrews (2010) describe five factors most relevant to violence risk:

- Past history of aggressive conduct;
- Dysfunctional family dynamics/parenting, including parents engaged in criminal activity;
- Antisocial and aggressive peer group companions/affiliations;
- Problematic traits (e.g., impulsivity, risk-taking, high aggressive emotionality); and
- Antisocial values, attitudes, beliefs—especially if they justify and promote violence.

They also describe potential strength and protective factors:

- Positive, prosocial attitudes;
- Good social skills;
- Good problem-solving skills;
- Strong academic skills and motivation;
- Interests in sports or other positive activities;
- Good physical health;
- Competent parenting, including adequate supervision, modeling, and guidance;
- Parents who are cooperative with school staff and other helping adults;
- Other supportive family members;
- Financial stability;
- Access to adequate community resources (e.g., mental health, medical, recreational, etc.);
- Stable neighborhood with minimal criminal activity; and
- Positive, supportive peers who are not persistently involved in delinquent misconduct.

Research identifying developmental trajectories toward misconduct in youth, risk and protective factors, and the desistance of violent misconduct with maturation has supported the development of approaches toward assessment and management of violent youth. This has included the development of specialized assessment tools which can be used once any potential or immediate threat has been contained for longer-term violence risk assessment and planning. This has now become a specialized area of practice in school and clinical psychology, which ordinarily requires additional focused training in violence risk assessment models and evaluation strategies. Note that psychological testing alone cannot reliably assess violence risk, and that multi-sourced information and specialized assessment tools are ordinarily required.

### *Operational Threat Assessment for School Settings*

A third development in recent years has been the refinement of *operational threat assessment*. Operational threat assessment occurs in "real time" in the wake of a student making a threat or reports by others of information that suggests a student may be threatening or preparing a violent attack.

The clear success of the piloting of the Virginia Threat Assessment Guidelines (VSTAG) in reducing threatened and actual violence led the Virginia legislature in 2013 to become the first state to mandate formation of threat assessment teams in all public schools in the state. It is highlighted here as a model for school-based threat assessment that is recognized as an evidence-based practice in the federal National Registry of Evidence-Based Programs and Practices.

The VSTAG model involves a multidisciplinary team of school personnel, including administrators, teachers, mental health staff, and resource officer(s), and can also include community-based mental health and/or law enforcement personnel. The principal or designee leads the team and makes threshold decisions at Step 1. The school resource officer or other law enforcement respond to illegal actions and emergencies and advise the team. School-based mental health personnel conduct mental health assessments and serve as team liaisons if follow-up mental health assessments or interventions are required. Other school personnel report threats and provide relevant threat assessment information to the team.

The VSTAG model works to place the threatener and the threat into a broader context. Factors to be considered include the age and capabilities of the student, prior history of discipline or legal involvement, the credibility of the student and their ability/willingness to provide information about the threat and its circumstances, and the details and credibility of information provided by witnesses and collateral informants.

Step 1 involves evaluation of the threat. Youth often make threats that may range from figures of speech or misguided humor to warnings of imminent and severe violence. However, making a threat in the absence of both *intent* and *capability* to carry out a threat suggests that the youth may not actually pose a threat.

Threats may be transient and reflect momentary frustration or a signal that some issue needs to be addressed or conflict resolved. Substantive threats signal *intent* that suggests some degree of risk the threat will be carried out, especially if there is also *capacity* to do so, such as access to weapons, plausible details and/or repetitions of the threat over time, and indications of planning and preparation for an attack. Indications of severe emotional distress, desperation, or thoughts of death or suicide should be taken very seriously. Substantive threats require a protective response that commonly includes warning the intended or potential victim(s) and the parents of the student of concern and victim(s), and may also require law enforcement consultation. The VSTAG model

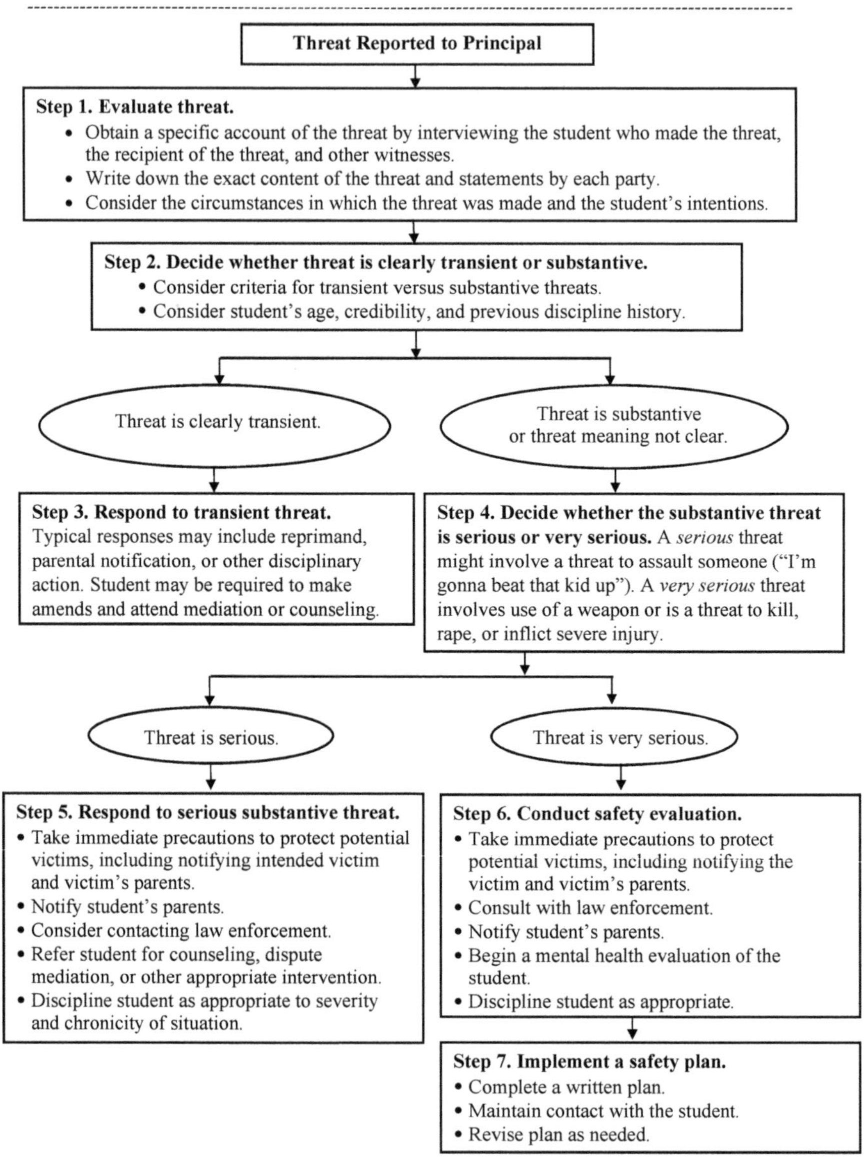


*Figure 17.1* Decision Tree for Student Threat Assessment.

Source: © Reproduced here with permission of Dr. Cornell.

advises that threats are presumptively treated as substantive if there is any doubt.

The VSTAG decision tree tracks the process once a threshold decision has been made about whether the threat is transient or classified as a serious or very serious substantive threat. All substantive threats involving a weapon are regarded as very serious. The process to respond to substantive threats involves making appropriate notifications, determining appropriate interventions, conducting safety evaluations and safety planning, and following up to ensure steps have been taken and the threat resolved pending further assessments or interventions.

JustChildren and Dr. Cornell (2013) offer seven recommendations for safe and fair use of the VSTAG model. The model has yielded lower overall suspension rates and lower racial disparities for longer-term suspensions, but "it must be carefully implemented and balanced with student rights, all with the goal of improving school safety and climate for everyone" (p. 15). The most relevant recommendations are:

- Don't overreact. Most threats are transient that can be quickly resolved safely and effectively without suspending a student. There are fewer more serious substantive threats. In these cases, the team takes protective steps to assure safety for all concerned while gathering additional information to identify emotional difficulties, victimization by bullying, or distress from other conflicts or problems. The goal is to address interventions that will diminish risk and avoid responses which may inadvertently increase risk. In the rare event of very serious substantive threats, the goal is again to assure safety for all concerned and, with consultation from law enforcement, determine if steps can be taken to diminish the threat in a manner that can help the student continue their education without unwarranted entanglement with the juvenile justice system.
- Protect confidential student information. Even when "health and safety" exceptions to FERPA or HIPAA are invoked to share information to assure safety when threats have been made, only that information that is necessary to assure safety should be disclosed.
- Clarify the role of law enforcement and use court referrals only as a last resort. Protocols that are mindful of relevant law and best practices should be in place between schools and law enforcement officials. Arrests and court involvement should be a last resort given research documenting the persisting negative consequences of court involvement on youth academic achievement, particularly for youth with low levels of delinquent misconduct.

Information about the VSTAG model, the research supporting its efficacy as an evidence-based model, and implementation issues is available through the Curry School of Education at the University of Virginia.

## Notes from the Field

The following brief vignettes illustrate a range of cases in which student threats prompted responses by school authorities with varying results for the youth and school.

### *Case 1*

*Timmy is a sixth-grade student with significant cognitive limitations. While being redirected away from a preferred activity by a classroom aide, he became very frustrated and said, "I'm gonna make a bomb and blow this place up!" He was suspended pending completion of a risk assessment by a community-based mental health professional that took two weeks to complete and cost the school district $3,000. The process of suspension and professional evaluation unfolded despite the fact that Timmy's cognitive limitations made it implausible that he had the skills to make an explosive device or even follow instructions to do so should he be able to access this information on the web.*

### *Case 2*

*Jules is an eighth grader who has had a tumultuous relationship with another girl, who alternates between being her "best friend" and worst enemy. During a disagreement over a boy in their class, Jules tells her, "I am going to f*** you up, cut your face with a knife!" The threat assessment process was initiated, and it was determined that Jules had uttered a transient threat in the heat of conflict with a peer. She was spoken to about the threat and her intentions, and its impact upon the girl and other classmates and students at the school. She was abashed and apologized for making the threat, acknowledging that she sometimes makes threats when she is angry, but she does not mean them, which makes it hard for her to keep friends. She is referred to a short-term intervention to develop emotional regulation and conflict resolution skills. She completes eighth grade successfully.*

### *Case 3*

*Jack is an adolescent in tenth grade. He has a very difficult living and family situation in a transient high-crime neighborhood and a history of arrest for graffiti and shoplifting. He is bright but underachieving. Five months ago, he affiliated with a neighborhood youth gang along with his best friend. His friend was killed in a drive-by shooting two weeks ago by some youths involved with a rival gang. Word on the street spread that he would be shot next and he began to suspect that a classmate in the rival gang was involved in his friend's shooting and would try to shoot him.*

*Jack confronted this classmate at school and told him in front of witnesses, "I am going to shoot you before you shoot me—sooner than you think!" When interviewed by the school resource officer and principal, he described in detail a pistol he said he had hidden near his home, declined to retract his threat "because this is just the world I'm in—it's him or me, no question."*

*His parents and those of his identified target were notified, and a mental health screen yielded no symptoms of significant mental illness. An urgent meeting with his parents, Jack, the school resource officer, school mental health professional, and gang outreach worker was held. A plan was developed with the outreach worker to attempt to diffuse the gang tensions, Jack agreed to surrender the gun to police through that worker, and short-term tutoring was initiated until Jack could begin in an alternative school out of his neighborhood. The gang tensions were resolved over the next two months and Jack learned that his classmate had not actually participated in the murder of his friend. With the support of the outreach worker, Jack gradually removed himself from his neighborhood gang and completed high school at the alternative school.*

### Case 4

*Bobby entered the twelfth grade after slowly declining grades and increasing social isolation over the previous nine months. He had long seemed "odd" to his peers and had been teased and bullied since middle school, but even peers who would spend time with him saw very little of him over the summer. At the end of September, Bobby was sitting by himself during a morning study period when he was joined by one of those peers. This peer asked Bobby what he was doing, and Bobby replied, "I'm just making my list of who I'm going to shoot today." The peer scoffed and then Bobby calmly showed him a pistol and several rounds of ammunition in the bottom of his backpack. The peer left and returned a few moments later with two other male peers, who joined him at the table and offered to work with him to refine his hit list. They worked with him, adding some new names to the list and having Bobby remove other names from the list, "because they're really good guys."*

*The study period ended, and they dispersed. Bobby was going to sit through one more class before shooting the youth on his list during lunch period. Shortly before that class ended, one of the peers had second thoughts and reported the gun and "the hit meeting" to a teacher, who immediately notified the principal who, in turn, called for a response from local police. The principal entered the classroom, calmly approached Bobby's seat, and swiftly picked up the backpack. He asked Bobby to follow him to his office and Bobby calmly complied. Asked what his intentions were, Bobby reported that he intended to shoot those students on the "hit list" and then shoot himself. Asked why, Bobby said, "Some need to die because they've been torturing me for years, some are just not lucky... but it doesn't matter. I'm not lucky, either." He then asked the principal for the backpack but sat calmly when the principal declined.*

*The police secured Bobby according to a protocol previously worked out with the school for urgent responses and took him to the emergency room where he was deemed to be "acutely psychotic, homicidal, and suicidal." He was psychiatrically hospitalized. As Bobby stabilized over the following weeks, the threat assessment team was involved with Bobby's parents, clinical care providers, and others, in crafting an educational plan, an overall safety plan, and a school re-entry plan. Bobby completed his senior year and would later successfully enter college.*

## Practical Tools for School-Based Professionals

The two most important steps for school-based professionals committed to level-headed responses to threats made by students are to: (a) investigate threats dispassionately and avoid over-reaction; (b) implement an evidence-based threat assessment model such as the VSTAG. This includes crafting internal protocols and confidentiality agreements, recruiting multidisciplinary team members, and establishing threat assessment and management protocols with law enforcement, other first responders, and community-based mental health professionals. Leaders should access technical support or training resources to make use of tools and written protocols that already exist and to address local obstacles to implementation. Additional recommendations are as follows:

- Establish mechanisms for identifying students in significant emotional distress and/or showing signs of acute psychiatric difficulty, especially depression, paranoia, or homicidal or suicidal thinking.
- Ensure responses to students with behavioral health needs rely upon mental health providers, with the goal of seeking evaluation and treatment rather than arrest and school exclusion.
- Encourage prompt engagement in conflict resolution mechanisms to diffuse tensions when conflict between peers arises. Peer mediation and conflict mediation strategies can help facilitate positive youth engagement and initiatives to challenge peer cultures of "no snitching" in favor of cultures of respect and safety.

## Take Home Ideas for Parents

Parents can facilitate the functioning of safe schools and level-headed responses to students by taking steps to:

- Talk to your children about the consequences of making threats, or engaging in violence, and emphasize the importance of sharing

information with responsible adults if they are aware of threatening statements or behaviors by peers. If you become aware of a possible threat made or posed by your child or another peer, do not delay in taking steps to assure safety and assess the situation.
- Model positive conflict-resolution strategies that do not rely on threats, intimidation, or emotional blackmail, and model and teach strategies for emotional regulation.
- Be aware of your child and their friends regarding their attitudes, values, and beliefs about respecting others, making threats or engaging in violence, and perceived justifications for intimidation, force, or assault.
- Be responsible about your child's access to firearms, particularly if your child is depressed, impulsive, using substances, easily angered, or perceives being in high conflict or threatening situations at school, or elsewhere. Trigger locks and use of special locking firearms storage cabinets are always recommended.
- Temporarily remove firearms from the home if your child makes threats to harm self or others, indicates s/he is in high conflict with peers and/or is receiving threats from peers, becomes preoccupied with violence, or shows signs of emotional dysregulation, including impulsivity or impaired judgment.
- Advocate for your child with school personnel if your child is being bullied, intimidated, or harassed, and insist that effective steps to address physical or emotional victimization be promptly taken by the school.
- Align and communicate in a candid and non-defensive manner with school personnel if your child is identified as being a bully, involved with problematic peers, making threats or behaving in ways that reasonably suggest your child may pose a threat, or showing signs of significant emotional distress. Be genuinely open to considering suggestions for assessment, treatment, or risk management planning.

## *Conclusion*

Level-headed responses to threats by students are most likely to occur when schools:

- Put into place threat assessment teams with clear policies and procedures;
- Avoid over-reaction to threats;
- Assure safety while protecting student privacy to the greatest extent possible under the circumstances;
- Respect the rights of students and families; and
- Take every possible step to avoid school exclusion or entanglement in the juvenile justice system.

Youth, families and schools working together with evidence-based models of threat assessment based upon mutual goals of safety and respect are most likely to successfully support student educational achievement while minimizing violence in schools.

Web resources are available in our eResource at www.routledge.com/9781138293571.

## References

American Broadcasting Corporation News (2013, January 20). *Kindergartner suspended over bubble gun threat.* Retrieved from http://abcnews.go.com/blogs/headlines/2013/01/kindergartner-suspended-over-bubble-gun-threat/

Centers for Disease Control and Prevention. (2007). *The effectiveness of universal school-based programs for the prevention of violent and aggressive behavior: A report on recommendations of the Task Force on Community Preventive Services.* (Publication No. MMWR 2007;56(RR-7): 1–12). Retrieved from www.cdc.gov/mmwr/PDF/rr/rr5607.pdf

Centers for Disease Control and Prevention. (2016). *Understanding school violence: Fact sheet.* Retrieved from www.cdc.gov/violenceprevention/pdf/School_Violence_Fact_Sheet-a.pdf

Council of State Governments (Justice Project) and Public Policy Research Institute (2011). *Breaking schools' rules: A statewide study of how school discipline relates to students' success and juvenile justice involvement.* New York, NY: Council of State Governments.

Cox, H. D. (2011). *Report on the Department of Education's effective schoolwide discipline initiative.* Retrieved from www.doe.virginia.gov/boe/meetings/2011/10_oct/agenda_items/item_k.pdf

Hoge, R. D. & Andrews, D. A. (2010). *Evaluation for risk of violence in juveniles.* New York, NY: Oxford University Press.

JustChildren & Cornell, D. (2013). *Prevention v. punishment: Threat assessment, school suspensions, and racial disparities.* Charlottesville, VA: University of Virginia (Curry School of Education) and Legal and Justice Center.

United States Secret Service & United States Department of Education (2002, May). *The report of the Safe School Initiative: Implication for the prevention of school attacks in the United States.* Washington, D.C.

United States Secret Service & United States Department of Education (2002, May). *Threat assessment in schools: A guide to managing threatening situations and to creating safe school climates.* Washington, D.C.

Zhang, A., Musu-Gillette, L., & Oudekerk, B. A. (2016). *Indicators of school crime and safety: 2015* (NCES Publication No. 2016–079/NCJ 249758). Washington, DC: National Center for Education Statistics, U.S. Department of Education, and Bureau of Justice Statistics, Office of Justice Programs, U.S. Department of Justice.

# 18 Home–School Collaboration

*Bruce Ecker*

The benefits of collaboration between parents and teachers are numerous: improved academic achievement, better school and home behavior, enhanced social skills, increased graduation rates, and decreased bullying (Henderson & Mapp, 2002; Jeynes, 2008, 2012). These benefits have been found from early preschool through high school graduation, in urban school districts as well as those that are suburban and rural, and with children of all races, both native-born and immigrant (Jeynes, 2007; Mapp, 2009; Quiocho & Daoud, 2006). When collaboration is close and consistent, children learn more, teachers feel supported, and parents feel engaged and effective. However, often, the kind of collaboration that yields such benefits is elusive. Opportunities for learning enrichment are squandered and children are lost without a consistent set of expectations. Teachers feel alone and unsupported. Parents feel cut-off and at times blamed. Yet, much is known about how to foster and maintain helpful home–school collaboration, and that topic is the focus of this chapter.

## Why It Matters

Collaboration between home and school is an important factor in ensuring a child's success both in and outside of school. Other factors are important as well, e.g., effective school leadership, dedicated teachers, high standards, curricula that are aligned with those standards, and an emotionally supportive school climate (Henderson & Mapp, 2002). Yet, home–school collaboration remains both a consistent and potent contributor, and one that can be enhanced by the efforts of both school personnel and parents.

### *Definitions*

Some definitions are in order. First, what is meant by home–school collaboration and by the related terms of parent involvement and parent engagement? The term *collaboration* connotes a process in which partners in a relationship have equal power, treat each other with respect, and work together toward a common goal. Collaborative partnerships are characterized by two-way communication, competence, commitment, trust, advocacy, and the aforementioned equality and respect (Turnbull, Turnbull, Erwin, Soodak, & Shogren, 2015). In *home–school collaboration*, these attributes apply to the relationship between a child's family members, typically parents but also grandparents, aunts and uncles, and at times unrelated caregivers, as well as school personnel.

*Parent involvement* refers to the participation of this same set of home caregivers in any school-related educational activity, such as attending parent–teacher conferences, monitoring homework, or leading a parent–teacher organization. *Parent engagement*, which is broader than parent involvement, describes the relationship between home-based caregivers and their children, as well as their relationship with other important adults in the child's life, such as teachers, all in the service of fostering the child's development. Thus, parent engagement encompasses the attachment between parent and child, the expectations that parents have for their children's achievement, parents' relationships with teachers, and many other factors.

### *Diversity and American School Children*

Ethnic, racial, economic, geographic, religious, and linguistic diversity is endemic in the U.S. population, as is variation in sexual orientation and gender identity. These are all aspects of culture. Just slightly more than half, 53%, of U.S. school-age children are White, 14% are Black, 24% are Latino, 5% are Asian, 1% are Native American or Pacific Islander, and 4% are two or more races (Musu-Gilette et al., 2016). Ninety-seven percent of school age children were born in the United States, although 23% have at least one foreign-born parent (U.S. Department of Health and Human Services, 2013). Nine percent of U.S. school children require assistance because English is not their first language (National Center for Education Statistics, 2017). A language other than English is spoken in 21% of U.S. homes (Ryan, 2013). Forty-one percent of children live in families designated as "low income" while, of those, roughly half live below the federal poverty line. While precise figures are not available, millions of American school children identify as either gay, lesbian, or transgender, and many have parents who identify in these ways. Home–school collaboration requires that we build bridges of acceptance and trust between parents and teachers. Among other actions, collaboration requires that we take time to understand each other's values, communicate in each other's languages, celebrate each other's joys, and support each other in times of conflict.

### *The Benefits of Collaboration*

The benefits of home–school collaboration have been found in study after study over nearly the past 50 years. They are evident from preschool through high school graduation, in cities, suburbs, and rural America, and with those who are White, Black, Latino, and Asian. These findings have been summarized in several lengthy reviews (Mapp, 2009; Miller & Kraft, 2014; Turnbull et al., 2015), indicating that increased collaboration is associated with:

- Higher scores on standardized achievement tests;
- Higher grade point average;
- Better attendance;
- Better work habits;
- Increased family confidence in educational outcomes;
- Better behavior at home and school;
- Better social skills;
- Higher rates of high school graduation;
- Lower rates of delinquency;
- Decreased bullying; and
- Decreased racial discrimination.

### *Types of Engagement*

There are several types of parental engagement, which here will be categorized as *direct* and *indirect*. Direct engagement includes activities in which parents and school personnel communicate with each other and pursue projects together, or when parents work with children at the behest of school personnel. These activities include teacher–parent conferences, volunteering in children's classrooms, attendance at parent–teacher organization meetings, helping children with homework, and home visits by teachers, among others. Indirect engagement includes activities, often with very powerful effects, in which parents support their children's education separate from specific contact from teachers. Such activities include parental practices that build children's self-confidence, holding high expectations for student achievement, reading to young children, and involving children in enriching extracurricular activities, be they in art, music, or athletics.

### *Effective Engagement*

Home–school engagement works when it improves outcomes for students and makes both parents and teachers feel more effective in their respective roles. Effective engagement is seen in a set of core attitudes as well as both direct and indirect activities. The foundational attitude is that relationships matter and that both school personnel and parents need to be welcoming, respectful, trusting, and open in their interactions (Jeynes, 2010). Second, parents and teachers need to believe that they both have much to offer, and they should focus on each other's resources and strengths rather than faults (Sheridan, Clarke, & Christenson, 2014). Third, parents and teachers must view each other as equals; each partner has a sphere of important knowledge, skills, and perspectives; these can complement each other, with neither being primary. Fourth, teachers and parents share one very important goal, i.e., advancing the development of each individual child, be that in the areas of academics, social relations, or emotional and behavioral adjustment. Successful collaborations maintain focus on this essential goal. Fifth, parents and teachers must appreciate cultural differences, i.e., the differences in ethnicity, race, language, economic resources, and gender identity that create the beautiful patchwork of U.S. society. Such appreciation builds bridges of understanding that then facilitate respectful collaborative relationships. Sixth, home–school collaboration has its greatest benefits when it fosters firm and supportive bonds between parents and their children (Sheridan et al., 2014). Teacher modeling of caring and emotionally responsive interactions with both students and families helps to foster these supportive bonds.

In addition to attitudes, several specific activities, both direct and indirect, have been found to foster the kind of engagement that yields good results for children. Some of these activities apply to children of all ages while others apply selectively. The first activity, or rather set of activities, involves inviting parents into schools. Invitations should come on a district-wide level, through letters from the superintendent and scheduled parent nights in every school; on a school-wide level, through frequent communication between school administration and parents and involvement of parents in school-wide governance committees; and on a classroom basis, through frequent letters home, regularly scheduled parent–teacher conferences, ongoing email access with prompt teacher replies, engaging parents as classroom helpers, an open-door visitation policy, and in some cases, home visits (Christenson & Carlson, 2005; Turnbull et al., 2015). It is highly effective for teachers and even principals to reach out and engage parents on an individual basis, through notes home, an email, a telephone call, or a brief conversation at the school door.

However, even when invited, many parents do not know how to engage with schools. It is the school professionals' responsibility to inform those parents who need to learn, for example, how to sign up to volunteer, what to ask in teacher–parent conferences, and how to serve on school committees. This process is termed *role construction* (Mapp, Johnson, Strickland & Meza, 2008). Role construction can be accomplished through emails or information sheets sent home with students (ideally in the native languages spoken by families in the school), classroom-based meetings, or school-based workshops.

The second area that has consistently been found to facilitate engagement, with benefits to students, is frequent two-way communication between home and school. All modes of communication should be used: newsletters, calendars, individual emails, and telephone calls. For communications to be effective, they need to accentuate the child's positive features while also discussing problems directly. Jeynes (2010) recommends the sandwich approach, in which teachers first present a positive feature, then discuss the problem-at-hand, and then finish with another positive aspect. The same holds for parents; they can start with something good that happened at school, then voice their concerns, and then finish with another positive aspect.

A third area of effective collaboration, decidedly indirect, has been found in some studies to have the most beneficial of all effects, and that is when teacher actions foster firm and supportive bonds between parents and their children (Jeynes, 2010; Sheridan et al., 2014). Teacher modeling of caring and emotionally responsive interactions with both students and families helps to foster these supportive bonds. Children feel cared about, parents feel cared about, and all are held, emotionally, by the bonds of respect and appreciation.

### *Developmental Differences*

While the basic principles of home–school collaboration, i.e., respect for the contributions of all partners—teachers, parents, and students, frequent back-and-forth communication, and joint activities that support the child's development in all areas, operate throughout the school years, there are developmental differences as well. In general terms, as children grow, they become more responsible for their work and more autonomous in completing it. There are also significant shifts in content. In the preschool years, teachers and parents work together to boost basic literacy and numeracy skills through talking together, shared reading, counting objects, and practicing letter–sound associations. In elementary school, parents express their interest in child learning by guiding and monitoring homework and participating in classroom activities. Concurrently, teachers and parents join in the task of boosting the child's confidence as a learner, teaching him that there is a wondrous world to learn about and that she will be a successful learner. Participating jointly in non-academic activities, such as cooking, building, and going to museums, has also been found to boost achievement. As in preschool, shared reading activities are beneficial.

In middle and high school, it becomes more important for parents both to have high expectations for their children's achievement and to be available to support children emotionally as they face increasingly complex academic and social challenges. In addition, it is useful to help children build the organizational skills that help them to manage having more classes and teachers at the secondary level, and also to monitor their academic and social activities. Adolescence is a complex developmental phase and schools can offer parents workshops on teen health, academic and social development, family relations, and the pitfalls of adolescence. As children progress in high school, it becomes important for school personnel to inform parents about the options and procedures for post-graduation activities, be they in college, the military, vocational training, or the workforce. Parents and teachers should actively discuss these matters with graduating teens. Developmental differences are described well by Mapp (2009).

### *Homework*

Homework is a key and at times controversial point of contact between teachers, parents, and students. Is homework useful? How much is the right amount? How can parents help? Should parents help? What kind of help is useful?

The answers to these questions are more complicated than one would expect, although some consistent themes emerge. Overall, parental involvement in child and adolescent homework results in higher rates of homework completion, fewer homework problems, and better academic achievement. However, parent homework involvement seems to benefit achievement at the elementary and high school levels, but less so in middle school, where parent involvement has been found to be associated with a decrease in achievement (Patall, Cooper, & Robinson, 2008). It is likely that parental help during middle school, when children both push for autonomy and are more emotionally vulnerable, is too risky an endeavor and too likely to lead to conflict. Further, in terms of areas of the curriculum, parent homework involvement has far better effects for language arts than for math. In addition, parent involvement benefits lower achieving students more than higher achieving students, who likely need the help less (Patall et al., 2008).

Some types of parent involvement work better than others, and it is worth underscoring that children are individuals with many differences, such that one strategy won't work for all. Nonetheless, it has been found to be helpful when parents believe both that homework is valuable and that their children are fully capable of completing it (Hoover-Dempsey, Whitaker, & Ice, 2010). In addition, it is beneficial when parents provide structure and clear guidelines for homework completion—communicating that homework needs to be done and then working out routines with each child individually regarding when and where (Patall et al., 2008). Incentives, even if only in the form of praise, are helpful as well. Requiring that a child finish homework before engaging in a preferred activity (e.g., video games, texting with friends, TV, etc.) is a natural way of building in incentives. Consistent monitoring of child performance is then needed; however, monitoring without the initial steps of providing structure and guidelines has been shown to decrease rather than increase achievement.

Parents should not become unduly involved in the work itself; that is the child's responsibility. Content help can be provided on occasion, at the child's request, but when parents take over, this detracts from the child's self-confidence and sense of responsibility. It also detracts from the teacher's awareness of what skills the child does and does not have. Similarly, it is not the parents' role to evaluate the quality of the child's homework; that is the job of the teacher.

Several teacher activities have been found to facilitate helpful parent–child homework experiences (Turnbull et al., 2015). First, teachers should invite parents in at the beginning of the school year to discuss the teachers' homework policies, including also conversation about parents' past experiences with homework. Second, as the primary benefit parents can offer is supporting their children in the process of homework completion, i.e., homework habits and study skills, teachers might provide instruction to parents regarding how to do that. This can be done via classroom parent workshops, regularly scheduled bulletins or emails sent home, or even video demonstrations. Third, teachers might make sure that students take home the materials they need to complete their homework, thereby avoiding the last-minute panic and frustration that can rock a household. Fourth, it is critical that teachers create ongoing parent–teacher modes of communication about homework, be these on websites on which homework assignments are listed or weekly newsletters. As noted previously, it is important that communications are available in the language that parents speak. While translation is a burden, it can be inordinately helpful in creating the school–family bonds that support student achievement. Fifth, on long-term assignments, teachers and families might jointly create contracts, specifying the student, teacher, and parent responsibilities. Finally, from the home perspective, parents should respect teachers' role in assigning the amount and type of homework and voice that support of the teacher openly to their children.

What should be done if a student repeatedly fails to complete homework? The first step should be for teacher and parent to reach out to each other and thereby start a process of problem solving. Is the work too difficult? Does the child possess the necessary prerequisite academic skills and self-discipline to complete the work independently? Can the family routine, with parental work schedules and sibling needs, provide the quiet space and regular structure that many children need to complete homework consistently? If not, an alternate setting, such as an after-school program, or a homework club at a library or community center, can be helpful. Or, does the lack of homework completion reflect a deeper problem; is it a sign of the child's high stress level, faulty confidence in himself as a learner, defiance toward the way life is treating him or her, or distraction due to emotional suffering? In every case, teacher, parent, and student should work together toward the goal of consistent homework completion, as this supports student achievement.

## Notes from the Field

*Aaron Copeland K-8 school, a public school in a small New England City, is a lively place, with adults and children of many sizes and colors, some dressed formally and others quite casually, rushing through its hallways. English is heard most often, but so is Spanish and occasionally Khmer. Parents are present in nearly all classrooms and also in the office. A colorful sign above the main school entrance announces, in three languages, "Children and Parents Welcome!" A bulletin board near the school entrance has pictures of school personnel as well as those of students and parents. There is a room in the main hallway, near the office, that serves as a family center; it contains couches and meeting chairs, with walls covered with vibrant artwork and notices of school and community activities. The space is used for regularly scheduled parent workshops, for parents and teachers to meet, for students and their parents to hang out, and for a homework club, staffed by a rotating roster of teachers, from 3:00 to 5:00 daily.*

*At Copeland, teachers reach out to all students and families with a hand-written welcoming note before the school year begins. The note describes the school year opening activities and also expresses the teacher's willingness to make a home visit, if invited. There is a classroom meeting within the first two weeks of school, during which parents are encouraged to share their wishes for the school year, the teacher describes classroom activities, and homework and discipline policies are discussed. Parents are invited to make appointments to meet with the teacher at any time. There are also two sets of parent–teacher–student conferences during the school year. Teachers send home weekly newsletters which detail classroom activities in positive terms and offer tips for managing homework. Teachers also maintain a class web-page on which school events and homework assignments are listed. There are two large parties for families at the school, one in December and the other in May, each with a different ethnic theme. Food is available at nearly every school function. The principal monitors all of this home–school collaboration activity and also sends home a monthly newsletter as well as other occasional communications. She is available to meet with parents whenever requested.*

*Families also have a central role in school governance. They participate fully in the School Council, where curricula are discussed, and many school policies are decided. Meetings are scheduled at convenient times for families and structured such that school personnel and parents have equal voices. Committees are created in important areas, such as school climate, core curricula, multiculturalism, school celebrations, and family–school relations; parents and teachers serve on all of these jointly.*

*Respect and collaboration were not always the watchwords of home–school relations at Copeland K-8. Prior to significant changes in teacher and parent attitudes, heralded by a change in school administration, many teachers believed that parents were weak and unsupportive partners in enforcing the standards and policies set by the school, and parents felt shut out and blamed. Parents who visited the school needed to leave their keys or a driver's license in the office as a reminder to return the visitor badge they received on entering. If children spoke in a language other than English, they did so quietly; when heard, they were told to speak English. Parents sometimes helped in classrooms, but they did only rote tasks at the teacher's direction. The principal held parent meetings during the school day, but few parents could attend in this working-class community. There were no notes of welcome at the beginning of the school year. There were no class web-pages on which to list homework assignments. School-to-parent communications were business-like and, when individualized, typically complained of student problems.*

*What caused the shift in these practices from home–school division to home–school collaboration? Two factors were key: dissatisfaction by teachers when parents didn't attend school functions and a decline in student homework completion. How did the shift in home–school relations occur? The appointment of a new community-oriented principal who then initiated a three-year process by which, step-by-step, teachers reached out to families and parent leaders were identified who were invited, personally, to take part in planning committees. School events were planned that appealed to both parents and teachers, with daycare provided. A community-based technical consultant helped in choosing software for classroom web-pages. Communications between school and home became more frequent and more positive. The family center was opened, funded in part by a grant. The School Council, previously weak and with little parent participation, become a powerful force for school betterment. The principal, both dedicated and determined, served as a model for reaching out and collaborating with families. There was more mutual understanding and less blaming. Parents and teachers became more satisfied and less frustrated. Student homework completion improved; overall achievement should follow.*

## Practical Tools for School-Based Professionals

While collaboration requires two willing partners, the primary responsibility for fostering collaboration lies with professionals, i.e., with schools. If not already doing so, school personnel might try some of the actions suggested in this chapter: writing to parents before the school year begins, discussing homework policies collaboratively, welcoming parents into the classroom, or working toward sponsoring a school-based family center. Changes should be made incrementally, one step at a time. Better yet would be to follow any one of the four insightful guides to fostering school–home collaboration listed here:

- Espstein and associates (2009) *School, Family and Community Partnerships: Your Handbook in Action.* This comprehensive guide focuses on all levels of partnership, from the classroom to the state education department, in providing the rationale, strategies, supporting materials, and evaluation measures for moving toward school–home collaboration. It includes a CD with PowerPoint slides to use in workshops as well as electronic copies of all program materials, some of which are translated into Spanish. This handbook is associated with the National Network of Partnership Schools, sponsored by the School of Education at Johns Hopkins University; additional materials as well as information about professional development programs can be found at http://nnps.jhucsos.com/.
- Similarly, broad in its vision, *Beyond the Bake Sale: The Essential Guide to Family-School Partnerships*, by Henderson, Mapp, Johnson, and Davies (2007), presents a strikingly clear vision of partnership accompanied by illustrative quotes from school personnel and parents, specific steps for action, expected obstacles, and ways of overcoming them. Among many valuable ideas, the authors describe the school-based family center, i.e., a designated space within a school in which activities are sponsored that engage parents, teachers, and students, both separately and together. This book is written in accessible language, with numerous concrete examples, needs assessment checklists, and action steps.
- More recent, *Powerful Partnerships: A Teacher's Guide to Engaging Families for Student Success*, by Mapp, Carver, and Lander (2017), is written specifically for use by K-12 teachers in classrooms. Its statement of four core beliefs is followed by well-detailed descriptions of practical collaboration-encouraging activities, such as letters of introduction from parents to teachers, describing how to manage phone calls, and even monthly potluck dinners. The text is supplemented by a website that offers downloadable forms and explanatory videos.
- Finally, Turnbull et al.'s (2015) *Families, Professionals and Exceptionality: Positive Outcomes Through Partnerships and Trust*, now in its seventh edition, is an excellent practical text on home–school collaboration, particularly for families who have children with special needs. This book presents the application of seven principles of partnership in evaluating, intervention planning, and measuring student outcomes. There is strong focus on understanding family interactions, functions, and the life cycle. There is also a strong emphasis on multiculturalism.

## Take Home Ideas for Parents

Even though schools carry the primary responsibility for home–school collaboration, parents have responsibility as well. Parents can do much to foster their children's school achievement. Far from an exhaustive list, the following recommendations are offered:

- Children's attitudes about school are, in part, a reflection of those of their parents. Tell your children how important school is to you. Ask them what happened in school, every day. Pay attention to the positive aspects. Accept their disappointments and annoyance but be careful not to blame school personnel, just as you wouldn't blame another parent or other family member.
- Make school activities a high priority. As much as work and other life demands allow, respond positively to teacher invitations; visit classrooms, serve on School Councils, join in teacher–parent nights. These are clear demonstrations of how you value school.
- Communicate often with school personnel. Tell them when there are major events in your child's life, especially those that might affect school performance. Tell teachers when you like what is going on in school and also when you don't. Teachers make mistakes; as do other school personnel. When disappointed, upset, or angry, discuss your feelings with teachers before sharing them with your children. Give teachers the benefit of the doubt.
- Enhance your children's educational experiences, both academic and recreational. Talk with them, read with them, build with them, cook with them. Take them to museums and sporting events. Share your thoughts on how the world works and listen to theirs.
- Provide your children with the structure and resources to complete their homework. Require that it be done, but don't do it for them. Help when you are asked, but not too much.
- Have high but reasonable expectations for your children's achievement; this conveys your assurance that your child will succeed, thus increasing his or her self-confidence.
- Finally, complement teachers' work by giving your child what research has shown is your greatest gift to their schooling, which is the combination of love and guidance. These provide the sense of security that enables children to persist in meeting the challenges they face in school.

## References

Christenson, S. L. & Carlson, C. (2005). Evidence-based parent and family interventions in school psychology: State of scientifically based practice. *School Psychology Quarterly,* *20*(4), 525–528. doi:10.1521/scpq.2005.20.4.525

Epstein, J. L., Sanders, M. G., Sheldon, S. B., Simon, B. S., Salinas, K. C., Jansorn, N. R. ... Williams, K. J. (2009). *School, family and community partnerships: Your handbook in action* (3rd ed.). Thousand Oaks, CA: Sage.

Henderson, A. T. & Mapp, J. L. (2002). *A new wave of evidence: The impact of school, family, and community connections on student achievement.* Austin, TX: National Center for Family and Community Connections with Schools.

Henderson, A. T., Mapp, K. L., Johnson, V. R., & Davies, D. (2007). *Beyond the bake sale: The essential guide to family-school partnerships.* New York, NY: The New Press.

Hoover-Dempsey, K. V., Whitaker, M. N. C., & Ice, C. L. (2010). Motivation and commitment to family-school partnerships. In S. L. Christenson & A. L. Reschley (Eds.), *Handbook of school–family partnerships* (pp. 30–60). New York, NY: Routledge.

Jeynes, W. H. (2007). The relationship between parent involvement and urban secondary school student academic achievement: A meta-analysis. *Urban Education, 4*(1), 82–110. doi:10.1177/0042085906293818

Jeynes, W. H. (2008). Effects of parental involvement on experiences of discrimination and bullying. *Marriage and Family Review, 43*(3–4), 255–268. doi:10.1080/01494920802072470

Jeynes, W. H. (2010). The salience of the subtle aspects of parental involvement and encouraging that involvement: Implications for school-based programs. *Teachers College Record, 112*(3), 747–774. Retrieved from www.researchgate.net/journal/0161-4681_Teachers_College_Record

Jeynes, W. (2012). A meta-analysis of the efficacy of different types of parental involvement programs for urban students. *Urban Education, 47*(4), 706–742. doi:10.1177/0042085912445643

Mapp, K. (2009). The evidence is clear. In S. Belway, M. Duran, & L. Spielberg (Eds.), *State laws on family engagement in education: National PTA reference guide* (pp. 5–7). Washington, DC: National Parent Teacher Association.

Mapp, K., Carver, I., & Lander, J. (2017). *Powerful partnerships: A teacher's guide to engaging families for student success.* New York, NY: Scholastic

Mapp, K. L., Johnson, V. R., Strickland C. S., & Meza, C. (2008). High school family centers: Transformative spaces linking schools and families in support of student learning. *Marriage and Family Review, 43*(3/4), 338–368. doi:10.1080/01494920802073205

Miller, D. D. & Kraft, N. P. (2014). Best practices in partnering with parents in school-based services. In P. L. Harrison & A. Thomas (Eds.), *Best practices in school psychology* (6th ed., pp. 479–490). Bethesda MD: National Association of School Psychologists.

Musu-Gilette, L., Robinson, J., McFarland, J., KewalRamani, A., Zhang, A., & Wilkinson-Flicker, S. (2016). Status and trends in the education of racial and ethnic groups 2016 (NCES 2016–007). U.S. Department of Education, National Center for Education Statistics. Washington, DC. Retrieved from https://nces.ed.gov/pubs2016/2016007.pdf

National Center for Education Statistics (2017). *English language learners in public schools.* Retrieved from https://nces.ed.gov/programs/coe/indicator_cgf.asp

Patall, E. A., Cooper, H., & Robinson, C. J. (2008). Parent involvement in homework: A research synthesis. *Review of Educational Research, 78*(4), 1039–1101. doi:10.3102/0034654308325185

Quiocho, A. M. L. & Daoud, A. M. (2006). Dispelling myths about Latino parent participation in schools. *The Educational Forum, 70*, 255–267. doi:10.1080/00131720608984901

Ryan, C. (2013). *Language use in the United States: 2011.* Retrieved from www.census.gov/prod/2013pubs/acs-22.pdf

Sheridan, S. M., Clarke, B. L., & Christenson, S. L. (2014). Best practices in promoting family engagement in education. In P. L. Harrison & A. Thomas (Eds.), *Best practices in school psychology* (6th ed., pp. 439–453). Bethesda MD: National Association of School Psychologists.

Turnbull, A., Turnbull, R., Erwin, E. J., Soodak, L. C., & Shogren, K. A. (2015). *Families, professionals and exceptionality: Positive outcomes through partnerships and trust.* Boston, MA: Pearson.

U.S. Department of Health and Human Services, HRSA, Maternal and Child Bureau (2013). *Children of foreign born parents.* Retrieved from https://mchb.hrsa.gov/chusa12/pc/pages/cfbp.html

# Index

Page numbers in **bold** denote tables, those in *italics* denote figures.

For Product Safety Concerns and Information please contact our EU representative GPSR@taylorandfrancis.com
Taylor & Francis Verlag GmbH, Kaufingerstraße 24, 80331 München, Germany

www.ingramcontent.com/pod-product-compliance
Ingram Content Group UK Ltd.
Pitfield, Milton Keynes, MK11 3LW, UK
UKHW022204190926
475702UK00003B/188

* 9 7 8 1 1 3 8 2 9 3 5 6 4 *